Mountaintop Theology

Mountaintop Theology

Panoramic Perspectives of Redemptive History

LARRY R. HELYER

CASCADE *Books* • Eugene, Oregon

MOUNTAINTOP THEOLOGY
Panoramic Perspectives of Redemptive History

Copyright © 2016 Larry R. Helyer. All rights reserved. Except for brief quotations in critical publications or reviews, no part of this book may be reproduced in any manner without prior written permission from the publisher. Write: Permissions, Wipf and Stock Publishers, 199 W. 8th Ave., Suite 3, Eugene, OR 97401.

Cascade Books
An Imprint of Wipf and Stock Publishers
199 W. 8th Ave., Suite 3
Eugene, OR 97401

www.wipfandstock.com

PAPERBACK ISBN: 978-1-4982-3768-0
HARDCOVER ISBN: 978-1-4982-3770-3
EBOOK ISBN: 978-1-4982-3769-7

Cataloguing-in-Publication data:

Names: Helyer, Larry R.

Title: Mountaintop theology : panoramic perspectives of redemptive history / Larry R. Helyer.

Description: Eugene, OR: Cascade Books, 2016 | Includes bibliographical references and indexes.

Identifiers: ISBN 978-1-4982-3768-0 (paperback) | ISBN 978-1-4982-3770-3 (hardcover) | ISBN 978-1-4982-3769-7 (ebook)

Subjects: LCSH: 1. Bible Geography. 2. Biblical Archaeology. 3. Bible Criticism, interpretation, etc. I. Title.

Classification: DS107 .H35 2016 (print) | DS107 (ebook)

Manufactured in the U.S.A.　　　　　　　　　　　　　　　AUGUST 18, 2016

To Jacob and Anna

"Should you be disposed to doubt it [the crucifixion], the very place which everyone can see proves you wrong, this blessed Golgotha . . . on which we are now assembled" (Cyril, *Cat.* 10.19).

"Deny not the crucified . . . Gethsemane bears him witness, where the betrayal took place" (Cyril, *Cat.* 13.38).

Contents

Preface ix

Acknowledgments xiii

List of Abbreviations xv

Chapter 1: Mount Ararat: Understanding God's Wrath and Mercy 1

Chapter 2: Mount Moriah and Mount Golgotha: Understanding the Cross 14

Chapter 3: Mount Sinai: Understanding Holiness: Part One 31

Chapter 4: Mount of Beatitudes: Understanding Holiness: Part Two 49

Chapter 5: Mount Nebo and Mount Gilboa: Understanding the Consequences of Sin 71

Chapter 6: Mount Ebal and Mount Carmel: Understanding Culture and Compromise 91

Chapter 7: Mount of Transfiguration and Mount of Olives: Understanding the Future 110

Chapter 8: Heavenly Mount Zion: Understanding Our Destiny 129

Bibliography 149

Appendix 153

Name Index 159

Scripture Index 161

Subject Index 168

Preface

MOUNTAINS POSSESS MAJESTY AND mystery. They inspire poets ("purple mountain majesties"), intimidate travelers, challenge climbers, and reassure the anxious ("as the mountains surround Jerusalem, so the Lord surrounds his people from this time on and forevermore" [Ps 125:2]). Whether appearing in a magnificent or mundane garb, mountains do what they've always done: they influence and shape the human story. Thus they function as boundaries and frontiers, as hindrances to travel and trade, as refuges for wild animals and havens for refugees, as sources of natural resources, as influencers of climate, as places to be avoided and feared or sought out and revered. Almost universally, great mountains are viewed as sacred places where deities dwell and sanctuaries and altars may be built in order to invoke their aid. Not surprisingly, scanning a Bible concordance turns up about 500 references to mountains and hills. Clearly, mountains played an important role in the lives of biblical characters and for multitudes today the same still holds true.

Mountains deeply touch the human spirit. They point to a power much greater than ours and portend a transcendent reality. They are reminders that planet earth appears to have had a long, even violent history, providing geologists with evidence of massive uplifting, tilting, or even explosive beginnings as volcanoes. In fact, human history is punctuated by volcanic eruptions of terrifying power and devastating consequences. These moments are wake-up calls: forces completely beyond our control impinge upon us daily—we are hardly masters of the house! There are, however, moments of incredible beauty and wonder, breathtaking vistas, whether viewed from the plains below or the slopes and summits above. As mountains reach heavenward, so too our thoughts are drawn upward. And from the summit, one gains a new perspective on familiar landscapes.

Preface

Some of the most significant events in the Bible occur on mountains. Recognizing this fact prompted me to write this book. I realized that a review of mountaintop experiences in Scripture was a virtual tour of its leading themes. Consequently, in this book, I adopt a twofold approach:

- Help the modern reader understand some basic information about a particular mountain or mountain range, including its location and the landmark events that occurred there.
- Suggest why what happened there and then is important here and now. In fact, this book places special emphasis on the continuing theological significance of these mountaintop experiences.

I invite you, my reader, to join me on twelve imaginary mountain climbs. The mountains chosen—it seems fitting the number should be twelve—play a significant role in the history of redemption. Each provides the geographical setting for a divine revelation or a divinely orchestrated event that accomplishes God's will on earth. The purpose of this literary exercise isn't frivolous; on the contrary, I want you to ponder afresh with me the theological truths underlying the stories that transpired on the slopes or summits of these storied mountains. Each mountain vista opens up new insights into God's plan and purpose or brings them into sharper focus. Though the book is primarily exposition, I deliberately aim at application throughout. In short, the book is intentionally designed to be devotional.

These selected mountaintop experiences provide panoramic views of biblical teaching:

- Character and nature of God
- Meaning of the cross
- Nature and consequences of sin
- Shape of Christian discipleship
- Hope of Jesus' second coming
- Ultimate destiny of believers in Christ
- Task of world missions

Together they constitute the essence and vitality of evangelical faith. Our contemporary culture bristles and pushes back against these core values and I detect a slow but steady erosion within the ranks of those who self-identify as Christians. In light of that, this book seeks to "keep on reminding

Preface

you of these things, though you know them already" (2 Pet 1:12) and to "contend for the faith that was once for all entrusted to the saints" (Jude 3).

We live in an era of increasingly narcissistic, entertainment-driven Christianity that tends to play down both the content and the setting of the faith. Against this historically ambivalent expression of Christianity, I want to insist that the drama of redemption didn't unfold in Camelot, Disney World, or a galaxy far, far away, but in the land of Israel. Events matter; God acted at a particular time, in a particular place, in order to save a particular people. The setting of redemptive history really matters, and when it is forgotten or ignored, historic Christianity begins to look like a fairy tale or a Hollywood movie. *Mountaintop Theology* provides Christian readers with essential historical-geographical-theological background necessary for better understanding the God who reveals himself in space-time and sacred Scripture. In short, I want the reader to grasp in a new, fresh way the historical basis of faith in Christ and the basics of that faith. I have written this book motivated by the conviction that these truths endure forever.

The reader may wonder whether I'm a mountain climber myself. I confess I'm not. I did climb Mount Sinai when I was in my twenties and have stood on the summits of all the mountains discussed except Ararat, Hermon, and Ebal, though I've been on the summit of Mount Gerizim directly across from Ebal. At this point in my life, I have neither the ambition nor energy to scale any of these unclimbed mountains—I'm quite content to sit in my recliner and view pictures of them. I should mention, however, that I'm still climbing Mount Zion—determined to reach the summit.

Acknowledgments

THIS BOOK GROWS OUT of a love affair with the land of Israel. It began in Sunday school in a small country church in Kent, Oregon. My aunt Nan, a gifted teacher, brought Bible stories to life. Of course, many of my mental images of these stirring episodes were greatly influenced by the terrain in which I grew up, the Columbia River plateau in Sherman County, Oregon. Later, after living and traveling in Israel, I realized, much to my delight, that there are several geographical similarities between Sherman County and Israel. For example, the elevation of the Mount of Olives is 2,700 feet above sea level, precisely the same as Kent. On our ranch we raised wheat and barley, just as they still do on the outskirts of Bethlehem in the Palestinian Authority and in many parts of Israel. We also had juniper trees and one of the relatively few areas of the world in which this species is indigenous is the land of Israel.

My fascination with Israel continued to grow during college years at Biola University. One day, while passing the library desk, I noticed a large plaster of Paris relief map of the land of Israel. The library was giving it away free to anyone who would kindly cart it off. Like a person who had discovered "treasure hidden in a field" (Matt 13:44), I took possession and it became part of the décor of our apartment—Joyce and I were newlyweds at the time There sat this six-foot-high map propped up against the wall of our living room. I spent hours carefully examining the geographical features of this unique land, "a land flowing with milk and honey", and a land "that the Lord looks after . . . from the beginning of the year to the end of the year" (Deut 11:9,12). Alas, I had to part with the map when we moved from Southern California to Portland, Oregon to attend Western Seminary. I donated it to Brea First Baptist Church. I fear it eventually wound up in a landfill.

Acknowledgments

During my senior year at Western, I saw a poster advertising a year abroad study program at the American Institute of Holy Land Studies (today called Jerusalem University College) in Jerusalem, Israel. Needless to say, that was the topic of conversation at dinner. Joyce shared my enthusiasm. We were excited about the prospect of living and studying in Israel and that is precisely what we did in 1968–69. Our lives have never been the same since. What a joy it has been over the years to have in Joyce a soul mate who shares the same passion for the land and people of Israel. We have returned numerous times and continue to host tour groups to Israel. It never gets old. The joy of seeing others excited about being in the land of the Bible is a constant reward.

I want to pay tribute to teachers who broadened and deepened my understanding of the land and its relationship to the Book. Chief among these is Anson Rainey, probably the leading authority in the world on the historical geography of the land of Israel when he passed away on February 19, 2011. His command of the sources was truly phenomenal and his legacy lives on in his magnum opus, *The Sacred Bridge*. In addition, I have also learned much from expert teachers and tour guides like James Monson (*Regions on the Run*), Bill Schlegel (*Satellite Bible Atlas*), and Paul Wright (*Greatness, Grace & Glory*), to name but a few of those whom I have personally known and studied with in the land of Israel.

Special thanks go to my literary agent, Karen Neumair, for her untiring efforts and encouragement in finding a publisher, and to the editorial team at Cascade Books who gave the book proposal a "thumbs up" and took on the task.

List of Abbreviations

Biblical Texts and Versions

ESV	English Standard Version
GNB	Good News Bible
HCSB	Holman Christian Standard Bible
KJV	King James Version
LXX	Septuagint
NASB	New American Standard Bible
NIV	New International Version
NRSV	New Revised Standard Version
REB	Revised English Bible

Other Ancient Texts

B. Bat.	*Baba Batra*
b.	Babylonian Talmud
Cat.	Cyril of Jerusalem, *Catechesis*
1 En.	*1 Enoch*
Hist. eccl.	Eusebius, *Ecclesiastical History*
J. W.	Josephus, *Jewish War*
1 Macc	1 Maccabees

List of Abbreviations

Šeqal.	Šeqalim
Sir	Sirach
y.	Jerusalem Talmud

Secondary Sources

ABD	*Anchor Bible Dictionary*. 6 vols. Edited by David Noel Freeman. New York: Doubleday, 1992.
ANET	*Ancient Near Eastern Texts Relating to the Old Testament*. Edited by J. B. Pritchard. 3rd ed. Princeton: Princeton University Press, 1969.
BAGD	Walter Bauer, W. F. Arndt, F. W. Gingrich, and Frederick W. Danker. *Greek-English Lexicon of the New Testament and Other Early Christian Literature*. 2nd ed. Chicago: University of Chicago Press, 1979.
BAR	*Biblical Archaeology Review*
BECNT	Baker Exegetical Commentary on the New Testament
BRev	*Bible Review*
DJG	*Dictionary of Jesus and the Gospels*. Edited by Joel B. Green and Scot McKnight. Downers Grove, IL: InterVarsity, 1992.
DOTHB	*Dictionary of the Old Testament: Historical Books*. Edited by Bill T. Arnold and H. G. M. Williamson. Downers Grove, IL: InterVarsity, 2005.
DOTP	*Dictionary of the Old Testament: Pentateuch*. Edited by T. Desmond Alexander and David W. Baker. Downers Grove, IL: InterVarsity, 2003.
DTIB	*Dictionary for Theological Interpretation of the Bible*. Edited by Kevin J. Vanhoozer. Grand Rapids: Baker, 2005.

List of Abbreviations

EDNT	*Exegetical Dictionary of the New Testament.* Edited by H. Balz and G. Schneider. 3 vols. Grand Rapids: Eerdmans, 1990–1993.
IDB	*The Interpreter's Dictionary of the Bible.* Edited by G. A. Buttrick. 4 vols. Nashville: Abingdon, 1962.
IDBSupp	*The Interpreters' Dictionary of the Bible: Supplementary Volume.* Edited by K. Crim. Nashville: Abingdon, 1976.
ISBE	*International Standard Bible Encyclopedia.* Edited by G. W. Bromiley. 4 vols. Grand Rapids: Eerdmans, 1979–1988.
MT	Masoretic Text
NIDOTTE	*New International Dictionary of Old Testament Theology and Exegesis.* Edited by William A. VanGemeren. 5 vols. Grand Rapids: Zondervan, 2012.
TDNT	*Theological Dictionary of the New Testament.* Edited by G. W. Bromiley. 10 vols. Grand Rapids: Eerdmans, 1964–1976.
WBC	Word Biblical Commentary
ZIDB	*Zondervan Illustrated Dictionary of the Bible.* Edited by J. D. Douglas and Merrill C. Tenney. Revised by Moisés Silva. Grand Rapids: Zondervan, 2011.
ZPEB	*Zondervan Pictorial Encyclopedia of the Bible.* Edited by Merrill C. Tenney. 5 vols. Grand Rapids: Zondervan, 1975.

1

Mount Ararat

Understanding God's Wrath and Mercy

"I have set my rainbow in the clouds." (Gen 9:13 NIV)

"Be mindful of your mercy, O Lord, and of your steadfast love, for they have been from of old." (Ps 25:6)

Introduction

MOUNT ARARAT, OUR FIRST climb, is an awesome mountain. Well, I need to qualify that a bit. Actually, the Bible never mentions a single peak called Ararat; it refers instead to a region called "the mountains of Ararat." This area, about the size of Kansas, was known as Urartu in biblical times and is located in northeastern Turkey near Lake Van.[1] Dominating the vicinity, however, is a volcanic mountain 16,854 feet in elevation called *Büyük* (mount) *Ağri Dağ* in Turkish and *Masis* by the Armenian population. Several "arkeologists" (folks who search for Noah's ark) think this is the mountain referred to in Genesis 8 in connection with the great flood of Noah.[2] From at least the eleventh century AD, it has been called Mount Ararat. In terms of elevation, this mountain towers above the others we

---

1. See map 1 in the appendix.
2. See Geissler, "Affirming Agri Dagh."

(metaphorically) climb. On a clear day, its snow-covered peak may be seen glistening from a great distance, a truly magnificent sight.

As you may know, a number of explorers have sought to discover, or have even claimed to see, a portion of Noah's ark on Mount Ararat.[3] It's not my purpose to investigate these claims. My interest lies in the theological message of the biblical narrative.[4] The story of the great flood makes a profound statement about who God is and how he deals with rebellious human beings. Before we start up, however, a word of caution. Physically climbing Mt. Ararat is a difficult and dangerous undertaking; but even an imaginary climb exacts an emotional and intellectual toll. The ascent forces us to reckon with a very dark moment in human history. But as I said in the preface, it's from the mountaintop that one truly sees the landscape. And the view from Mt. Ararat is stunning.

Setting of the Flood Story

Noah's flood didn't just happen "out of the blue." Warning signs were clearly visible; tremors signaled the coming of "the big one." The flood story is part of a larger block of narrative material, Genesis 1–11, the so-called primeval history, stories about the origins of life and human civilization. It functions as important background material, informing ancient Israel about her prehistory, her place in the world.

Understanding the Structure of the Larger Story

Following the story of the fall in Gen 3, Gen 4–11 depicts what happens after the first human couple disobey God and are driven out of the garden of Eden. This section consists of several discrete episodes each vividly illustrating the tragic consequences of sin. What we have is almost like an ancient Israelite version of the top rated American TV soap operas of the early 2000s: *The Young and the Restless, The Bold and the Beautiful, Days of Our Lives, General Hospital,* and *As the World Turns*!

For example, in Gen 4, the narrator relates two stories, the first featuring the family and the second featuring both family and society. Sin wreaks

---

3. If you are interested in pursuing this, see the website www.noahsarksearch.com/. See also Bailey, *Noah, the Person and the Story.*

4. See Walton, "The Flood," 322.

havoc in both spheres. Life can never be the same as it was in Eden; we now live east of Eden (Gen 3:24). In the story of Cain and Abel, we have an alpha male (Cain) who thinks he can handle sin by himself and doesn't need God's grace. He ignores the Lord's pointed warning: "Sin is lurking at the door; its desire is for you, but you must master it" (Gen 4:7), and detests his younger brother Abel who recognizes his need for grace and thereby gains God's favor (Gen 4:4). Cain's intense jealousy and pride drive him to commit the first murder in human history. What shouldn't be overlooked in this story is the sobering fact that, in the United States, a family member or an acquaintance kills the victim in about 78 percent of all murders.[5] Clearly, all is not well in the family, then or now.

Lamech can't control his anger or his lustful pride. In taking more than one wife, he violates a creation mandate.[6] When injured, he takes justice into his own hands and avenges himself by killing his adversary. In effect, this primeval vigilante becomes a warlord who dominates those weaker than he. Predictably, this leads to violent turf wars. It's no surprise that the preflood world "was filled with violence" (Gen 6:11). The current culture of carnage in the United States may be traced back to the same fundamental problem that confronted Lamech.

Understanding the Prequels to the Flood Story

These stories illustrate a dreadful reality: sin shatters the harmony of the garden. All human relationships are now broken. Vertically, humans are alienated from God; horizontally, they are alienated from each other and from their environment. Genesis 3:14–19 succinctly summarizes the dire consequences of the fall. Perpetual enmity exists between Eve's offspring and the serpent's seed, that is, a state of spiritual warfare exists between the kingdom of Christ and the kingdom of the Dark Lord.[7] As for women, their lot in a fallen world has often been unhappy—besides the pain of childbirth and the stresses of child-rearing women suffer, husbands have tended to bully their wives and then blame them for their own failures![8] Adding to

---

5. This is according to a study by the U.S. Department of Justice. See www.bjs.gov/content/pub/pdf/htus8008.pdf.

6. Gen 4:23; cf. Mark 10:2–12.

7. Gen 3:15.

8. Gen 3:12, 16.

the misery, the earth, out of which Adam was formed, lies under a curse and suffers environmental disharmony.[9]

Most distressingly of all, human beings undergo a dissolution of body and spirit. The genealogy of Gen 5 underscores this grim reality about post-Edenic life: we're all going to die. Punctuating the genealogy is that unsettling refrain: "and he died." It's not a question of whether; it's only a question of when. As Benjamin Franklin reminds us: "Nothing is certain except death and taxes."[10] According to Gen 3–9, physical death is a direct consequence of the first sin of Adam. The Apostle Paul seems to agree: "Sin came into the world through one man, and death came through sin, and so death spread to all because, all have sinned"(Rom 5:12).[11]

These stories illustrate what happens when sin gets a foothold and demonstrate the explosive force of sin in the human heart and society. Like a deadly virus, sin works in stealth. No aspect of human existence is immune from its pernicious influence. To change metaphors, sin is like an avalanche bearing down upon us with irresistible force. The pristine world, pronounced very good by the Creator, is now very bad—it's a very dangerous place to live and no one is safe. Violence becomes the operative word. Powerful bullies like Lamech prowl the 'hood and intimidate the weak. They contend for dominance with other wannabes and turf wars erupt everywhere. By the way, the two stories narrated after the flood, Noah's drunkenness and the tower of Babel, demonstrate that the flood didn't wash away human sin.[12] It's still very much present.

Another disturbing scenario adds to the disheartening situation. According to Gen 6:1–13, the sons of God "saw that they [the daughters of men] were fair [beautiful (NIV)], and they took wives for themselves of all that they chose" (Gen 6:2). The context makes clear that this wasn't a good thing, but exactly why isn't instantly clear. Crucial for understanding this episode is the precise meaning of the phrase "sons of God" and the clause "they took wives for themselves."

One explanation for this mysterious episode is that the sons of God are the godly line of Seth who compromise their spiritual legacy and intermarry with the ungodly line of Cain. Another interpretation equates

---

9. Gen 3:17–18.

10. Written in a letter to French scientist Jean-Baptiste LeRoy on November 13, 1789.

11. As Daane puts it, "Original sin is the first sin of Adam, the source of all *other* sins . . ." ("Sinner," 5:445 [italics his]). See also Blocher, "Original Sin," 553–54.

12. Gen 9:20–27; 11:1–9.

the term with powerful warlords like Lamech who acquire large harems as status symbols to satisfy their egos and lust. Finally, some equate the sons of God with fallen angels who cohabit with human women and procreate hybrid beings called the Nephilim ("fallen ones") (Gen 6:4).

In spite of the perplexing questions it raises, I think the third view is the one intended. In short, a demonic invasion descends on the planet featuring cohabitation with mortals. This is a ghastly Ghostbusters scenario without any humor whatsoever. From these unholy unions come "heroes of old, men of renown" (Gen 6:4).[13] Nightmarish images of Orcs, Ringwraiths, Lord Voldemort, and Dementors flash before my mind. Doesn't sound like a place where I'd like to live!

But is such a thing possible? Would God permit a blurring of the lines between the demonic and the human? Consider the following: The expression "sons of God" is used of angelic beings in the Bible, some of whom are hostile to God.[14] Both Jewish and Christian traditions call them fallen angels and typically identify them with demons. Furthermore, Scripture treats demonic possession as a reality in both Testaments.[15] Decisive in this regard is the view of Jesus and his apostles.

Options two and three could be combined in such a way as to relieve the difficulty of holding that demons actually cohabited with women. Perhaps demons took possession of wicked individuals like Lamech, who in turn married Sethite women. This could account for both the superhuman strength of their offspring and their utter depravity.

On the other hand, both Jewish and Christian traditions hold that there was an angelic revolt and intermarriage with humans resulting in a superrace. This blurring of the creation order necessitated the great flood of Noah. This notion is found, for example, in a book called *1 Enoch*, dating to

---

13. Ancient Greek mythology preserves a tradition about an age of monstrous giants called the Titans—not to be confused with the NFL team in Nashville, Tennessee! The Olympian gods led by Zeus overthrew these primordial gods. Besides their great strength, the Titans were brutish and callous. The Greek poet Hesiod says: "Ouranos (heaven) . . . gave to . . . his sons, the name of Titans, the Stretchers, for they stretched their power outrageously and accomplished a monstrous thing, and they would some day be punished for it" (Hesiod, *Theogony*, 207–210). Hittite mythology (the Hittites were an ancient people of Anatolia, or central Turkey) has a similar tradition and remnants of this myth also appear in the Babylonian myth *Enumah Elish* (*ANET*, 61).

14. Job 1:6; 2:1; 38:7; cf. 1 Kgs 22:19–22; Job 15:8; Pss 82:1; 89:7; Jer 23:18; Rev 12:7–9; Jude 6.

15. Deut 32:17; 1 Sam 16:14–16, 23; Mark 1:23–27, 34; 5:1–20; 6:7; 9:17–29; Acts 16:16–18; 19:12–16; Jas 2:19.

the second century BC.¹⁶ The NT contains at least two passages that could be interpreted along similar lines.¹⁷ Several leading church fathers held that the sons of God were indeed fallen angels (Justin Martyr, Clement of Alexandria, Tertullian and Irenaeus, among others).¹⁸ At any rate, Genesis 6 implies that what happened was so serious it forced God to step in and stop it. Thankfully, he intervened.¹⁹

Significance of the Flood Story

The wrath of God is real. This sinks in when you stand atop Mt. Ararat. It's like surveying the scene of a historic battlefield like Gettysburg. From the heights of Ararat, one recalls the great flood of Noah as recorded in Genesis 6–8. You try to comprehend the awful loss of life. You ask yourself, why? Grappling with this question is what our imaginary climb is all about.

Understanding the Wrath of God

Judge Judy puts things to right and people in their place with panache. But I'd rather not think of God sitting on the bench, because, frankly, he knows too much incriminating stuff about me. He's got me dead to rights. Anyone

---

16. *1 En. 6–16*. For background, see Helyer, *Exploring Jewish Literature*, 77–92.

17. 2 Pet 2:4–5; Jude 6.

18. For a discussion of "one of the most controversial and difficult passages of the OT," see Walton, "Sons of God, Daughters of Man," 793–98.

19. The biblical story of the great flood of Noah is not unique. In fact, anthropologists attest to about sixty-eight different flood stories deriving from diverse cultures stretching literally across the planet. In terms of the Bible, however, the most important of these originate from the ancient Near East. There are three major versions of a great flood: 1) the oldest is a Sumerian account featuring the hero Ziusudra who escapes a divinely decreed flood. 2) In a later Akkadian account, called the *Atrahasis Epic*, the creator-god Enki warns the hero Atrahasis to build a boat and escape a flood sent by the gods. 3) Tablet XI of the *Gilgamesh Epic* narrates a flood episode clearly indebted to the *Atrahasis Epic* in which the hero, Utnapishtim, likewise escapes a flood sent by the gods. There are a number of explicit parallels between this account and that of Genesis. But the theological differences are profound. In the pagan flood stories the reason for the mass destruction is trivial: human beings were making too much noise and disturbing the sleep of the gods! In Genesis there is a deep moral and ethical crisis: "Now the earth was corrupt in God's sight, and the earth was filled with violence" (Gen 6:11; cf. 6:5). As Lewis points out, "The Genesis story attests the mercy and the judgment of the Lord. Its religious interpretation of the cataclysm contrasts with the more obscure message of the Mesopotamian stories" ("Flood," 2:799). See also Hunt, "Noah," 605–11.

who's in their right mind admits the same. And God carries a lot more clout than Judge Judy. For obvious reasons, I'd rather focus on God's love and forgiveness than his righteous wrath against sin.

Ascending Mt. Ararat, however, reminds me that God gets angry and sometimes he lets that be known—big time. The landscape of redemptive history is pockmarked by some pretty large divine craters, the biggest being Noah's flood. Readers may be familiar with the as-yet–unsolved mystery that occurred in Siberia, Russia on June 30, 1908, called the Tunguska Event. A vast area (about 830 square miles) of this isolated (thankfully!) landscape was devastated by something extremely powerful. The majority opinion is that a huge meteor or comet slammed into earth's atmosphere and exploded over this region. The resulting explosion, the equivalent of 1,000 Hiroshimas, obliterated everything, leveling about 80 million trees in the process. As extensive as that destruction was, it pales in comparison to the flood. The Bible uses expansive terms to describe its extent: "all the high mountains under the whole heaven were covered . . . all flesh died . . . and all human beings . . . . Only Noah was left, and those that were with him in the ark" (Gen 7:19, 21, 23).[20] On any reckoning, it involved a massive loss of life.

Several modern explorers recount harrowing stories of near disaster on the slopes of Mt. Ararat. But on a vastly larger scale, this mountain recalls a very close call for the entire human race—we are fortunate to be alive on planet earth! Noah's flood didn't happen because of global warming; it happened because of global sinning. The movie *Evan Almighty* trivializes the biblical account. Make no mistake about it; God was really upset: "it grieved him to his heart" (Gen 6:6). He decreed a deluge capable of wiping out all living things. This terrifying moment in redemptive history raises a hard question about the personality and character of God. Can we justify what God did? Was it the right thing? What kind of God is he?

So, why did God do it? The short answer is: he had to. Had he not intervened and started over, Satan would have achieved his aim, which was to distort and disfigure God's image in human beings. God wouldn't let him get away with it. His mercy and goodness compelled him to act on behalf of his unique creation, *homo sapiens*.

---

20. On the extent of the flood, see Walton, "The Flood," 320–22. "All agree on the theological teaching and significance of the passage, regardless of the geographical extent of the flood" (ibid., 322).

Mountaintop Theology
Understanding the Mercy of God

God is merciful. The Scripture resounds with this truth. Here's a sneak preview of another mountain we're going to climb. On Mount Sinai, Moses asked the Lord, "Show me your glory, I pray" (Exod 33:18). Here is the Lord's reply:

> "I will make all my goodness pass before you, and will proclaim before you my name, The Lord; and I will be gracious to whom I will be gracious, and will show mercy on whom I will show mercy. But," he said, "you cannot see my face, for no one shall see me and live." (Exod 33:19–20)

The Lord then placed Moses in the cleft of a rock to protect him from this awesome display of his glory. When the Lord passed by, these words rang out:

> The Lord, the Lord, a God merciful and gracious, slow to anger, and abounding in steadfast love and faithfulness, keeping steadfast love for the thousandth generation, forgiving iniquity and transgression and sin, yet by no means clearing the guilty, but visiting the iniquity of the parents upon the children and the children's children, to the third and the fourth generation. (Exod 34:6–7)

In the mystery of God's sovereignty and grace, Israel becomes one of those "on whom I will show mercy." After thirty-eight years of wandering in the wilderness—because of their disobedience—Moses reminds the new generation of Israel: "the Lord has taken you and brought you out of the iron-smelter, out of Egypt, to become a people of his very own possession, as you now are" (Deut 4:20). That's mercy.

David was a recipient of the Lord's mercy multiple times. Once, after foolishly insisting on a census of Israel's fighting men (the sin of pride and militarism), he was faced with three alternative punishments: famine, flight from his enemies, or falling into the Lord's hands. David wisely chose the last option: "Let us fall into the hand of the Lord, for his mercy is great" (2 Sam 24:14; 1 Chr 21:13). David knew that it's the very nature of God to be merciful: "Be mindful of your mercy, O Lord, and of your steadfast love, for they have been from of old" (Ps 25:6). So did the prophet Micah: "He does not retain his anger forever, because he delights in showing clemency" (Mic 7:18). Nehemiah understood this truth. In a moving prayer of contrition, he reflects back on the devastation of Judah's destruction and the exile. With a heart full of gratitude, he says, "But in your great mercy you did not put an end to them or abandon them, for you are a gracious and merciful God" (Neh 9:31).

The flood story highlights this wonderful attribute. The human family in the person of Noah and his immediate family were the recipients of God's mercy. We still are.

Harmonizing God's Wrath and Mercy

So how do we reconcile God's wrath with his mercy? The flood story forces us to consider an essential attribute of God: he is holy. Holiness entails the complete absence of sin and evil. Holiness and evil can't coexist in God's presence. Holiness obliterates all that is evil, just like light dispels darkness.[21]

This is dramatically illustrated in the sacrificial cult of Israel. When an Israelite brought a sacrificial animal to the tent of meeting, a priest first inspected it and, if it was acceptable and without blemish, the worshiper laid his hands on the innocent animal's head. A symbolic transfer of guilt took place. Then the worshiper slit the animal's throat while a priest caught the blood in a basin. The blood served as a cleansing agent. The priest took the bowl of blood over to the great bronze altar. There he poured the blood out at the base of the altar.[22] The intense heat vaporized the blood. What a graphic picture of what happens to our sin when we accept God's forgiveness! This recalls what the writer of the book of Hebrews says: "our God is a consuming fire" (Heb 12:29). The Psalmist says, "as far as the east is removed from the west, so far he removes our transgressions from us" (Ps 103:12).

Holiness means that God can't nonchalantly deal with sin like a dotting grandfather on his darling grandchildren. Sin is contrary to his very nature. He must react against it or he wouldn't be God—he'd be the devil. Consequently, God displays his righteous indignation, his wrath, against sin. The preflood civilization progresses to the point of no return; the only remedy is to destroy it and start over. Like a surgeon dealing with a completely mangled leg, God must amputate in order to save the patient. It would do no good to utter benign platitudes and earnest exhortations to be better and do better. He must judge sin summarily and decisively in order to redeem fallen humanity. And that is what he did.[23]

21. Chapters three and four will explore God's holiness in more depth.
22. Lev 1.
23. The two sequel stories to the flood (Noah's drunkenness and the Tower of Babel)

The wrath of God is a muted theme in modern theology and most pulpits. It is, however, a prominent theme in both Testaments of the Bible. To be sure, there have been theologians and churchmen who wanted to jettison the OT and emphasize only the New. In their opinion, the OT pictures God as wrathful and vengeful, a sub-Christian view. For others, it's simply too negative and obscures the love and forgiveness of God.

Theologians struggle to understand God's wrath and so do ordinary Bible readers. Is God's wrath a settled aspect of his personality? Or is it a momentary fit of rage that comes over him? Is wrath an attribute of God like his power and love? The ancient Greeks compounded the problem by thinking that wrath was either a sign of irrationality or weakness. When early Christian theologians in the post-NT era tried to harmonize Greek thought with the Bible, this presented a problem. How could they be faithful to the biblical view of God and yet admit that God was either irrational or occasionally displayed a character defect? This may partially explain why an early churchman named Marcion (ca. AD 140) rejected the OT, with its supposedly sub-Christian view of God, and excluded it from his list of sacred Scriptures. The church roundly rejected Marcion's approach and he was banished for his efforts.

But some Christian theologians, overly influenced by Greek philosophy, went to another extreme. In order to protect God from any defect, they reasoned that God was impassible, that is, he doesn't experience emotions at all. When the Bible speaks of God showing emotion—and it does this a lot—this should be understood as a literary convention called anthropopathism (from *anthropos*, man and *pathos*, passion). Thus God is described *as if* he experiences emotions and feelings like human beings and the biblical passages in which such depictions occur are said to be accommodations to the limitations of mere mortals.

The issue of anthropopathism is related to the larger question of God's immutability. Does God change? For Aristotle, behind everything stands the unmoved mover, the first cause of all causes. Aristotle's unmoved mover was immutable and therefore impassible. Some Christian theologians followed suit: God too is immutable and therefore impassible. The reasoning is that the first cause of all things can't experience any real change without

---

make a common point. The great flood didn't wash away sin from the human race. On the contrary, sin is deeply embedded in the very nature of humanity. The important thing to observe is the institution of human government as an absolutely essential institution for preventing a return to the anarchy of the preflood generation. For further discussion see Helyer, *Yesterday*, 78–84.

ceasing to be the first cause. Aristotelian thought put God in a logical straitjacket. In my view, the Bible presents a truly dynamic, interacting being who, though not changing in his fundamental attributes like self-existence, omnipotence, omniscience, omnipresence, and holiness, does experience emotions and does change in his response to human attitudes and actions. I feel much more secure praying to a heavenly Father, in whose image I exist as a self-conscious, rational, feeling and deciding being, rather than to an impersonal ground of all being or unmoved mover.

"But Noah found favor in the eyes of the Lord" (Gen 6:8). This has to be one of the great verses of the Bible. So much packed into a little. God does something that no one else in the universe can: he exercises mercy and justice with perfect concord and equilibrium. Think of what happens when one or the other is absent or imbalanced. Mercy without judgment lapses into sentimentalism. Sentimentalism can only wring its hands and lament, "How sad!" Judgment without mercy is indifferent to the human plight. It allows spiritual cripples no space for repentance and restoration and can only intone: "How bad!" One of the supreme glories of Christian faith is to be able to proclaim a God who perfectly embodies the two essential attributes of mercy and justice: "How glad!" We survived as a race because of it and our hope for the future depends on it.

Living under the Sign of the Rainbow

In the aftermath of the flood, God gives assurance that never again will he destroy the earth by means of a flood. This promise, a binding obligation the Creator willingly assumes, is ratified by a marvelous phenomenon now regularly appearing in earth's atmosphere. The shimmering rainbow serves as a perennial reminder of God's character. God is merciful and just. God's covenants all demonstrate outward signs that speak of inward spiritual realities. For example, the Abrahamic covenant featured the outward sign of male circumcision.[24] The Sinai covenant featured the paschal lamb and Sabbath.[25] The new covenant has two signs: water baptism and the Lord's Supper. These simple but evocative actions symbolize profound spiritual realities: new birth and a new covenant community created through the body and blood of Jesus.

---

24. Gen 17:9–14.
25. Exod 12; 20:8–11; 23:12.

Mountaintop Theology

Every time you see a rainbow in the sky, a short word of thanksgiving is in order: God is merciful and his mercy endures forever.[26] And Abraham's question receives an affirmative answer: "Will not the Judge of all the earth do right?" (Gen 18:25). Yes, you can count on it! He punishes sin but provides a sacrifice for sinners: wrath and mercy embrace in perfect harmony.

The rainbow is a fitting symbol for God's entire redemptive activity, but it's especially appropriate for the new covenant.[27] The new covenant, anticipated by Jesus on the evening of the Last Supper and inaugurated the next afternoon on the cross, stands under a resplendent rainbow. That is, from our vantage point in redemptive history, as we look backwards to Mount Calvary, a glorious rainbow appears above the cross.

At the time Jesus was crucified, of course, no such rainbow appeared: "When it was noon, darkness came over the whole land until three in the afternoon" (Mark 15:33). For a while, Jesus even felt utterly abandoned by God: "My God, my God, why have you forsaken me?" (Mark 15:34). The Apostles Peter and Paul bring us as close to the meaning of this profound mystery as is humanly possible: "He himself bore our sins in his body on the cross, so that, free from sins, we might live for righteousness" (1 Pet 2:24). "God made him who had no sin to be sin for us, so that in him we might become the righteousness of God" (2 Cor 5:21).

Jesus didn't die a disappointed and despairing man. The Gospels are quite clear on that point. Mark tells us that just before he died, "Jesus gave a loud cry and breathed his last" (Mark 15:37). But Dr. Luke sets our minds at ease. Before he died, Jesus said: "Father, into your hands I commend my spirit" (Luke 23:46). These aren't the words of a derelict. The Apostle John, who was present at the foot of the cross, heard the very last words of Jesus: "It is finished" (John 19:30). These aren't the words of a defeated man; they're the words of a victor! Just read John's gospel and the book of Revelation—you'll be convinced.

The sun came up on the first day of the week; the age of resurrection began that morning (Mark 16:2; 1 Cor 15:20–24). So now a rainbow adorns the cross. The rainbow continually reminds us of God's character and how he puts sinners right with himself. Under the new covenant mercy and justice come together and the cross is where they embrace. There believers are

---

26. Ps 136.

27. On the meaning of the rainbow in redemptive history, see Branch, "Rainbow," 667–68.

the recipients of mercy beyond reckoning. The chorus of a hymn captures the truth:

> Mercy there was great, and grace was free,
> Pardon there was multiplied to me;
> There my burdened soul found liberty—At Calvary.[28]

But there too God acts justly and pours out his wrath on sin: "God presented Christ as a sacrifice of atonement, through the shedding of his blood—to be received by faith. He did this to demonstrate his justice at the present time, so as to be just and the one who justifies those who have faith in Jesus" (Rom 3:25–26, NIV). And because of that we have confidence in "Jesus, who rescues us from the wrath that is coming" (1 Thess 1:10). We no longer live in dread of God's wrath.[29] The reason is truly good news: "We have peace with God through our Lord Jesus Christ" (Rom 5:1) and "there is therefore now no condemnation for those who are in Christ Jesus" (Rom 8:1). Grace, a twin of mercy, punctuates the NT and is sometimes paired with mercy and peace. The latter results from the former two and together they constitute a trinity of blessings: "Grace, mercy and peace from God the Father and Christ Jesus our Lord" (1 Tim 1:2; 2 Tim 1:2). Fittingly, the Apostle John, when describing his vision of the heavenly throne room, draws attention to this particular detail: "around the throne is a rainbow that looks like an emerald" (Rev 4:3).

---

28. Lyrics by William R. Newell, "At Calvary."
29. Rom 1:18; 2:5.

2

Mount Moriah and Mount Golgotha

Understanding the Cross

"God himself will provide the lamb for a burnt offering, my son." (Gen 22:8)

Introduction

WE CLIMB TWO MOUNTAINS in this chapter. Once again, I need to make a qualification. Folks who live in mountainous regions of the world must readjust their thinking. In terms of elevation, Mount Moriah and Mount Calvary are scarcely mountains. Compared to Mount Ararat, these two mountains are mere molehills. After all, they only rise to about 2,500 feet—hardly nosebleed height! No need for oxygen, mountain climbing gear, or any special preparations whatsoever. In fact, more than a million people visit the site annually.[1] And yet, these twin peaks offer a spiritual panorama unequaled among the mountains we climb.

Locating Mount Moriah and Mount Calvary

First, let's get our bearings: Where are these two mountains located and what happened there that significantly shaped salvation history?

---

1. The Central Bureau of Statistics and Tourism Ministry in Israel tallied 3.5 million tourists in 2013 and 3.4 million in 2014, despite the Gaza War. Of this number, a majority visits Jerusalem.

Mount Moriah

Geographical Setting

As was the case with Mount Ararat, the first time the Bible mentions a place called Moriah, it actually refers to "the land of Moriah" (Gen 22:2). In this vicinity, Abraham climbs to the summit of a ridge or hilltop and prepares to sacrifice his son. In biblical tradition, this high point was later called Mt. Moriah, the location of Solomon's splendid temple.[2] The episode narrated in Genesis 22, the near-sacrifice of Isaac, is, by any reckoning, one of the most powerful and poignant stories in Scripture. But before unpacking it, we need a little more background on the location itself.[3]

Mount Moriah is most likely the summit of a ridge surrounded on three sides by deep valleys, or *wadis*, as they're called in Arabic. On the east is the Kidron Valley; on the south and curving around to the west is the Valley of Ben Hinnom. Slicing between these two valleys is an intermediate valley, during NT times called the Tyropoeon Valley, traditionally understood to mean "the valley of the cheese makers."[4] This intermediate valley separates Moriah from the higher western hill on which lies the present day Old City of Jerusalem, compacted into a maze of narrow streets and alleys.

Below and to the south of Mount Moriah lies the ancient City of David. Visitors are surprised—and perhaps a bit disappointed—to learn that the storied capital of the United Kingdom of Israel isn't even within the Old City walls! These walls actually date back to the period of the Ottoman Turks. In the sixteenth century AD, the Ottoman Sultan, Suleiman the Magnificent, ordered the reconstruction of Jerusalem's walls (AD 1537–41). His chief engineer decided to leave out the area of the ancient City of David (a decision which cost the engineer his head, by the way!), and so, we have this strange happenstance: the earliest and most famous portion of the city now

---

2. 2 Chr 3:1. The elevation of this site, the so-called Temple Mount, is 2,435 feet (courtesy of Google Earth).

3. See map 2 in the appendix.

4. This designation comes from the first century Jewish historian, Flavius Josephus (*Jewish War* 5.4.1). Ronny Reich argues that the place name really means "the Valley of the Tyrians," named after a community of Phoenicians from the city of Tyre (located in modern Lebanon, not far from the northern border of Israel). Solomon employed Tyrians in the construction of the First Temple (1 Kgs 5) and, in the time of Nehemiah, Tyrians sold fish in Jerusalem on the Sabbath (Neh 13:16). In light of that, there was probably a colony of expatriate Tyrians living in this area of Jerusalem, thus bequeathing their name to this venerable city. Reich, *Excavating the City of David*, 327–28.

lies outside the walls. Actually, this oversight has an upside. Archaeologists have been able to excavate a few areas in the City of David and have made some exciting discoveries, which probably wouldn't have been possible had it been incorporated into Suleiman's Jerusalem.

Historical Importance of Mount Moriah

Here are the salient historical facts for our climb. Near the end of his storied career, King David purchased the area from Araunah the Jebusite. The high point had previously served as Araunah's threshing floor.[5] Exposed to the prevailing westerly winds, it provided an ideal location for winnowing the chaff from the grain. David laid plans for building a magnificent temple in which Yahweh, the God of Israel, would be honored as the one, true, and living God.

As narrated in 1 Kings 6–8, Solomon constructed and dedicated the First Temple. It stood on the summit of Mount Moriah from about 967 BC until August 14, 586 BC, when it was burned to the ground by the Babylonian army of Nebuchadnezzar. On the ruins of the First Temple, a small Jewish remnant, led by Zerubbabel and Joshua, dedicated the Second Temple on March 12, 516 BC.[6] This temple, enhanced by the Hasmoneans (ca. 142 BC–63 BC)[7] and greatly enlarged and adorned by Herod the Great, beginning in 20 BC—though still not completely finished in Jesus' day—stood until AD 70.[8] On *Tish'ah b'av* (the ninth of Av, occurring in either July or August according to the Jewish calendar), Roman legionnaires burnt it to the ground. This was part of Titus's sack of Jerusalem, the coup de grâce

---

5. 2 Sam 24:18–25; 1 Chr 21:18–22:1.

6. Ezra 6:15–22.

7. This is the name of a priestly family that led the Jewish resistance movement against the attempt of Antiochus IV to stamp out Judaism and Hellenize Jews during the crisis of 175 BC–167 BC. Mattathias had five sons who followed his exhortation to resist the Hellenizing program. They are sometimes called the Maccabees after a nickname given one of the sons, John. Maccabeus probably means something like "hammer" and aptly describes the violent character of his resistance. These brothers successfully led a revolt that, remarkably, succeeded in gaining political freedom. The book of 1 Maccabees is essential reading for background on this turbulent period. Two of the sons, Simon and Jonathan, also served as high priests. They thus combined political and religious leadership roles, a move that set off dissent and division within the Jewish community. Because they weren't from the priestly line of Zadok, some priests and laypersons rejected this usurpation of the high priesthood. See further, Helyer, "The Hasmoneans," 38–53.

8. John 2:20.

Mount Moriah and Mount Golgotha

that crushed the first Jewish revolt against Rome. No Jewish temple has stood on this site since.[9]

There is, however, a splendid Islamic shrine, the Dome of the Rock, dating back to the seventh century AD, standing on precisely the same location as the First and Second Temples.[10] The area on which this shrine stands is considered holy to the three monotheistic faiths: Judaism, Christianity, and Islam.

Not surprisingly, given the Middle Eastern conflict between Israel and her Arab neighbors, especially the Palestinians—the majority of whom are Muslims—great tension surrounds the site today. Access to the Temple Mount, as Jews refer to it, or the *al Haram al-Sharif* ("the Noble Sanctuary"), as Muslims call it, is strictly regulated. For non-Muslims, access to the *Haram* is restricted to certain days and hours and no non-Muslim prayers are allowed. Also, the Muslim religious council in charge of the *Haram*, the *Waqf*, remains vigilant against visitors focusing on the *alleged* first and second temples. Their official stance flies in the face of reality: they flatly deny there ever was a Jewish temple on the site.

Of course, Christians are drawn to this site because of Jesus' association with it. From the Gospels, the following incidents come to mind:

- Jesus was dedicated in the Second Temple precincts and proclaimed as the promised Messiah by Simeon and Anna (Luke 2:22– 38).
- He regularly visited it as a child and confounded the religious teachers by his wisdom when he was twelve (Luke 2:41–47).
- He was tempted by the devil on a high point of the temple (Matt 4:5).[11]
- He denounced the money changers and purchasing policies of the High Priests and Sadducees who had jurisdiction over its precincts (Mark 11:15–17).

---

9. There is some evidence that Bar Kochba may have erected some sort of edifice on the site during the Second Revolt against Rome (AD 132–135) since sacrifices were offered on an altar in that area. See Mare, *Archaeology*, 205–7.

10. Some contest this point. For a convincing demonstration that the Dome of the Rock does indeed rest over the site of the Jewish temples, see Ritmeyer, *Secrets*, 65–97.

11. This high point was probably a tower or parapet from which a priest blew a trumpet signaling the beginning of evening and other religious feasts such as the new moon. A portion of a platform with a Hebrew inscription reading "to the place of trumpeting" was found by archaeologists excavating at the foot of the western wall. See Murphy-O'Connor, *Holy Land*, 112.

- He regularly taught in its porticoes when he visited Jerusalem during religious festivals (John 2:13–25; 5:1; 7:14; Luke 19:47).
- He healed people there who were blind and lame (Matt 21:14).
- He prophesied its total destruction: "not one stone here will be left on another; every one will be thrown down" (Matt 24:1–2).
- In the temple precincts, Jesus prophesied that his physical body, likened to a temple, would be raised up after its destruction, that is, after his death on the cross (John 2:19–21).

After the Second Jewish Revolt (AD 132–35), Hadrian built a pagan temple, Jupiter Capitolinus, on the site of the Second Temple. Jerome tells us that Hadrian erected a statue of himself on horseback on the very site of the Holy of Holies.[12] This structure was probably removed when Byzantine Christians assumed control of the area (ca. AD 324). Eusebius (ca. AD 325) mentions that the Temple Mount lay in ruins and stones were regularly pillaged and reused in other construction projects. In AD 560, however, the Byzantine emperor Justinian built a basilica style church to the south of the temple site named the Church of St. Mary. In AD 710, after the Islamic conquest of Palestine, the Muslims converted it into a mosque and named it *al Aqsa*.[13] The cross atop the church was replaced with a golden crescent, a symbol of Islam.[14]

Prior to this, however, in about 690 AD, Caliph Abd al-Malik built the beautiful Dome of the Rock, directly over the site of the Second Temple, sending a clear message of the superiority of Islam over both Judaism and Christianity. According to Islamic tradition, Muhammad ascended to heaven from the rock now lying beneath the gilded dome of this shrine.

---

12. Cited in Mare, *Archaeology*, 214.

13. The Arabic name means "at the farthest" and has been taken to mean that by this time the mosque at Jerusalem was reckoned as the third most holy site of Islam after Mecca and Medina. This interpretation, however, has been challenged by researchers who claim that this understanding can't be documented prior to the 1930s, during the time of the Mufti of Jerusalem, Amin al-Haj. They claim he invented this interpretation as part of an ideological and propaganda struggle against the Zionists.

14. Peretz Reuben claims that the *al Aqsa* mosque may have actually reused cedar beams from the Second Temple and even the First Temple. See Reuven, "Wooden Beams," 40–47. See also a YouTube video of some beams that may be remnants of these beams being burned at the Golden Gate area. Online: http://www.israelnationalnews.com/News/News.aspx/161686#.ULeSlYZgEok.

An indentation on the rock formation is revered as the very footprint of Muhammad.[15]

When the Crusaders invaded the Holy Land and recaptured Jerusalem for Christendom in AD 1099, they converted the Dome of the Rock into a church and called it the *Templum Domini* ("Temple of the Lord"). The Knights Templar (you may recall the sensational and erroneous allegations made about them in the book and movie, *The Da Vinci Code*), were entrusted with the protection and maintenance of this holy site and it became their headquarters. But the Muslims under Saladin reconquered the Holy City (*al Quds* in Arabic) in 1187 and expelled the Crusaders. They tore down the cross and once again raised the golden crescent over the Dome of the Rock and *al Aqsa*. These two structures remain to this day, though not without repeated refurbishing, remodeling, and repairs.[16]

Mount Calvary (Golgotha)

The Temple Mount, however, is not the prime attraction for most Christian tourists. Instead, they gather at the Garden Tomb or cram into the Church of the Holy Sepulcher, two rival sites for the place of Jesus' crucifixion, burial, and resurrection. Herein lies a long-standing controversy. In the NT, the site of Jesus' crucifixion was known in Aramaic as Golgotha, the hill of the skull.[17] It was a morbid place, a place of execution located outside the city

---

15. It is quite clear that Abd al Malik was not dependent upon the tradition that Muhammad ascended to heaven at this location. That was a later tradition. Rather, he was countering Jewish and Christian truth claims by taking over this holy site and Islamizing it. This was the first public attempt by Islam to project their ideology through architecture. Remember that at this time magnificent basilicas and religious structures graced Jerusalem and the Holy Land. In order to counter the propaganda value of such buildings, Islam launched a new era in its history by emphasizing through tangible, visual evidence the triumph of Islam over its two predecessors. One subtle way this was achieved was by building a mosque near a Christian holy site with its minaret higher than the church's dome. Thus, for example, the minarets of both mosques flanking the Church of the Holy Sepulcher soar higher than the church. Another was through even more magnificent architecture and art. Ironically, Abd al Malik and succeeding caliphs often adapted and borrowed Christian techniques and even employed Christian architects and artists in constructing their shrines and mosques.

16. For a brief survey of the many refurbishings, see Beatrice St. Laurent, "The Dome of the Rock and the Politics of Restoration," bridgew.us/Review/Archives/1998/December/dome.htm.

17. Matt 27:33; Mark 15:52; John 19:17.

walls.[18] The name "Calvary" comes from the Latin translation of Golgotha, *Calvaria* ("skull"). According to John's gospel, there was a garden nearby.[19] But precisely where was it?

Church of the Holy Sepulcher

The first candidate, the Church of the Holy Sepulcher, sits a mere quarter of a mile to the west of the Temple Mount, on the slightly higher western hill of the Old City.[20] In its favor is the weight of Christian tradition. In AD 326 local Christians identified this area as the place of the crucifixion and resurrection. Accordingly, Constantine built a magnificent rotunda, open courtyard, and basilica as a memorial and place of worship. Modern archaeological excavations and soundings have confirmed that, in the first century AD, the site was indeed outside the city walls and functioned both as a rock quarry and garden.[21] Today, the Greek Orthodox, Roman Catholics, Armenians, Syrian Orthodox, Copts, and Ethiopians grudgingly share portions of this complex and confusing structure. The cacophony of sounds, clouds of incense, and garish décor are a bit much for most Protestants.

Gordon's Calvary and the Garden Tomb

In the nineteenth century, when Protestants began in earnest to explore the Holy Land, Otto Thenius (1842) and Claude Conder (1879) suggested that a rocky eminence overlooking and just east of the modern Garden Tomb was a more appropriate site for the crucifixion. Then in 1867, Conrad Schick, another Protestant, discovered the Garden Tomb. Because as yet there was no evidence that the Church of the Holy Sepulcher rested outside the city walls in the first century and, owing to dislike of Roman Catholicism, many Protestants fastened on to the new location. This preference was strengthened in 1883 by the advocacy of the famous British general Charles Gordon.[22] In 1894 a group of British Protestants formed the Garden Tomb

18. Matt 27:32; John 19:17; Heb 13:12.

19. John 19:41.

20. According to Google Earth, the elevation of the Holy Sepulcher is just over 2,500 feet. See map 2 in the appendix.

21. See Wilkinson, ed., *Egeria's Travels*, 39–46 for diagrams and discussion.

22. Gordon's arguments are based more on sentiment and mysticism than archaeology and geography. See Frantzman and Kark, "General Gordon."

Association to promote this location and to this day it remains one of the most frequently visited sites in the Holy Land. Indeed, the Garden Tomb does provide a wonderful setting in which to meditate and worship.

Probable Location

But let me cut to the chase. The Church of the Holy Sepulcher has stronger support. The combination of early tradition and modern archaeological findings tip the scales in its favor. The Garden Tomb has a major problem: the tomb shown as Jesus' tomb actually dates back to the time of the kings of Judah, Iron Age II in archaeological terminology.[23] The Gospels state that Jesus was buried in a *new* tomb that had not been used.[24] It's hard to imagine that Joseph of Arimathea's new tomb departed from the standard type used in the Second Temple period and reverted back to a type used centuries earlier in the Iron Age.[25]

Significance

The significance of this place for Christians can hardly be overestimated. It is literally and spiritually the bedrock of our faith. As you enter this venerable church and turn right, you ascend stone steps leading up to a chapel perched fifteen feet above the main floor level, on top of a rock formation. This is the chapel of Golgotha. Christian tradition identifies this site as the place of the crucifixion. Descending from Golgotha, you proceed to the very center of the basilica, beneath the refurbished rotunda ceiling. Here stands an ornate structure, called the aedicule. This carved stone and marble edifice is flanked and bedecked by numerous incense censers, candles, and icons. Inside is the single most holy site of Christendom: the empty tomb of Jesus. If you've never visited it, I hope you'll get the opportunity, if only for a brief moment of prayer and meditation. You'll never get closer to where it really happened than right there.[26]

---

23. Barkay, " Garden Tomb"; Bahat, "Holy Sepulchre Church."
24. Matt 26:60; Luke 23:53; John 20:41 [italics mine].
25. See Mare, *Archaeology*, 185–89; Ritmeyer, *Jerusalem*, 57–63.
26. For a virtual tour of this revered church that takes you back in time from the present structure to the reconstructed garden tomb, see www.proterrasancta.org/holy-sepulchre-a-3d-journey-back-in-time/.

Theologically Understanding Mount Moriah and Mount Calvary

It's time to take a spiritual climb up these two mountains and catch a vision of the theological landscape that stretches out before our eyes. Mt. Moriah is forever linked to the story of Abraham's near-sacrifice of Isaac, called the "binding of Isaac" in Jewish tradition. In order to make sense of this troubling, mysterious story, you need to see it in the context of the entire Abraham cycle of stories narrated in Genesis 12–25.

Literary Setting of the Binding of Isaac

The Abraham cycle of stories (Gen 11:27—25:11) is a skillfully told obstacle story. That is, the plot revolves around a series of crises each of which threatens to undermine a grand promise given to Abraham right at the outset of the story.[27] In Gen 12:1–3, 7, the Lord essentially promises Abram three things:[28]

- An heir and many descendants
- A heritage
- An inheritance

The Lord promises Abram that he will become a great nation and the father of many nations.[29] In fact, his descendants will be as numerous as the stars in the sky and the grains of sand along the seashore.[30] The Lord promises Abram a priceless privilege: to know the true and living God and to be a channel of blessing for all the nations.[31] He also promises to give Abram's descendants the land of Canaan, later granted to them as an everlasting possession.[32]

These glowing promises are repeatedly threatened. Crises arise in which the promise is cast in doubt. Abraham and Sarah must simply trust

27. See further Helyer, "Abraham's Eight Crises."

28. Abram is his name as we initially meet him in the biblical narratives. It means "exalted father." Later the Lord changes his name to Abraham, "father of a multitude," in keeping with the Lord's promises to him (Gen 17:5).

29. Gen 12:2; 17:5.

30. Gen 15:5; 22:17.

31. Gen 12:2–3.

32. Gen 12:7; 17:8.

that the Lord will fulfill what at times seems humanly impossible. In fact, in Gen 18:14, a question by the Lord himself brings us to the real heart of the entire cycle of stories: "Is anything too hard for the Lord?"[NIV] Abram sometimes wavers and he doesn't always come out smelling like a rose, but the Lord is faithful. Several times the Lord intervenes and bails Abram out of a jam. In my view, the Abraham cycle goes through a series of eight crises:

- Famine in the land and a descent to Egypt where Pharaoh takes Sarah as a wife (Gen 12:10–13:1).
- Lot, Abram's apparent heir, separates and strikes out on his own outside the land of promise (Gen 13:2–18).
- Abram intervenes in a Middle Eastern war and risks retaliation (Gen 14:1–16).
- Abram accepts Sarah's advice and tries to secure an heir by means of a concubine (Gen 16:1–16).
- Abimelech takes Sarah into his harem about the time she is pregnant with Isaac (Gen 20:1–18).
- Abraham disinherits Ishmael and makes Isaac the sole heir (Gen 21:8–14).
- The Lord asks for Isaac back as a burnt offering (Gen 22:1–19).
- Abraham acquires a bride for Isaac to continue the line of promise (Gen 24).

In the midst of these crises, the Lord reaffirms his basic promise six times. The result is that Abraham and Sarah live out their lives in the tension between promise and fulfillment. They must cling to the promise as they face ever-new crises. In the end, Abraham and Sarah demonstrate a faith that endures. This is a major purpose of the cycle of narratives. Abraham and Sarah serve as role models; not perfect but persevering.

Our interest centers on crisis seven in Genesis 22. Fitting that it should be number seven—seven is a number that is often used with symbolic significance to represent what is complete or perfect. In this case, we have a crisis that is completely mystifying! The Lord commands Abraham to sacrifice his only son, Isaac. The story is like a blow to the solar plexus. It comes out of nowhere, completely unexpected. Our immediate response is: You're kidding me! How could the Lord do such a thing! You may recall we had a similar reaction to the story of the flood. This story too requires patient rereading and reflection. There has to be an explanation for the unthinkable. But what is it?

If the art of good storytelling lies in omission, this story is as good as it gets. Questions surge to the surface. But the narrator won't permit access into the inner thoughts of the leading characters. These can only be inferred from their actions and brief snippets of dialogue. In order to appreciate this story, each detail must be examined and then plugged back into the whole, since each piece only makes sense when seen in relation to the whole. And, as I will argue, the whole includes the whole Bible.

The narrator informs the reader what this episode is all about. It's a test. And what a test it is! Of course, Abraham doesn't know this. So, as disturbing as the incident is, at least the reader knows what's going down. Once again, you, the reader, are called upon to exercise faith that the Lord always does the right thing, even if the evidence seems contrary.

The Lord directly summons him: "Abraham!" Then the Lord commands him: "go to the region of Moriah." This reminds us of Abram's initial call to leave his fatherland.[33] In both instances, the Hebrew is *lekh lekha* (literally "go for yourself!"). Both summons require an extraordinary act of commitment. Leaving one's family and sacrificing one's only son, the heir, are unthinkable in ancient Near Eastern culture. Western culture doesn't think twice about the former, but the latter turns our stomach. In both cases, however, Abraham responds promptly. No remonstrance; no request for restatement in view of possible misunderstanding or mishearing; no attempt to bargain with the Lord —as was the case earlier with Sodom and Gomorrah.[34] Abraham set out early the next morning (Gen 22:3).

There can be no doubt what is demanded. The words are painfully clear. They permit no equivocation. "Offer him there as a burnt offering" (Gen 22:2). Archaeological evidence confirms that Canaanites occasionally sacrificed their firstborn children. At Canaanite sites in the Holy Land, jars with tiny infant skeletons have been found and they clearly didn't die of natural causes. This depraved practice was part of a warped conception concerning how the deity relates to human beings. In order to secure blessings such as many children, fruitful seasons, and protection from enemies, Canaanites sought to demonstrate their devotion to their god by giving their firstborn in sacrifice. This act of supererogation was calculated to

---

33. Gen 12:1.
34. Gen 18.

Mount Moriah and Mount Golgotha

place the deity under obligation. The deity must reward such commitment. In truth, it's nothing more than crude magic, a genie-in-a-bottle religion. In Latin there's a phrase that well describes this twisted mentality: *Do ut des.* "I do [this] in order that you may do [this for me]." In short, the worshiper says, "You owe me one."

Some scholars think our story is really a tale designed to reinforce a prohibition against child sacrifice in ancient Israel. Surely, something much more profound is going on than that. Child sacrifice was never required of loyal worshipers of Yahweh. He doesn't delight in this kind of monstrous ritual.[35] But doesn't the story say just the opposite? I don't think so. Let me further unpack the story and make my case.

The narrative art of this story is exquisite. With a bare minimum of words, the narrator sketches a scene of rising emotional intensity. A build-up of words and phrases identify Isaac:

- your son
- your only son
- Isaac (whose name ironically means "laughter")
- whom you love

These are like nails driven into the heart. What was going through Abraham's mind? Try to imagine the anguish of his heart. The reader is forced to climb the mount with Abraham, step by tortuous step. The cadence and phrasing of the story in Hebrew (and even in English translation) builds to the incredible climax. At the very last moment, after it's clear Abraham is going through with it, a substitute ram is provided.

Did Abraham inform Sarah about this strange command from Yahweh? No way! She would defend her beloved Isaac to the death. Did Abraham let his servants in on what was going down? Once again, it's unthinkable. They too would have vigorously protested and defended Isaac the heir apparent against an old man who had suddenly gone daft. No, this terrible assignment must be carried out alone. Only a father and his beloved son ascend Mount Moriah *together*.

Isn't there something haunting in the fact that Isaac carries on his back the wood for the sacrifice? Does Isaac suspect something sinister when he inquires of his father: "Father! . . . The fire and wood are here . . . but where is the lamb for a burnt offering?" (Gen 22:7). Abraham's response is difficult

---

35. Isa 57:4–5; Jer 32:35; Ezek 16:20–21.

to measure: "God himself will provide the lamb for a burnt offering, my son" (Gen 22:8). Was this just Abraham's way of keeping Isaac in the dark until the last possible moment? Or was this an amazing act of faith on Abraham's part. Somehow, some way, the Lord will provide. I think it was the latter.

There's another feature to the story that's hard to fathom. Why doesn't Isaac protest or resist or beg his father to change his mind? He's mute; he's passive. It doesn't make sense; it seems surreal. Isaac completely trusts his father's intentions.

The Story Behind the Story

Haven't we heard this story before? Don't we hear echoes of something familiar? There's more going on here than meets the eye. This is a preview of another father and son drama that will unfold just a short distance away on Mount Calvary. In both cases, a father gives up an only son, a well-beloved son. Just as Isaac carried the wood on which he would be consumed, so Jesus carried his cross.[36] And just as Isaac doesn't resist his father, so Jesus is silent before his accusers[37] and entrusts himself completely to his father while on the cross.[38] The similarities can hardly be a coincidence. In short, the story of Isaac anticipates the story of Jesus.

My attempt to make sense of this episode relies on typology. Typology is a method of biblical interpretation that demonstrates how the Old and NTs form one, connected story. It sees intentional associations between persons, things, events, and institutions that link both Testaments. These typological links are not mere fabrications; they grow out of the very fabric of salvation history. A helpful way of expressing this relationship is to say that certain features of the OT anticipate or foreshadow the person and work of Jesus Christ in the NT. Isaac's near sacrifice on Mount Moriah is a preview of Jesus' actual sacrifice on Mount Golgotha.

I don't think I'm just imagining this typological connection—many ancient and modern Christian interpreters of the Bible affirm this link as well. In fact, if you get an opportunity to visit the Church of the Holy Sepulcher, climb the stairs to the Chapel of Golgotha. To the right, on the south wall of the Latin Chapel, is a striking mosaic depicting Isaac's near sacrifice. The thematic links with Jesus' death are unmistakable and Christians

---

36. John 19:17; Mark 15:21.
37. Mark 14:61; Acts 8:32–35.
38. Luke 23:46.

throughout the generations have heard them resonate in their hearts. The NT encourages us to make precisely this kind of connection. In his wonderful chapter eight of Romans, the Apostle Paul uses language that clearly echoes that of Genesis 22: "What, then, shall we say in response to this? If God is for us, who can be against us? He who did not spare his own Son, but gave him up for us all—how will he not also, along with him, graciously give us all things"(Rom 8:31–32)?

Struggling with the Story

Now I ask some hard ethical and theological questions. Why did the Lord put Abraham through such an emotional wringer? Any parent who tried this in our society today would be locked up for child abuse! Would the Lord ever actually require a parent to sacrifice a child?

No, the Lord will *never* command you to sacrifice a child as Abraham nearly did. This is not to say that you will never experience the most piercing inner pain imaginable—losing a child in death. This *could* happen. In fact, multitudes of parents have suffered this agony. Of course, in the overwhelming majority of cases, the circumstances didn't involve the parent actually delivering an intentional deathblow. My heart goes out to those parents who accidentally kill a child. This has to be one of the most devastating experiences imaginable.

But this isn't the same thing as what Abraham was ordered to do. He was commanded to slay Isaac with his own hand and then burn his body completely. This stops us in our tracks. I'm aware that occasionally mentally deranged parents have actually murdered their children and even burned their bodies afterwards. But no parent in his or her right mind can even contemplate such an act.

So why am I confident that God would never ask you to do what he ordered Abraham to do? The answer goes back to our typological approach. Abraham's experience on Mount Moriah has no counterpart in ordinary history. It was a moment when time and eternity came together. It was a preview of Jesus' death on the cross, *a one time only event in salvation history.* These two unique moments in redemptive history are tightly linked—there will be no repeat performances.

The Lord granted Abraham a preview of the central event of redemptive history. Abraham glimpsed what it would take to atone for the sins of the whole world.³⁹ A father must give up his son in sacrifice. In Genesis 22, the Lord spared Abraham the agony of killing his son Isaac. But God the Father had to let his Son go. What could possibly induce him to do such a thing? I can do no better than cite perhaps the most widely known verse in the Bible:

> For God so *loved* the world that he *gave* his only Son so that everyone who believes in him may not perish but have eternal life." (John 3:16 [italics for emphasis])

We are now staring at a deep mystery. I won't pretend to have answers beyond this stage. I'm reminded of Ben Sira, a Jewish sage of Jerusalem, who said: "Neither seek what is too difficult for you, nor investigate what is beyond your power" (Sir 3:21). Theologians have sought to plumb the depths of the cross but invariably admit they are out of their depth. But all Christians can rejoice and praise God for what is revealed. At the cross, the Lamb of God took away the sin of the world.⁴⁰ The righteous one became sin for us in order that we might become the righteousness of God in him.⁴¹ This great exchange puts us right with God. We can now call God our heavenly Father, Jesus our firstborn brother, and the Holy Spirit our counselor and friend. Because we are in communion with the triune God, we have no fear of his wrath against sin. In Paul's words:

> There is therefore now no condemnation for those who are in Christ Jesus. For the law of the Spirit of life in Christ Jesus has set you free from the law of sin and death." (Rom 8:1–2)

Did Abraham understand what had happened? Perhaps not completely; but I think he grasped the essential meaning. Here's why I think so. In chapter eight of John's gospel, there's an account of a bitter controversy between Jesus and the religious leaders. Not without interest, it takes place in the vicinity of the Second Temple on Mount Moriah. In the midst of swirling debate and acrimonious charges, the Jewish religious leaders insinuate that Jesus is illegitimate.⁴² They proudly boast that they are Abraham's children. To this Jesus replies: "If you were Abraham's children, you would be doing what Abraham did" (John 8:39). Riled, they retort: "Are you greater than our father Abraham, who died? The prophets also died. Who do you claim

---

39. 1 Jn 2:2.
40. John 1:19; 1 Jn 2:2; Rev 5:9–10.
41. 2 Cor 5:21.
42. John 8:41.

to be?" (John 8:53). Jesus' answer shocks them: "Your ancestor Abraham rejoiced that he would see my day; *he saw it and was glad*" (John 8:56 [italics mine]). They can't fathom how this can be: "You are not yet fifty years old," the Jews said to him, "and have you seen Abraham?" (John 8:57). Jesus' answer is a stunner and I think provides an answer to my question: "Very truly, I tell you," Jesus answered, "before Abraham was, I am" (John 8:58).

The pre-incarnate Lord Jesus Christ was already there during Abraham's sojourn in Canaan. He was there on Mount Moriah and saw Abraham's finest hour. He witnessed this exercise of amazing faith and trust. Abraham believed God would provide an offering or, in the case of Isaac's death, raise him from the dead. The author of Hebrews concurs: "He considered the fact that God is able even to raise someone from the dead—and figuratively speaking, he did receive him back" (Heb 11:19). On Mount Moriah, the pre-incarnate Lord previewed his own forthcoming role on Mount Calvary. He is the offering that the Father provides and raises victoriously from the dead. We might say, then, that Abraham participated in a dress rehearsal for the forthcoming performance of the "Greatest Story Ever Told." Yes, God will provide! And Abraham "was glad."

And so are we. God in Christ reconciled us to himself through the death of his beloved Son. I'm quite at a loss to plumb the rationale for this self-giving love. Why was it necessary? Could not another remedy have been found? We try to use analogies to explain this singular event, but in the end, they all seem inadequate and incomplete. A hymn by Frederick M. Lehman perhaps says it best:

> The love of God is greater far
> Than tongue or pen can ever tell;
> It goes beyond the highest star,
> And reaches to the lowest hell . . .
>
> Could we with ink the ocean fill,
> And were the skies of parchment made,
> Were every stalk on earth a quill,
> And every man a scribe by trade,
> To write the love of God above,
> Would drain the ocean dry.
> Nor could the scroll contain the whole,
> Though stretched from sky to sky.

Mountaintop Theology

This must be the only way it could be. I can only accept the benefits of the cross and offer my profoundest thanks for a love that knows no bounds. Mount Moriah and Mount Calvary invite us into the very heart of God.

3

Mount Sinai

Understanding Holiness: Part One

"You shall be holy for I the Lord your God am holy." (Lev 19:2)

Introduction

TWO MOUNTAINS, DRAMATICALLY DIFFERENT in altitude and appearance, confront us in the next two chapters. Though outwardly dissimilar, their theological significance is remarkably similar: both summon believers to a life of holiness.

Holiness is in short supply in Christian circles. Several reasons account for this. For one, there's a good deal of confusion over the meaning and concrete expression of holiness. A second is the perception that it requires far more time and effort to achieve than we're willing to invest. Third, it isn't particularly glamorous or exciting; there are just too many other things we'd rather do. Contemporary Christian discipleship emphasizes activism. That's not necessarily a bad thing; it's just that tangible results tend to trump the intangible notion of holiness. Being rather than doing is not very appealing to most North American Christians. If we're anything, we're doers![1]

---

1. "God did not make us human doings, but human beings" (Jay Kesler, Taylor University chapel address).

Mountaintop Theology

Climbing Mount Sinai and the Mount of Beatitudes is essential because these two peaks provide a panoramic view of holiness. Paradoxically, a new vision of holiness enhances Christian activism.[2]

Problem of Location

Our first task is to locate these two mountains, easier said than done. That they carry enormous theological freight becomes apparent simply by the space in Scripture devoted to what happened or was proclaimed on their summits. No fewer than 63 out of 186 chapters of the Pentateuch (33 percent) feature Mount Sinai as the setting where the Lord established his covenant with Israel and spelled out the terms for relationship in what we call the law of Moses. The Gospel of Matthew devotes three of its twenty-eight chapters to the Sermon on the Mount (approximately 10 percent), chapters that function as the fundamental charter for the new covenant between Christ and his church. Curiously, in spite of the importance of these two sites in redemptive history, their precise locations are contested.

Locating Mount Sinai

Church tradition locates Mount Sinai at Jebel Musa ("mount of Moses") in the southern portion of the Sinai Peninsula, but modern scholarly support for this tradition is far from unanimous: "The problem of identifying the route of the Exodus and Mount Sinai itself is one of extraordinary difficulty, far more difficult than any other problem of Palestinian Biblical Topography."[3] So, what are the options? They fall into three different geographical areas: 1) Saudi Arabia/south Jordan, 2) central/northern Sinai,

---

2. Charles Ringma offers this reflection:
   In our time of religious uncertainty, in this post-Christendom age, we need to recapture the art of waiting, and to emulate the ministry of watchmen. Our descralized world does not, *first of all*, need the ministry of our evangelical activism. It needs the plaintive cry of God's people. It needs the women and men who will, in prayer, probe the heart of God, while discerning the heart of the world. (*Whispers*, 104 [italics mine])

3. Aharoni, "Kadesh-Barnea and Mount Sinai," 118. This is echoed by Beitzel: "Few OT geographical questions have been more vigorously debated than the location of Mt. Sinai," *New Moody Atlas*, 109. See also Horn, "What We Don't Know."

and 3) southern Sinai.⁴ I follow the majority view of historical geographers in placing Mount Sinai in the southern peninsula of Sinai.⁵

As early as the fourth century AD, Christian pilgrims considered Jebel Musa in southern Sinai to be biblical Mount Sinai and I see no good reason to dissent. Egeria, the indefatigable nun from Western Europe, climbed to its summit "where the divine glory itself, God Almighty, condescended to abide whilst Moses was given the holy Law."⁶ She also described a monastery at the foot of Mount Sinai.⁷ In the sixth century, Justinian rebuilt the monastery. Later in the ninth century it was named in honor of Saint Catherine (ca. AD 287–305), a Christian martyr under Roman Emperor Maxentius.

Today, thousands of pilgrims visit the monastery and tread its silent alleys (the monks at the monastery take a vow of silence). The monastery library is world famous for its ancient biblical manuscripts. Taking pride of place is the oldest, extant version of the entire Bible in Greek, the Codex Sinaiticus. Constantin von Tischendorf, a German Christian scholar and explorer, discovered it among discarded manuscripts when visiting the

---

4. For those who are interested in the historical-geographical arguments for and against the proposed locations, see the addendum at the end of this chapter.

5. See Aharoni and Avi-Yonah, *Macmillan Bible Atlas*, 46; Rainey and Notley, *The Sacred Bridge*, 120; Wright, *Greatness*, 18; and Beitzel, *The New Moody Atlas*, 109–113. See map 3 in the appendix.

6. Valerius, a Galician monk, describes her exploit in a seventh-century letter. "[T]his woman, once having heard the voice of the gospel, hastened to the Mount of the Lord, and went, you may be sure, joyfully and without the slightest delay. They, while Moses was receiving the Law of the Lord, could not wait forty days, and made themselves a graven image to take God's place; but she awaiting the Lord's coming as though she could perceive it already, forgot her female weakness, and went on to the holy Mount Sinai. . . . With unflagging steps, and upheld by the right hand of God, she hastened to that beetling summit with its top almost in the clouds; and thus, borne onwards by the power of her holy zeal, she arrived at the rocky mountain-top where the divine glory itself, God Almighty, condescended to abide whilst Moses was given the holy Law. There her joyful exultation burst forth in paeans of prayer, and she offered to God the sacrifices of salvation, and giving heartfelt thanks to his glorious Majesty . . . ." (Wilkinson, ed., *Travels*, 176).

7. Egeria also mentions "the Burning Bush out of which the Lord spoke to Moses . . . . The Bush itself is in front of the church in a very pretty garden which has plenty of excellent water" (ibid., 96). Sure enough, when my wife and I visited the monastery in January of 1969, one of the monks identified a shrub in the courtyard as the burning bush of Moses. This is highly unlikely. Almost certainly, this identification owes more to convenience for pilgrims and tourists than historical fact!

monastery in 1844. This priceless Bible now resides in the British Museum in London.[8]

Jebel Musa is an awesome mountain, a marvelous location for a theophany:

> On the morning of the third day there was thunder and lightning, as well as a thick cloud on the mountain, and a blast of a trumpet so loud that all the people who were in the camp trembled. . . . Now Mount Sinai was wrapped in smoke, because the LORD had descended upon it in fire; the smoke went up like the smoke of a kiln, while the whole mountain shook violently (Exod 19:16, 18).

What makes it so magnificent is its composition and structure: a granite massif that rises almost vertically off the surrounding desert floor. Its twisted granite rocks take on differing hues of russet, orange, red, and mauve, depending on the time of day and the amount of sunlight bathing its slopes.[9] Climbing it before dawn to arrive at the summit by sunrise is an unforgettable experience.[10] It's easy to understand why the Lord chose it as a rendezvous with his people Israel. Here he enters into a covenant with liberated slaves, the descendants of Abraham, Isaac, and Jacob, along with a mixed multitude, and chooses them as his very own people.[11]

Theological Significance of Mount Sinai

The importance of the revelation at Mount Sinai can hardly be overstated. Three monotheistic religions comprising about 54 percent of all the people living on the planet look to Mount Sinai as foundational for their belief

---

8. See Porter, "Hero or Thief?" 45–53, 66.

9. I resonate with Aharoni's description of the entire southern tip of the Sinai peninsula: "The ever-changing, ever-deepening colours of the mountains in this part of Sinai, alike of the Nubian sandstone mountains in the northern section of the range and of the granite peaks in the south, invest this indescribably beautiful region with an aura of sanctity, and one can well believe that here God appeared to Moses" ("Kadesh-Barnea and Mount Sinai," 126).

10. Personally climbing the mountain adds a dimension of realism to the biblical account that is simply unmatched. About halfway up the mountain, one observes a fascinating, twisted rock formation. It requires little imagination to envision it as the place where Moses stood "in a cleft of the rock" as the glory of the Lord passed by (Exod 33:22) and where Elijah "stood at the entrance of the cave" and heard the voice of the Lord (1 Kgs 19:13).

11. Exod 12:38; Num 11:4; Exod 4:22; 19:5–6.

Mount Sinai

concerning God's standard for morality and ethics. For Orthodox Judaism, Moses is the great Teacher and the Torah binds the conscience of observant Jews. Even nontraditional Jews acknowledge the importance of the Torah as a moral and ethical guide. Muslims also accept Moses as a true prophet and so incorporate the essential teachings of the Ten Commandments into their code of ethics. Christians follow their Lord in taking seriously God's revelation to Moses on this mount. Indeed, Jesus' response to implied criticism of his view on the law speaks for itself:

> Do not think that I have come to abolish the law or the prophets: I have not come to abolish but to fulfill. For truly I tell you, until heaven and earth pass away, not one letter, not one stroke of a letter, will pass from the law until all is accomplished. Therefore, whoever breaks one of the least of these commandments, and teaches others to do the same, will be called least in the kingdom of heaven, but whoever does them and teaches them will be called great in the kingdom of heaven. (Matt 5:17–19)

No surprise then that the revelation on Mount Sinai has continuing significance for Christians.

Structure of the Sinai Revelation

Trying to make sense of the Mosaic law is daunting given the large number of detailed prohibitions and prescriptions.[12] According to Jewish tradition, there are 613 commandments in the Pentateuch divided into 365 prohibitions (one for each day of the year!) and 248 positive commandments. Keeping all this in mind is no small undertaking.

As a helpful starting point, carefully note the structure of the book of Exodus. I'm going to suggest that the narrative flow makes a significant theological statement. Here's an outline:

- The Lord liberates his people from bondage (Exod 1–19).
- The Lord delivers to his redeemed people a detailed way of life (Exod 20–23).

---

12. "Most Bible readers make as least one attempt in their lives to read the Bible cover to cover. The enterprise is surprisingly successful at the beginning . . . carried along by the smooth flowing narrative to the feet of Mount Sinai (Horeb) but [they] are then unexpectedly dumped into an incomprehensible heap of case laws and curtain measurements. It is like reading *Moby Dick*, a thrilling narrative, interrupted by a taxonomy of whale species" (Waltke, *OT Theology*, 445).

- The people of Israel agree to enter into a covenantal relationship with the Lord based on these stipulations (Exod 24). They promise: "All the words the Lord has spoken we will do" (24:3).

- The Lord reveals specific directions for constructing the tabernacle in which his presence dwells and he is worshiped (Exod 25–40).

The sequence of the narrative flow isn't coincidental; it's intentional. In other words, it points to the only way one may approach a holy God. You can't skip to point four, the worship part, without first experiencing point one. Only those redeemed from bondage to sin begin the journey of holiness. No shortcuts allowed! Neither can you bypass points two and three. Redemption requires transformation. This is where the Ten Commandments and their elaboration come in. Worship that ignores the divine standards of morality is hypocrisy.[13] The prophets of Israel rail against ritual without righteousness.[14] Only those who commit themselves to the divine standards of righteousness and holiness dare darken the doors of the tabernacle. In principle, what was true then is true now. As the author of Hebrews expresses it: "Make every effort to live in peace with everyone and to be holy; without holiness no one will see the Lord" (Heb 12:14, NIV). Worship without holiness is abhorrent to God.

That brings us to perhaps the most important observation of all. The revelation on Mount Sinai is predicated upon this fundamental theological fact: God is holy and he requires that his people reflect his holiness. Notice how the entire Sinai revelation is framed and punctuated by this enduring reality. It begins at the burning bush episode. Moses is warned: "Come no closer! Remove the sandals from your feet, for the place on which you are standing is holy ground" (Exod 3:5). The song sung after the crossing of the Red Sea strikes the same keynote: "Who is like you, majestic in holiness, awesome in splendor, doing wonders?" (Exod 15:11). Furthermore, this holy God is leading his people to his "holy abode" (Exod 15:13) and during the trek to Mount Sinai they are reminded that the seventh day is "a holy sabbath to the Lord" (Exod 16:23). When the people of Israel finally arrive at the sacred mountain, the Lord announces his agenda for his

---

13. Walter Eichrodt observes that the Decalogue "is the expression of a conviction that moral action is inseparably bound up with the worship of God" (*Theology* 1:76). Waltke agrees: "piety and ethics have priority over external expressions of religion . . . [and are] embedded in the Torah's narrative" (*OT Theology*, 449).

14. Isa 1:12–20; Amos 4:4–5; 5:21–27.

treasured possession: "you shall be for me a priestly kingdom and a holy nation" (Exod 19:6).

But the Lord also reminds Moses: "Set limits around the mountain and keep it holy" (Exod 19:23). The people remain at the foot of the mountain; the priests and seventy elders may come up halfway; but only Moses may ascend to the very presence of the holy God. This same recognition of degrees of holiness is also reflected in the tabernacle in that ritually clean Israelites may enter the courtyard, but not the holy place. The priests perform their ministrations in the holy place, but only the high priest may enter the most holy place, and that but once a year. When we get to the so-called Holiness Code, chapters 17–26 of Leviticus, a repeated refrain runs through the entire section: "You shall be holy, for I the Lord your God am holy" (Lev 19:2). All of this to say that holiness is the most pervasive theme of the revelation of God at Mount Sinai.[15]

Definition of Holiness

Clearly, holiness is essential. But what is it? In the English-speaking world, the word *holy* can be used in a wide range of meaning, especially in slang. If you're a Chicago Cubs fan, you still remember the trademark exclamation of the late, beloved Cubs announcer, Harry Cary: "Holy cow!" On the silver screen, Robin exclaims, "Holy socks, Batman!" And from the movie *Grumpy Old Men* comes this gem: "Holy moly!" These expressions, involving not a little irreverence and euphemism, are unlikely to be helpful in discovering biblical holiness. Adding to the confusion, English speakers occasionally use the word *holy* in a quite negative way. Have you ever criticized someone for acting "holier than thou"? This implies that holiness is next to hypocrisy and thus to be avoided like the plague.

Most often, however, English speakers reserve the word "holy" for sacred realities like the "Holy Bible" or God himself. One thinks of the hymn "Holy, Holy, Holy." Protestants join Catholics and Orthodox Christians in reciting the creed: "I believe in the holy, catholic church." In these contexts, holy or holiness is an attribute belonging to God and to individuals and institutions standing in close association with him. This is a helpful point of departure for our biblical exploration.

---

15. "God preserves holiness at the tabernacle by appointing sacred times for meeting him, a priestly caste who enter his dwelling and sacred rituals for consecrating the priests and the people to worship him" (Waltke, *OT Theology*, 447).

Mountaintop Theology

The Hebrew notion of "holy" or "holiness" (*qodesh*) fundamentally denotes that which is set apart from ordinary, common use and devoted to God and his service. A person, object, location, set time, or institution may thus be set apart and consecrated to God.[16] Priests, through an act of ordination, are set apart for special service to God. Because they serve as mediators between God and people, they are entrusted with the task of ministering in the sanctuary. They both intercede for and bless God's people. To do the former, they stand with their backs to the people, lift up their hands in supplication to heaven, and intercede for the needs of the worshipers. They then turn to face the people and, with arms raised and hands spread open, they bestow God's blessing upon the people.[17] In miniature, this symbolizes what it means to be holy. Holiness entails being a channel of God's blessing to all people: "You shall be my treasured possession out of all the peoples. Indeed, the whole earth is mine, but you shall be for me a priestly kingdom and a holy nation" (Exod 19:5–6).

The Heart of Holiness

The essential core of the Mosaic law is embodied in the Ten Commandments, in Jewish tradition called the "Ten Words," introducing the covenant terms and stipulations.[18] Imagine all the various laws as a series of concentric circles in which the innermost circle is the Ten Words. Everything else is an elaboration and elucidation of these primary moral principles. Further reflection reveals that the character of God underlies these principles; in short, morality is rooted in the essence of who God is. Above all else, God is holy.[19]

Further inspection shows that the Ten Words fall into two main divisions: commandments one through four relate to God; commandments five through ten relate to one's neighbor. It's no surprise that Jesus, when

---

16. Holy refers to "that which is marked off, separated, withdrawn from ordinary use" (Eichrodt, *Theology*, 1:270).

17. Indeed, one of the signs of an old synagogue consists of two outstretched hands above the lintel of the door. This recalls the famous priestly benediction of Num 6:24–26.

18. Exod 20:1–11.

19. "God is considered to be the source of holiness. . . . It is first of all associated with the Lord and can be used almost as a synonym of deity . . . God's holiness thus becomes an expression for his perfection of being that transcends everything creaturely" (Naudé, "קדש," 3:879).

asked to identify the greatest of the commandments, responded with this answer:

> The first is, "Hear, O Israel: The LORD our God, the LORD is one. Love the LORD your God with all your heart and with all your soul and with all your mind and with all your strength." The second is this, "You shall love your neighbor as yourself." There is no other commandment greater than these. (Mark 12:29)

Jesus read the first four commandments as part of loving God; the last six involve loving one's neighbor. This implies that our vertical relationship is fundamental to our horizontal relationship. We can't really love our neighbor without first loving God. And we don't really love God unless we show love to our neighbor. Though the two divisions of the Ten Words are inseparable, the sequence is not accidental.

A moment's reflection makes it abundantly clear that these basic moral principles are still binding on the people of God today. Holiness entails adhering to these fundamental stipulations and adhering is essentially a matter of the heart. This is true in both Testaments. As a matter of fact, the NT reiterates nine of the Ten Commandments.[20] The Sabbath commandment, the only one not restated, is fulfilled in the work of Christ on behalf of his people.[21]

Expressions of Holiness

A sanctuary possesses the quality of holiness because this is where God's presence is especially manifested and where he is approached in worship by his people.[22] It's not a place of ordinary or workaday activity—not intended for idle chitchat, texting, or tweeting. The sanctuary is supremely a place where the vertical relationship with God is reaffirmed and maintained. Central to the sanctuary is the liturgy. Sacred actions set the sanctuary apart from the realm of the secular and give expression to what it means to be set apart as God's holy people.[23]

---

20. Mark 12:28–34; Rom 13:8–10; James 2:8–13.

21. Heb 4:1–13; cf. Rom 14:5–6; Col 2:16.

22. "God's presence determines the location of the sacred sites, not the other way around" (Waltke, *OT Theology*, 459).

23. Brueggemann observes that "the Jerusalem temple was the locus of dramatic activity whereby all of life—cosmic, political, personal—was brought under the rule of Yahweh. In coming under the rule of Yahweh, moreover, all of life was made whole and

Mountaintop Theology

Sacred seasons are those occasions in which the people of God withdraw from the ordinary, common pursuits of life and focus on God's person and works. Worship in a variety of forms characterizes sacred seasons. The Sabbath is in many respects the fundamental sacred season that forces Israel to cease its labors and to reflect on the Creator of all things. In addition, the year is punctuated by three pilgrimage festivals that link the agricultural year with key moments in salvation history:

- Feast of Unleavened Bread (barley harvest and liberation from Egypt)
- Feast of Weeks (wheat harvest and, in later Jewish tradition, the giving of the law at Mount Sinai)
- Feast of Tabernacles (summer fruits and remembrance of Sinai wanderings)

Standing in singular solemnity, the Day of Atonement (Yom Kippur) annually addresses the defilement of the sanctuary by Israel's accumulated inadvertent and unintentional sins. These must be atoned for in order for a holy God to continue to dwell in the midst of his people. It was a time of introspection and confession.

In both the OT and the NT, holiness is cultivated and maintained by regularly meeting with God's people in sacred spaces and in sacred seasons.[24] But holiness in the OT also demands separation. This brings us to the many regulations in the Pentateuch having to do with ritual uncleanness. How do these relate to holiness? This is a very complex and controversial question. I offer a few general observations.

These regulations appear to embody a symbolic world view in which certain material things or conditions mirror spiritual realities.[25] Fundamental for understanding this system is the meaning of "unclean." To be unclean means to be disqualified or unfit to participate in the communal and worship life of Israel; conversely, "clean" means that someone or something is qualified and fit. The words *kasher* or *kosher* convey this meaning in Judaism. The notion of wholeness and integrity lies at the core of these regulations. That which deviates from a cultural, religious norm or standard

---

safe" (*Theology*, 661).

24. See Exod 20:8; 23:14–17; 1 Cor 11:17–34; Heb 10:24–25. "The God of the Christians . . . acts in time and space: his power and his love are encountered by particular people at particular times in particular places" (Hill, *Christianity*, 67).

25. "All these visible things were soaked with symbolic meaning" (Eichrodt, *Theology*, 1:99).

is considered unclean. Related to this is the desire to prevent a mixing of distinct kinds or a blurring of boundaries. This may account for the various food laws, prohibition about wearing garments of mixed origin, and planting one's field with different kinds of crops. Specific occasions rendering one unclean include:

- contact with a corpse (Lev 21:1–12; Num 6:6–12)
- consumption of forbidden food (Lev 11)
- contracting contagious skin diseases (Lev 13)
- processes connected with sexual intercourse and procreation (Lev 12, 15)

Cleanness was restored by following certain actions (such as temporary separation, immersion in water, washing one's clothes, offering a prescribed sacrifice) that qualified those affected to rejoin and participate in the communal life of Israel. For example, sexual intercourse between a husband and wife rendered both of them unclean until the following day and after immersion in water. This meant a regular alternation between unclean and clean for married couples. It should also be noted that it effectively barred Israelites from participating in cultic activities like sacred prostitution as practiced by the Canaanites and other pagans.

Much more could be said on this matter. Here is my take on how the ritual purity system functioned in the OT:

- symbolizes the effects of sin in the world (e.g., death and disease)
- seeks wholeness and integrity in all of life (food, clothing, sex, and work)
- serves to protect the sanctity of Israel from pagan contamination (sacred prostitution, pagan sacrificial practices, and cultic rites for the dead)

OT Holiness and the Christian

This raises a rather important question: Are Christians still required to observe the ritual purity regulations given at Mount Sinai? The short answer is no. Having said that, however, one must next ask, Is there anything of importance to be gleaned from these ordinances? The short answer is yes.

One discerns a clear counterpart in NT ethics and morals.[26] To be sure, the NT transposes ritual impurity into a higher key, namely, spiritual impurity, described as "works of the flesh" (Gal 5:19), "every kind of impurity," (Eph 4:19; Rom 1:24), and "whatever in you is earthly" (Col 3:5). These impurities are understood as the by-product of the nature if sin and inevitably result in a lack of wholeness and integrity.[27] Paul reminds his readers that "the wages of sin is death" (Rom 6:23), a spiritual death that separates one from God.[28] In short, the symbolic world view of the OT points to a profound disordering of human existence, a reality the NT takes with utmost seriousness.

Of course, the NT proclaims the good news that sins have been atoned for in Christ's death on the cross on our behalf and that a response of faith and repentance removes the uncleanness of sin.[29] But even after conversion, failure to maintain the required norm and standard of holiness disrupts fellowship with a holy God and requires heartfelt confession.[30] Trespasses also disrupt harmonious relationships with neighbors, requiring reconciliation to restore fellowship on the horizontal level.[31]

The ongoing theological significance of the ritual purity system lies in its powerful reminder that sin affects all aspects of human existence. The NT, following the teaching of Jesus, locates the problem in the very core of our being, in biblical language, the heart (Mark 7:14–23). What the uncleanness laws required of ancient Israelites was careful discernment and discrimination. They must discern what was clean and unclean, what was permissible and impermissible across a wide range of choices. Many of these regulations served as a prophylactic against pagan practices, protecting the people of God from behaviors that seriously harm and ultimately destroy spiritual life.

The NT significantly modifies but does not entirely jettison the ritual purity system; careful discernment and discrimination are still essential for living a life of holiness. The Apostle Paul prays for the Philippian believers that their "love may abound more and more in knowledge and depth of insight, so that [they] may be able to *discern* what is best and may be pure

---

26. See further Thielman, *Theology*, 291–301.
27. Rom 6:12; 1:18–25; Eph 2:1–3; 1 Pet 4: 2–4.
28. Rom 1:28–32; Eph 2:1–3.
29. 1 Cor 6:9–11.
30. 1 Jn 1:9.
31. Matt 5:23; Jas 5:16.

and blameless until the day of Christ " (Phil 1:9–10 NIV [italics mine]). The author of Hebrews agrees. He defines mature believers as those "who by constant use have trained themselves to *distinguish* good from evil" (Heb 5:14, NIV [italics mine]). The Apostle Peter chimes in with this exhortation: "Like obedient children, do not be conformed to the desires that you formerly had in ignorance. Instead, as he who called you is holy, be holy yourselves in all your conduct; for it is written, 'You shall be holy, for I am holy'" (1 Pet 1:14–16). Finally, the Apostle John makes the same point using his distinctive imagery: ". . . if we walk in the light as he himself is in the light, we have fellowship with one another and the blood of Jesus his Son cleanses us from all sin" (1 Jn 1:7). Make no mistake about it, NT holiness requires precisely what the OT demanded: separation from the unclean (2 Cor 6:17 citing Isa 52:11; Ezek 20:34, 41).[32] The message of Mount Sinai reappears reconfigured on another mountain, our next climb.

Addendum: In Search of the Historical Mount Sinai

Saudi Arabia/South Jordan

On April 18, 1984, Ron Wyatt appeared on the CBS morning news program and announced his discovery of the real Mount Sinai at Jebel al-Lawz in the Saudi Arabian peninsula.[33] In 1998–1999, he was interviewed on *Dateline NBC*, *Larry King Live*, and *The 700 Club*, where he gave further details about his remarkable claim. It was even rumored that Tom Cruise and Sean Penn had signed to star in a movie about this discovery—a rumor that failed to materialize. Wyatt supports his identification with the following arguments and evidence:

- Jebel al-Lawz is the highest peak in western Saudi Arabia rising to 8,465 feet, and the first-century AD historian Josephus says that Mount Sinai was "the highest of all the mountains that are in the country" (*Ant.* 3.5.1 [76]). In contrast, Jebel Musa only reaches 7,363 feet and is even topped by adjacent Jebel Katarin at 8,536 feet.

---

32. Cf. 1 Pet 1:14–16. ". . . [L]ike Israel of old, the Corinthians need to pay careful attention to the boundaries of holiness that God prescribed for his people so that they might be separate from the peoples around them" (Thielman, *Theology*, 291).

33. See the following website for photos and arguments supporting this identification: www.arkdiscovery.com/mt-sinai_found.htm.

Mountaintop Theology

- Jebel al-Lawz lies in the ancient territory of Midian and, according to the Bible, Moses tended the flock of Jethro, "the priest of Midian" (Exod 3:1). Wyatt thus argues that Mount Sinai should be located in Midian (Saudi Arabia), not the Sinai peninsula. Crucial to his case is his contention that the pharaohs of the New Kingdom considered the Sinai peninsula part of Egypt.
- The Apostle Paul says that Mount Sinai is in Arabia and therefore sites in the Sinai peninsula are automatically disqualified (Gal 4:25).
- Jebel al-Lawz gives evidence of volcanic activity with the top 200 feet of its peak appearing to have been scorched black, in keeping with Exod 19:18: "Now Mount Sinai was wrapped in smoke, because the Lord had descended upon it in fire; the smoke went up like that smoke of a kiln, while the whole mountain shook violently."
- Various structures, rock carvings, and unusual features are said to correlate with the biblical narratives about Mount Sinai.

At first glance, Wyatt's arguments carry considerable weight. Even Hershel Shanks, editor of *Biblical Archaeology Review*, inclines toward Jebel al-Lawz as the most probable site for Mount Sinai, a view also held by Frank Moore Cross, one of the foremost experts in ancient Hebrew inscriptions.[34]

On closer examination, however, the biblical and historical-geographical arguments unravel. Several scholars have carefully answered Wyatt's arguments point by point.[35] The reader will find a convenient and concise rebuttal in the *New Moody Atlas*.[36] Here is a summary rebuttal of Wyatt's claim:

- Almost certainly, Josephus himself never visited Mount Sinai. He is relying on the biblical description of Mount Sinai and Jewish traditions. Reflecting a thinly disguised apologetic emphasis in his writings, he enhances the features of the mountain as part of his overall argument for the superiority of the law of Moses over against Greek and Roman philosophical and religious traditions.
- The Midianites were a nomadic people and appear in the biblical narratives in places as far afield as northern Israel, Ammon, Moab, the Negev, and northern Sinai. Moses's pasturing of Jethro's sheep in

---

34. See Shanks, "An Interview."
35. See Franz, "Mount Sinai," 101–13.
36. Beitzel, *New Moody Atlas*, 109–10.

southern Sinai is quite in keeping with this nomadic lifestyle. Furthermore, Wyatt's claim that Sinai was reckoned as part of Egypt is simply wrong, as a close study of Egyptian sources makes clear.[37]

- Paul's mention of Arabia as the location of Mount Sinai fails to take into account that in the first century AD, the term Arabia designated an area stretching from Sinai all the way to the outskirts of Damascus in Syria.

- The language of the Exodus account is theophanic, not geographic. That is, the mention of thunder, lightning, thick clouds, smoke and fire, trumpet blasts, and tremors characterize an appearance of God regardless of where he manifests himself. It should be noted, however, that as recently as 1982 a significant earthquake occurred in the southern Sinai.

- The various geological and geographical features Wyatt appeals to are supported more by vivid imagination than careful examination and often reflect misunderstanding of what they actually are.[38]

Other sites suggested in Saudi Arabia, such as Jebel el-Bedr, Jebel Manita, Jebel Baqir, as well as Petra in Jordan, all share the same shortcomings of Jebel al-Lawz. These sites can only be correlated with the biblical texts, especially the itineraries in Exodus, Numbers, and Deuteronomy, by taking considerable liberties or by ignoring them. In my view, it is highly unlikely that Mount Sinai was located in either Saudi Arabia or southern Jordan.

Northern Sinai

Har Karkom

An Israeli scholar, Emmanuel Anati, identifies Har Karkom in the north-central part of the Sinai Peninsula as the biblical Mount Sinai, about halfway between Kadesh-Barnea and Petra. He bases his proposal on rather doubtful interpretations of some Proto-Sinaitic inscriptions[39] and cultic

---

37. "[A]ncient Egyptian hegemony never extended into south central Sinai" (Beit Arieh, "Route Through Sinai," 28–37).

38. Franz, "Mount Sinai," provides particulars.

39. Most scholars believe these inscriptions are a very early form of what later became the Semitic languages of Hebrew, Aramaic, and Phoenician.

installations found on the site. According to Anati, Har Karkom was a "mecca" for cultic activity in the third millennium.[40] The main problem here, of course, is that this is about a millennium too early to fit the Israelite sojourn! This doesn't faze Anati because, in his view, the biblical stories of the Exodus are literary creations composed of allegorical, mystical, legendary, and emotional elements.[41] But even scholars who likewise doubt the historicity of the Exodus place the emergence of the Hebrew tribes in the Palestinian hill country somewhere during the last half of the second millennium BC. Consequently, Anati's proposal has garnered little support.[42]

Jebel Sin Bisher

Another Israeli historical geographer, Menashe Har-El, opts for a site called Jebel Sin Bisher in west-central Sinai not far off the Darb el-Hajj, the famous pilgrimage route to Mecca.[43] His primary argument is its suitability in being a three days' journey from Egypt. The main problem here is the assumption that Mount Sinai was the destination Moses had in mind. In fact, the name of the destination isn't mentioned and, at this point in the negotiations, Moses requests only a temporary leave, not a permanent departure from Egypt. Consequently, this passage doesn't really help us locate Mount Sinai. Even more telling, one must discount the itineraries in Exod 15:22—19:2 and Num 33:1—15. To be sure, Jebel Sin Bisher does fit nicely with the notice in Deut 1:2 about the eleven days journey from Horeb to Kadesh Barnea, but one must then pick and choose which texts to privilege in this sort of approach. Better to find a site which best fits all the relevant texts. Finally, in terms of physical features, Jebel Sin Bisher pales in comparison with Jebel Musa. In my view, it's unlikely to be the biblical Mount Sinai.

---

40. For a list of the similarities Anati alleges between Har Hakarkom and the biblical accounts of the Exodus, see Franz, "Mount Sinai," 105–6. Several of these are so general they could apply to any number of locations and a couple are of dubious interpretation.

41. Ibid., 105.

42. For a helpful overview, see Enns, "Exodus Route."

43. Har-El, "Exodus Route."

Mount Sinai

Jebel Khasm el-Tarif

The American archaeologist Bryant Wood proposes a site in the northern Sinai called Jebel Khasm el-Tarif, located about twenty-two miles north-northwest of Eilat on the Gulf of Aqaba and some seventy miles from Kadesh Barnea (Ein Qudeis and Ein Qudeirat).[44] Even though it lacks the impressive features of Jebel Musa, Wood argues that the biblical itineraries and narratives eliminate Jebel Musa and other southern sites from consideration and point to a northern view. He assumes that Mount Seir lies on the way from Sinai to Kadesh-Barnea. Relying especially on Deut 1:2, he estimates that families with herds cover about seven miles a day. This places Horeb/Sinai some seventy miles distant from Kadesh-Barnea, thus eliminating Jebel Musa (at least twice that distance away). This then places Mount Sinai just off the Trans-Sinai Highway (Darb el Hajj), linking Midian with Egypt by way of Jebel Khasm el Tarif. According to Wood, Moses's grazing Jethro's sheep at the mountain of God and his reunion with Aaron at the same location dovetails nicely. He concludes that "Gebel Khasm et Tarif is the only site thus far proposed that meets all of the Biblical requirements for Mt. Sinai."[45]

Wood's assumption, however, that Mount Seir is located in the wilderness of Paran is problematic. He arrives at this by questionable exegesis of several poetic texts in the OT. These texts indicate only that the Lord comes from the general direction of the south, for that is the common denominator in all the place names. Locating Mount Seir west of the Arabah flies in the face of a long-standing consensus that it should be situated somewhere in southern Jordan, the ancient homeland of the Edomites.

More problems surface. The Hajj route crosses some of the most barren and forbidding terrain in the entire Sinai. Water and vegetation are more scarce than in the southern peninsula and would have required even more miracles to sustain the Israelites and their animals than is recorded in Scripture. Furthermore, how could a trek along the well-known Dharb el-Hajj not result in at least one site being remembered in Jewish, Christian, and Islamic tradition? This strains credibility.[46]

---

44. See Wood, "In Search of Mt. Sinai." See also Wood, "Beneath the Surface."

45. Wood, "In Search of Mt. Sinai."

46. Wood says nothing about 1 Kgs 19:8 in which Elijah traveled forty days from Beersheba to Mount Sinai. Jebel Khasm el Tarif is only about fifty miles south of Beersheba, in which case Elijah averaged less than a mile a day—slow progress indeed! If the forty-day trek is taken literally, admittedly a moot point, the elapsed time comports

Southern Sinai

I still think Jebel Musa in southern Sinai best fits the biblical and geographical evidence.[47] We know from Egyptian annals that, on average, their army could maintain marches of about fifteen miles per day. Modern Bedouin with their flocks and herds average between six and seven miles per day.[48] These averages provide realistic ranges by which to gauge Israelite movements in the desert. According to the itinerary in Num 33:5–15, once the Israelites passed through the sea and into the wilderness, they journeyed three days in the wilderness before camping at Marah. After that they camped at five other places before arriving in the wilderness of Sinai. If there were no other stopping points, there must have been extended stays at each camping site because Exod 19:1 says it took two months to travel from Egypt to the wilderness of Sinai. Taking the itinerary at face value points to southern Sinai as Israel's initial destination and the location of Mount Sinai. This is more likely than a trek across the barren wastes of central and northern Sinai.

---

better with a southern Sinai location than with Gebel Khasm et Tarif.

47. For further discussion and a defense of the traditional view, see Brisco, "Exodus"; Harrison and Hoffmeier, "Sinai"; Andersen, "Sinai"; Davies, "Sinai"; and Mattingly, "Sinai." Anson Rainey, widely recognized authority on the historical geography of the OT, concludes: "An eleven-day journey from Kadesh-barnea can only point to a place in southern Sinai and rules out most alternatives, especially the Hejaz" (Rainey and Notley, *Sacred Bridge*, 120).

48. Beitzel, *New Moody Atlas*, 112.

4

Mount of Beatitudes

Understanding Holiness: Part Two

"Be perfect, therefore, as your heavenly Father is perfect." (Matt 5:48)

Introduction

THE LOCATION OF THE Mount of Beatitudes is even more difficult to pin down than Mount Sinai. In Matthew's gospel, the evangelist simply says, "When Jesus saw the crowds, he went up *the mountain*; and after he sat down, his disciples came to him. Then he began to speak . . ." (Matt 5:1–2 [italics added]). Eugene Peterson deftly paraphrases the moment: "When Jesus saw his ministry drawing huge crowds, he climbed a hillside. Those who were apprenticed to him, the committed, climbed with him. Arriving at a quiet place, he sat down and taught his climbing companions."[1] As already stated, my intent in this book has been to view you, my readers, as committed climbing companions and to revisit together some of the significant mountaintop moments of Scripture. But in this instance, what was the name of the mountain and where was it located? Matthew doesn't say. When he wrote his Gospel, his primarily Jewish-Christian readers perhaps knew the location so no identification was needed.[2] The author of the

---

1. *The Message*, 18.
2. Most scholars suggest Syria, Galilee, or Transjordan as the setting for the composition of the Gospel. See Hagner, *Matthew 1–13*, lxxv.

Gospel of Luke, not being a Palestinian Christian and writing for a primarily Gentile audience, either didn't know or didn't feel it necessary to locate the mountain precisely.[3]

Locating the Mount of Beatitudes

Modern Site

The modern site of the Mount of Beatitudes affords a lovely view of the northern end of the Sea of Galilee. Situated on the summit of a hill, the Church of the Beatitudes serenely overlooks the lake. Below and along the lakeshore to the east lies Capernaum, Jesus' headquarters for his Galilean ministry. The Franciscan Sisters built the church in 1938 with financial assistance from the Fascist dictator Benito Mussolini—probably the only thing for which we can be grateful to him! For all its grace and serenity, however, the site is admittedly a Johnny-come-lately. What other options are there?

The Arbel

Two other candidates deserve mention. The most impressive heights overlooking the northwestern end of the Sea of Galilee are the rocky cliffs called the Arbel. Its summit provides a panoramic view of the entire lake.[4] And directly to the north and below the Arbel lies the valley of Arbel, also known as the Valley of the Doves. According to a Jewish legend, the Messiah of Israel will be revealed here. What we can say with near certainty is that Messiah Jesus did indeed pass through this valley because this is the location of a road linking Cana and Nazareth with Capernaum.[5] And just maybe, he also delivered his famous sermon from the lofty heights of the Arbel. At least some of Napoleon Bonaparte's soldiers who participated in the invasion of Palestine thought so.[6] The main problem is its difficult loca-

---

3. See map 4 in the appendix.

4. I'll never forget sitting on its rocky crags with a group of students in 1993. As we gazed out over the lake below us, our tour guide brought out his boom box and the majestic strains of Handel's Hallelujah Chorus rang out over the vista—a truly inspiring moment.

5. Luke 4:16, 30–31

6. Several French battalions engaged the Turkish forces in the Jezreel Valley and

tion for the multitudes. It's hard to imagine that the Savior would choose such a difficult, potentially dangerous, spot to deliver the most famous sermon of all time.

Horns of Hattin

The Horns of Hattin hover above the Arbel about three miles farther to the west and about 400 feet higher in elevation. Lying just off the road already mentioned between Nazareth and Capernaum, and much more accessible to the general public, this site punctuates the western skyline. Visitors to the Sea of Galilee's northern shore can't miss its distinctive peak standing like a silent sentinel. The summit offers a panoramic view of upper and lower Galilee, the Golan Heights, and majestic Mount Hermon in the distance. The Crusaders identified the Horns of Hattin as the site for the Sermon on the Mount.[7]

Problem of Identification

An objection to identifying either the Arbel or the Horns of Hattin as "the mountain" is the relative distance of both from Capernaum (approximately six miles and nine miles respectively), since the latter is clearly the headquarters of the early Jesus movement. On the other hand, the immediate context of the Sermon on the Mount in Matthew's gospel describes Jesus teaching in the synagogues of Galilee, an area encompassing some 650 square miles.[8] There are, accordingly, a number of possible locations and certainty eludes us.

Tradition and History

You may wonder why I accept the traditional site of Mount Sinai but demur on the location of the Mount of Beatitudes. The short answer is that historical traditions are not of equal value. In this case, the Church of the

won a decisive victory in 1799.

7. Ironically, a major military defeat leading to the demise of Crusader domination of the Holy Land occurred on its slopes and summit. On the fourth of July 1187, the Ayyubid Sultan Saladin (Salah al-Din Yusuf ibn Ayyub) crushed a Crusader army, already grievously suffering from the intense summer heat and thirst.

8. Matt 4:23.

Beatitudes is a twentieth-century building not built over an older site. We must also remember that the two Jewish revolts against Rome in AD 66–74 and AD 132–135 resulted in a major displacement of Jewish Christians from the Holy Land. With them also went the historical memory of some of the sites associated with Jesus' ministry. The vacuum was filled with Gentile Christians who took over leadership and constituted the majority of the ongoing church. The major sites, of course, especially in the Jerusalem area, were remembered and venerated, but since the Gospel tradition doesn't actually pinpoint the location of the Sermon on the Mount, it was no longer known. In fact, a former teacher of mine, Dr. G. Douglas Young, founder of Jerusalem University College, used to say with a twinkle in his eye that the only site connected with the ministry of Jesus in Galilee about which there can be no doubt is the Sea of Galilee!

What we can say is that as early as the fourth century AD, Byzantine Christians identified the location of the Sermon on the Mount at a site much closer to the lake than the present Church of the Beatitudes. They erected a small chapel in close proximity to the present day churches of the Multiplication of the Loaves and Fishes and the Primacy of Peter at a place called Tabgha.[9] It should be noted that the latter two churches are built upon earlier churches dating to the fourth century AD. Just below the Byzantine church of the Beatitudes was a cave. Once again our indomitable Christian pilgrim, Egeria, mentions this cave and church in her journal.[10] This more ancient church was destroyed sometime during the Islamic conquest of the seventh century and was never replaced.

As already mentioned, the present day Church of the Beatitudes, located higher up on the summit, was built in the mid-twentieth century. For this reason, I leave the location of the Mount of Beatitudes an open question. It is certainly possible that the Byzantine tradition locating it relatively close to the shore is correct, but that is the most that can be said. Nonetheless, the modern church provides pilgrims with a wonderful panorama from which to ponder Jesus' words. I always feel spiritually refreshed when

---

9. Tagbha is an Arabic corruption of the Greek word *heptapēgon*, meaning seven springs. These springs empty into the Sea of Galilee making the area a favorite feeding spot for the local fish called *musht*. The area was certainly well known and fished by Peter, James, and John (cf. Luke 5:1–11). In July 2015 arsonists caused considerable damage to this lovely chapel. See http://www.reuters.com/article/2015/06/18/us-israel-church-fire-idUSKBN0OY0FW20150618.

10. "Near there [i.e., the area around Capernaum] on a mountain is the cave to which the Saviour climbed and spoke the Beatitudes" (Wilkinson, ed., *Egeria's Travels*, 200.)

visiting the site. In the end, the exact location is not the essential thing; it's the message: "Everyone then who hears these words of mine and acts on them will be like a wise man who built his house on rock" (Matt 7:24). "The words that I have spoken to you are spirit and life" (John 6:63).

Theology of the Sermon on the Mount

Some understand the Sermon on the Mount as radically different from the message of Mount Sinai. In this, they are radically wrong! Properly understood, the Mount of Beatitudes simply transposes the theme of Mount Sinai into a higher key.

Structure of the Sermon

The message of the sermon is better grasped in light of its overall structure.[11] Here's a way of seeing the sermon in one sweep:

- Kingdom principles: Eight words 5:2–12
- Kingdom mission: Salt and light 5:13–16
- Kingdom righteousness: Be perfect 5:17–48
- Kingdom piety: Prayer and priorities 6:1–34
- Kingdom cautions: Golden rule and warnings 7:1–27

What shouldn't be missed in this outline is the striking parallel with the legislation on Mount Sinai. Just as the great law code of Moses begins with ten core principles (the Ten Words), the Sermon on the Mount begins with eight core qualities—the Eight Words.[12] The beatitudes define the character of those who comprise the kingdom of God. These are characteristics that should be reflected in all the people of the kingdom, just as the Ten Words defined the conduct (and by implication, the character) of the old covenant people of the kingdom.[13] As in the Mosaic law code, so in

---

11. For interpretative approaches to the sermon, see Wilkins, *Matthew*, 191–200.

12. I'm taking what could be considered the ninth Beatitude (5:11–12) as, in fact, an elaboration and expansion of the eighth.

13. "The Beatitudes (5:3–12) describe the divinely approved lifestyle of those who have repented at the arrival of the rule of God in Jesus's words and works" (Turner, *Matthew*, 143).

Jesus' sermon we have some core principles that are then expounded and fleshed out in daily living.

Some might object to my insistence that holiness is fundamental to the Sermon on the Mount as it was in the Sinai covenant. The word *holy* scarcely occurs in the sermon, being mentioned only in connection with a warning about giving what is holy (or sacred [NIV]) to dogs and swine.[14] Rather, what seems uppermost in the sermon is the notion of righteousness. For example, the fourth beatitude describes a person who hungers and thirsts for righteousness.[15] Then, when Jesus defends his view of the law and prophets, he insists that not even the least of the commandments should be broken and warns his followers that their righteousness must exceed that of the scribes and Pharisees.[16] Chapter six of the sermon sets out how one expresses true righteousness in matters of charitable giving, public and private prayer, fasting, and personal piety, climaxing with this charge: "But strive first for the kingdom of God and his righteousness, and all these things will be given to you as well" (Matt 6:33). So what place is left for holiness?

This objection ignores the intimate relationship between righteousness and holiness in both Testaments. As the law of Moses makes clear and Jesus repeatedly affirms, the essence of holiness consists in being rightly related to God and neighbor.[17] Furthermore, the climax of Matthew 5, which showcases what true righteousness consists of, concludes with this statement: "Be perfect, therefore, as your heavenly Father is perfect" (Matt 5:48). The Greek word *telios* rendered into English as "perfect" is very close in meaning to the Hebrew word *qadosh* in the holiness code: "You shall be holy to me; for I the Lord am holy, and I have separated you from the other peoples to be mine" (Lev 20:26).[18] The notion of being whole, complete,

---

14. Matt 7:7.

15. Matt 5:6.

16. Matt 5:18–20. Apparently, Jesus was accused of dismissing some aspects of Torah as unimportant or no longer binding. What may be lurking behind this accusation is the likelihood that Jesus did in fact dismiss some of the oral traditions, scribal interpretations of written Torah. Jesus puts his emphasis on what is written ("not one letter, not one stroke of a letter, will pass from the law until all is accomplished"[Matt 5:19]).

17. Matt 19:16–21; 22:23–28.

18. "Being 'whole' manifests itself in concrete behaviour; to be undivided in relation to God includes detaching oneself from that which separates from God" (Delling, τέλειος).

and undivided is what provides an unmistakable bond between righteousness and holiness. You can't have one without the other.

Beyond this semantic affinity lies a deeper structural connection between the Sinai revelation and the Sermon on the Mount. This has to do with a conscious comparison and contrast Matthew creates between the figures of Moses and Jesus. Matthew's markedly Jewish portrayal of Jesus utilizes typology to draw attention to these links. In short, Jesus is a new and greater Moses. Even the way Matthew structures his Gospel draws attention to this association by inserting five large blocks of teaching material into his Gospel:

- The Sermon on the Mount (Matt 5–7)
- Instruction to the Twelve (Matt 10)
- Parables of the Kingdom (Matt 13)
- Church Discipline (Matt 18)
- Olivet Discourse (Matt 24–25)

The five discourses recall the five books of Moses, the Pentateuch. But more than a debatable structural parallel exists: a typological link between Moses and Jesus lies deeply embedded in the Gospel. Matthew deliberately highlights key moments in Jesus' life that recall similar events in Moses's life. The birth narrative is a case in point. Jesus is born during the reign of the despot Herod the Great. This paranoid potentate seeks to destroy the infant Jesus after eastern magi arrive in Jerusalem in search of the newborn king of the Jews.[19] This echoes a life-threatening crisis for the infant Moses. He too was born during the reign of a ruthless ruler who decreed the death of all Hebrew male children.[20] Moses is providentially spared; so is Jesus.[21] This is but one of several instances of Moses typology in Matthew's gospel. Here are some others:

- Just as the book of Exodus presents Moses as a divinely ordained savior from oppression, so also an angel promises Joseph that his son will save his people from their sins.[22]

---

19. Matt 2:1–18.
20. Exod 1:8–22.
21. Exod 2:1–10; Matt 2: 12–18.
22. Exod 2:1–25; 3:7–10; Matt 1: 23.

Mountaintop Theology

- Just as the people of Israel left the land of Egypt bound for the promised land, so too the Holy Family left Egypt and returned to the land of Israel.[23]
- Both Moses and Jesus are tested in the wilderness.[24]
- Both minister to the twelve tribes of Israel, the people of God.[25]
- Moses mediates the old covenant on Mount Sinai; Jesus mandates the charter of the new covenant on the Mount of Beatitudes.[26] Jesus also institutes the Last Supper on Mount Zion to commemorate the new covenant and utters his Great Commission on an unnamed mountain (Mount of Beatitudes?) in Galilee.[27]

Matthew's gospel doesn't merely compare these two figures: Jesus is much greater than Moses. In fact, Jesus' authority is such that he even modifies or cancels certain aspects of the Mosaic law in the so-called antitheses.[28] His authority, while recognized by all, is rejected by most, and results in judgment, both historical and eschatological.[29]

Much of the conflict between Jesus and the religious authorities of his day centers on competing views of what it means to be the holy people of God. That is why the Sermon on the Mount is so crucial: it is Jesus' bold declaration defining what it means to be holy. The law of Moses teaches us much about holiness; but the law of Christ takes us to an entirely new level of sanctity.

Jesus and Holiness

According to Jesus, holiness is essentially a matter of the heart. This is by no means a novel insight; after all, the central creed of the Mosaic law addresses each Israelite: "You shall love the Lord your God, with all your heart, and with all your soul, and with all your might" (Deut 6:5). Unfortunately, by

---

23. Exod 12:40–42; Matt 2:13–15, 19–23.
24. Exod 15:22–17:15, Matt 4:1–11 par. Mark 1:12–13; Luke 4:1–13.
25. Exod 24:4; Matt 10:1–6; 19:28.
26. Exod 19:20–23:33; Matt 5–7.
27. Matt 26:27–29; Matt 28:16.
28. Matt 5:21–48.
29. Matt 7:28–29; 21:23; Matt 9:34; 12:14; 13:13–17; Mark 13:24–37; Matt 24:29–25:46; Matt 24:15–22; Luke 21:20–24; Mark 13:24–37; Matt 24:29–25:46.

the time of Jesus, this requirement tended to be obscured by punctilious observance of particular regulations. In order to prevent transgression of the written statutes, scribal authorities created supplemental laws, the so-called oral tradition, designed to prevent inadvertent wrongdoing.[30] The upshot was an ever-growing body of burdensome legislation.[31] Jesus cuts away the legalistic overgrowth and brings us back to the core principles.

According to Jesus, there are eight qualities of the heart that lead us into the holiness God intended. Each beatitude, a statement of joy and spiritual well-being, is connected with a certain mental and spiritual mindset that both characterizes a kingdom citizen and results in a present and eschatological reward. Here is what holiness looks like.

Humility

The first quality is a recognition of one's spiritual poverty.[32] This radically overturns common perceptions about what holiness is and how one becomes holy.[33] Christendom has far too often redefined holiness in terms of behavioral performance and good deeds production—a striving to increase one's spiritual net worth. Apparently, this was also the case in some first-century Jewish circles as well. Jesus' stinging critique of external piety without accompanying heart attitudes is still relevant.[34]

The first Beatitude speaks of a profound recognition that we bring nothing to the spiritual table. We must humbly confess like Peter, "Lord, I am a sinful man!"(Luke 5:8). Spiritual brokenness and emptiness is where

---

30. The Oral Law was legitimized by the tradition that on Mount Sinai Moses received two forms of the law: written and oral, the latter preserved and passed along to succeeding generations. Here is how it is stated in the Mishnah (written down ca. AD 200): "Moses received the Law from Sinai and committed it to Joshua, and Joshua to the elders, and the elders to the Prophets; and the Prophets committed it to the men of the Great Synagogue. They said three things: Be deliberate in judgement, raise up many disciples, and make a fence around the Law" ('Abot 1.1). The oral law served as the fence.

31. Matt 11:28–30; 15:1–20; 23:1–26; Acts 15:10; Phil 3:7–11.

32. Peterson paraphrases it this way: "You're blessed when you're at the end of your rope. With less of you there is more of God and his rule"(*Message*, 18).

33. "[T]he Beatitudes . . . define reality in such a way that the usual order of things is seen to be upside down in the eyes of God" (Hays, *Moral Vision*, 321).

34. "[F]or all who exalt themselves will be humbled, but all who humble themselves will be exalted" (Luke 18:14; cf. Mark 7:6–7 [cf. Isa 29:13 LXX]; Luke 11:37–52).

the path to holiness begins. There are no shortcuts and no exemptions.[35] Here is where our journey with Christ begins; but it doesn't stop there. Holiness always exists in the realm of humility. When pride enters, holiness exits. We never advance in holiness to a place where humility may be safely set aside. Even after years of following the Savior, each Christian knows deep down in his or her heart that it is all of grace. As the Apostle Paul memorably states: "But by the grace of God I am what I am, and his grace toward me has not been in vain" (1 Cor 15:10).[36] This means that holiness is only cultivated through dependency—dependency on the grace of our Lord Jesus Christ. How ironic that much of modern psychology seeks to liberate individuals from all sorts of dependencies and codependencies![37] The freedom to be all that we're meant to be begins at the foot of the cross and continues as we carry our cross all the way to the New Jerusalem.[38]

Note the promise attached to this heart attitude of spiritual humility: "theirs *is* the kingdom of heaven"[italics added]. The use of the present tense is important and points to an important theological truth about the Beatitudes: the kingdom of God is both a present and future reality. Briefly stated, Jesus has already inaugurated the kingdom by his incarnation, ministry, death, burial, resurrection, and ascension. But this is just the first phase of an ongoing process, the initial installment of a program that includes ZIP files that are finally unzipped and activated at the second coming of Christ. All believers in Christ live in a "now but not yet" state of existence. Already we experience sins forgiven, the indwelling of the Holy Spirit, and the fellowship of the saints. But we are also painfully aware of our continuing vulnerability to sin and an ongoing spiritual warfare with the powers of darkness.[39] Only at the second coming of Christ do we arrive at the last stage of salvation, glorification—the total and everlasting eradication of our sin nature, sometimes called the beatific vision. Glorification

---

35. Recall our discussion of the structure of the book of Exodus in the previous chapter. One cannot truly worship without first having been truly redeemed.

36. Echoed constantly by Mother Teresa: "Humility is nothing but the truth . . . the surest way to be one with God . . . because we know we have nothing in ourselves. You see what God has done. I think God is wanting to show His greatness by using our nothingness" (Rai and Chawla, *Faith and Compassion*, 98).

37. This is not to deny that many dependencies and codependencies are emotionally crippling and need to be confronted. But being liberated from psychological dependencies is not a panacea for true integration and fulfillment. That comes only as we acknowledge our deep dependency upon the grace of Christ.

38. Mark 8:34–38.

39. Eph 6:10–20.

is accompanied by a thoroughgoing transformation of the universe, what Jesus calls "the renewal of all things" (Matt 19:28) and the Apostle Paul the liberation of creation "from its bondage to decay" (Rom 8:21). In the meantime, the Christian lives "between the times." Consequently, Beatitudes two through seven depict the eschatological fulfillment of our present salvation *in the future tense*.

Penitence

The second Beatitude is also counterintuitive. Mourning is not something we relish nor is it something we immediately connect with being holy. Why is there blessing in a state of mourning and why is it a prerequisite to holiness? The short answer is that spiritual contentedness coexists with sorrow over the consequences of our many sins and that of the society in which we live. Furthermore, suffering for one's faith is also an inevitable consequence of walking the Via Dolorosa.[40] This paradox requires unpacking.[41]

Sin is not trivial nor is it conducive to holiness. So long as we live in this body we must wage war with our sin nature; so long as we live in this world we must resist its allure, "the desire of the flesh, the desire of the eyes, the pride in riches" (1 Jn 2:16–17), and stand against the stratagems of the one who dominates it, the Dark Lord.[42] In short, though characterized by joy[43] and the celebration of all that is good,[44] Christians never forget from whence we came and where we now live.[45] We continue to mourn over the lingering effects of sin and, on occasion, to suffer from the backlash of the sons and daughters of darkness against the sons and daughters of light.[46]

Unfortunately, penitence has nearly disappeared from the vocabulary of modern North American Christianity and is in acute need of rehabilitation. We live in a fallen and fractured world and penitence expresses the

---

40. A point repeatedly made by the Apostle Peter in his first epistle. See further Helyer, *Peter*, 162–83.

41. Hauck observes, "the NT Beatitudes often contain sacred paradoxes" ("μακάριος"). See also Garland, "Blessing and Woe."

42. 2 Cor 2:11; Eph 6:12, 16;1 Pet 5:8–11; 1 Jn 5:19.

43. 1 Thess 5:16; Gal 5:22; Phil 4:4.

44. Phil 4:8.

45. Eph 2:1–3; 5:8; Phil 4:8; Rom 8:18–26; 1 Pet 1:6.

46. Eph 5:9–16.

necessity to confess our sins.[47] It doesn't mean being morbid killjoys who specialize in being dour and dull, but it does mean we exercise self-judgment and are accountable to the Lord and his church.[48]

Christian worship services typically begin with confession; it can scarcely be otherwise.[49] Penitence jolts us back into reality and shatters our spiritual smugness. Penitence takes seriously the most oft-repeated prayer in Christendom: "Forgive us our debts [sins], as we also have forgiven our debtors" (Matt 6:12). By God's grace, we are enabled to pray, "Lord, do not hold this sin against them" (Acts 7:60).[50] Penitence restores humility and thus is essential to true holiness.

Penitence is not pointless; sin shall be no more—this is an eschatological promise. Beyond mourning now lies everlasting comfort in the not yet. The use of the passive voice, "they will be comforted" is another instance of a divine passive, that is, God himself is the one who does the comforting. The Apostle Paul picks up on this: "Blessed be the God and Father of our Lord Jesus Christ, the Father of mercies and the God of all consolation, who consoles us in all our affliction, so that we may be able to console those who are in any affliction with the consolation with which we ourselves are consoled by God" (2 Cor 1:3-4). Though not often thought about in these terms, the book of Revelation is supremely a book of comfort. From the opening to the concluding vision, the book resonates with the assurance of everlasting comfort in the presence of God.[51]

---

47. 1 Jn 1:9; Jas 5:16.

48. 1 Cor 11:27-32.

49. In the Roman Catholic Mass, after the greeting comes the Penitential Act in which the congregants recall their sins and put their trust in God's mercy. It includes reciting the *Kyrie Eleison*, "Lord, have mercy," which is also the most frequently sung prayer in the Eastern Orthodox Church. In morning and evening prayer services of the Anglican and Episcopal churches, confession of sin immediately follows the opening sentences from Scripture: "And so that we may prepare ourselves in heart and mind to worship him, let us kneel in silence, and with penitent and obedient hearts confess our sins, that we may obtain forgiveness by his infinite goodness and mercy" (*The Book of Common Prayer*, 41). Congregational or gathered churches likewise include a time of introspection and confession before partaking of communion.

50. Which follows the pattern set by the Lord (Luke 23:34).

51. Rev 1:17-18; 7:15-17; 14:13; 21:3-4. A point emphasized by Helyer and Cyzewski, *Good News*.

Mount of Beatitudes

Meekness

This Beatitude is clearly drawn from Psalm 37:11: "But the meek shall inherit the land, and delight themselves in abundant prosperity." Once again, the Master overturns cultural expectations and norms. Meekness was not valued in the ancient world nor is it high on our list of spiritual attainments. For many, meekness is weakness. Special Agent Leroy Jethro Gibbs's rule number six, "Never say you're sorry, it's a sign of weakness," speaks for many.[52] In fact, meekness involves an inner strength worthy of admiration. Meekness exhibits a courage that controls our natural (and fallen) instincts to put ourselves first and domineer over others. We prefer a muscular mode of operation: retaliate for wrongdoing and respond to force with force. Meekness moves in an entirely different direction, demonstrating forbearance and forgiveness.[53] Above all, it displays a servant's heart and ministers to the needs of others.[54]

The Master modeled meekness and exhorted us to live likewise.[55] The problem is that meekness runs against the grain of both human nature and contemporary culture; consequently, we must be constantly reminded "to speak evil of no one," "avoid quarreling," "be gentle," and "show every courtesy to everyone" (Titus 3:2). In the final analysis, being meek is neither an acquired skill nor a genetic predisposition—it's a grace bestowed by God.

Paradoxically, the eschatological blessing attached to meekness vastly exceeds our overweening ambition to control our tiny speck of the cosmos. This Beatitude promises nothing less than the entire world. If Abraham was promised that his descendants would inherit the land of Canaan, Jesus promises his followers an inheritance commensurate to the extent of his reign, literally, to the ends of the earth.[56] Paul picks up on this promise when he reminds the contentious Corinthians, "For all things are yours, whether . . . the world or life . . . or the present or the future—all belong to

---

52. He is the main character on the popular TV program NCIS.

53. Eph 4:31–32; 1 Pet 3:9, 16.

54. Cultivating a servant's heart has long been part of the mission statement of Taylor University. At commencement, each graduate receives a servant's towel along with a diploma as a way of symbolizing the ideal of servant leadership.

55. Matt 11:28–30; Mark 8:34; 2 Cor 10:1; 1 Pet 2:21. Meekness is a hallmark of the Servant of the Lord in Isaiah. See especially Isa 42:2–3; 50:6; 53:7. NT writers identify Jesus as the Suffering Servant.

56. Matt 19:28; 25:34; 28:18.

you" (1 Cor 3:21–22).[57] Peter chimes in with this breathtaking prospect: "in accordance with his promise, we wait for new heavens and a new earth, where righteousness is at home" (2 Pet 3:13). And the Apostle John caps it off with a promise from the risen Lord: "I will give a place with me on my throne" (Rev 3:21).

Lest there be any lingering misunderstanding about meekness—as if it were a sort of *quid pro quo* bargain with God—let it be clearly stated: a courteous, gentle, respectful attitude toward others is not a temporary expedient in order to finally have our own way in the New Jerusalem. Meekness is an everlasting characteristic of kingdom citizens. We never outgrow it nor advance beyond it. It is an essential aspect of our extreme makeover in the image of Christ.[58] In short, it is an indispensable requirement for holiness.

Hunger for Righteousness

The fourth Beatitude takes us right to the heart of the fierce controversy between Jesus and the religious authorities and leadership of his day. They fundamentally differ on the definition of righteousness, and consequently, of holiness. The question comes down to this: What constitutes true righteousness and how does one acquire and demonstrate it? This question has continued to be debated in Judaism and Christianity. Indeed, major rifts in both religions have developed as a result of the dispute.

The term *righteousness* carries several shades of meaning.[59] It may refer to justice, that is, fairness in dealing with people, "getting a fair shake." The gold standard in this regard is the way God relates to his creation, especially human beings. His dealings with us are always just or right. Closely connected to justice is the concept of relationship. Someone who is righteous is someone who is rightly related to God and neighbor. Being in the right entails living in accordance with God's revealed will and issues in ethical or righteous behavior.[60] Matthew's gospel places great emphasis on "the *doing* of righteousness . . . realized in proper conduct . . . which consists of a

---

57. See also Rom 4:13 where Paul reinterprets the original promise of the land (of Canaan) as the world.

58. Col 3:5–17.

59. See Kertelge, "δικαιοσύνη."

60. Kertelge speaks of righteousness as the "program of Jesus . . . the content of the will of God" (ibid).

relationship of brotherhood to each other . . . ."[61] No unresolved disputes and grievances threaten the relationship.[62] Clearly, the various nuances of righteousness overlap.

Jesus pronounces a blessing upon those who hunger and thirst for righteousness. The intensity of this probably escapes most of us who live in an affluent society. We loudly proclaim "we're starved" if we miss a single meal! Jesus was addressing an audience who, for the most part, existed on a subsistence diet; they were able to eat just enough to survive. The listeners knew from firsthand experience what it's like to be parched with thirst and tortured by hunger. This degree of longing for righteousness in the innermost being of a disciple is what Jesus elevates to the level of blessedness: to be rightly related to God and experience ethical perfection. Kingdom citizens are consumed by this passion.

Once again, God delivers big time in the "not yet": "they will be filled." The filling, of course, has nothing to do with a gourmet delight, but rather a relationship with God that results in an A+ standard of righteousness—nothing short of perfection or holiness. The Apostle Paul describes this blessedness as "the surpassing value of knowing Christ Jesus my Lord . . . found in him, not having a righteousness of my own that comes from the Law, but one that comes through faith in Christ, the righteousness from God based on faith" (Phil 3:8–9).

Mercy

The prophet Hosea reminds Israel what the Lord highly values: "For I desire steadfast love [or mercy] and not sacrifice" (Hos 6:6).[63] The Master agrees and attaches a codicil: ample reward awaits those who exhibit this attitude and its accompanying behavior toward others. They will be repaid in kind, that is, in kindness.

---

61. Ibid.
62. Matt 5:23–26.
63. The NRSV and ESV usually render the Hebrew word *hesed* as "steadfast love." In Hos. 6:6, the REB, NASB, HCSB render *hesed* as "loyalty," the JPS as "goodness" and the NAB as "love." The NIV, however, translates it as "mercy," perhaps influenced by the LXX that usually translates *hesed* as *eleos*. Most English versions translate *eleos* in Matt 5:7 as "mercy."

Mountaintop Theology

Mercy is an obligation for all disciples of Jesus because it reflects the character of God our heavenly Father.[64] The OT celebrates the Lord as "a God merciful and gracious, slow to anger, and abounding in steadfast love."[65] The book of Lamentations, paradoxically, celebrates the fact that "the steadfast love of the Lord never ceases, his mercies never come to an end; they are new every morning" (Lam 3:22–23).[66] The story of King David's great sin and his confession in Psalm 51 highlights this amazing attribute of God: "Have mercy on me, O God, according to your steadfast love; according to your abundant mercy blot out my transgressions"(Ps 51:1). The Lord did indeed have mercy on David: "Then I acknowledged my sin to you, and I did not hide my iniquity; I said, 'I will confess my transgressions to the Lord,' and you forgave the guilt of my sin" (Ps 32:5).

The NT story of redemption explodes in praise of the mercy of God. The Virgin Mary extols this enduring feature of God's dealings with his people: "His mercy is for those who fear him from generation to generation" (Luke 1:49). The Apostle Paul, a man who "received mercy,"[67] never tires of reminding his believing readers and listeners that they too are the beneficiaries of God's undeserved mercy.[68] The capstone of Paul's reflection on God's mercy appears at the conclusion of his theological tour de force: the problem of Israel's unbelief (Rom 9–11). He bursts out in rapturous praise and wonder: "For God has imprisoned all in disobedience so that he may be merciful to all. O the depth of the riches and wisdom and knowledge of God!" (Rom 11:32–33). No wonder he begins his exhortation to the Romans with an appeal to "the mercies of God" (Rom 12:1).

Mercy received requires mercy repeated. In fact, failure to extend mercy, after experiencing God's mercy, puts one at spiritual risk.[69] Jesus illustrates how mercy is fleshed out in human relationships by the provocative parable of the Good Samaritan—provocative because the model of mercy is none other than a hated Samaritan! The lawyer who baited Jesus with the question: "And who is my neighbor?" is prompted to supply

---

64. See our earlier discussion of God's mercy in chapter one.

65. Exod 34:6; Num 14:18; Ps 25:6–7; 103:8–10; Jer 32:18.

66. I say paradoxically because, at the time Lamentations was written, the people of Israel had reached their historical nadir. The state no longer existed and they were a people in exile far from their beloved home and bereft of their sacred temple.

67. 1 Cor 7:25; 2 Cor 4:1;1 Tim 1:13, 16.

68. Gal 6:16; Eph 2:4; 1 Tim 1:2; 2 Tim 1:2; Titus 3:5.

69. Matt 18:23–35.

the correct answer to Jesus' counter-question: "The one who showed him mercy" (Luke 10:37). As the parable of the Good Samaritan so palpably portrays, mercy refers to the feeling of one who is not only moved by the sight of another's suffering ("when he saw him, he was moved with pity" (v. 33), but also moved to alleviate the suffering ("He went to him . . . and took care of him"(v. 34).

According to the Apostle Peter, mercy begets believers: "Blessed be the God and Father of our Lord Jesus Christ! By his great mercy he has given us a new birth into a living hope . . ." (1 Pet 1:3). Paul emphatically agrees.[70] The Apostle James takes it further by appealing to "full mercy" as genuine evidence of God's operative grace in one's life (Jas 3:17). In a more specific sense, Paul's list of grace gifts includes showing tangible acts of mercy: "if it is to show mercy, do it cheerfully" (Rom 12:8, TNIV). Jesus' half-brother Jude captures the now-but-not-yet character of this Beatitude by describing believers as waiting for the eschatological mercy of the Lord Jesus Christ all the while showing mercy to those caught in the web of doubt and sin.[71] The garment of holiness is woven with threads of mercy.

Pure in Heart

We come to an expression easily misconstrued. Our immediate perception of purity probably envisions sexual purity. Purity involves sexuality, but only as part of a larger concept. The essential idea is that of undivided loyalty. "Pure in heart" refers to someone who places the Lord at the center of his or her life. Nothing takes his place; nothing overshadows him. Obviously, sexual purity will be but one aspect of the overarching moral and spiritual purity Jesus demands. Loyalty entails obedience to the express will of the sovereign Lord, something revealed not veiled.

Once again, we encounter no revolutionary idea per se. The OT summoned Israel to undivided loyalty. Indeed, the Ten Words opens with this charge: "You shall have no other gods before me" (Exod 20:3). Israel's national history can be summarized as a persistent failure to be loyal to the sovereign Lord.[72] The Master makes the same demand of his disciples: "You cannot serve God and wealth" (Matt 6:24). This can be restated: "Strive first for the kingdom of God and his righteousness" (Matt 6:33) or dra-

---

70. Eph 2:4.
71. Jude 21–23.
72. Neh 9:16, 26, 29; cf. Acts 7:39, 51–53.

matically reformulated: "If any want to become my followers, let them deny themselves and take up their cross and follow me. For those who want to save their life will lose it, and those who lose their life for my sake will find it" (Matt 16:24–35). The bottom line, however, is the same: disciples have a primary and overriding obligation to be loyal to their covenant Lord and obedience is the litmus test of loyalty. "They who have my commandments and keep them are those who love me" (John 13:21).[73]

The rest of the NT reinforces the link between undivided loyalty and being pure in heart—perhaps nowhere more eloquently expressed than in the Epistle of James. The half-brother of Jesus clearly remembered the Master's call for loyalty and recognized what is at stake. James's opening meditation on divine wisdom warns against the peril of doubt: "for the doubter, being double-minded and unstable in every way, must not expect to receive anything from the Lord" (Jas 1:8). Doubts beset the undecided and anemic allegiance adversely affects one's prayer life. Contrariwise, complete commitment to the Lord drives doubt away. James is also wary of worldliness. Worldliness at its core displays disloyalty because it mistakes the source of genuine security. James calls this condition being "double-minded" (Jas 4:8).

The eschatological fulfillment of this Beatitude is the beatific vision: "for they will see God" (Matt 5:8). Commentary fails. The experience transcends anything we can conceive or imagine.[74] A problem arises here in that the OT is quite insistent that no one can actually see God.[75] The Apostle Paul continues to hold this view[76] and yet here we have Jesus affirming the contrary and the Apostle John says the saints "will see his face" as he sits on his throne (Rev 22:4). Perhaps, however, the resolution lies in the incarnation. Jesus Christ is truly God with us.[77] As the Master reminds Philip, "Whoever has seen me has seen the Father . . ." (John 14:9; cf. 1:18). In the New Jerusalem, the invisible Father God may not be visible even to glorified eyes; but the incarnate Son forever embodies and displays his essence and glory. Or perhaps, the glorified do at last see the Father. We shall *see*.

---

73. Cf. 1 John 2:3–6; Rev 12:17; 14:12.

74. "Matthew describes the greatest possible eschatological reward, one that by its nature includes all else" (Hagner, *Matthew 1–13*, 94).

75. Exod 33:20.

76. 1 Tim 6:16.

77. Matt 1:23.

Peacemakers

This state of blessedness is in short supply. Whether on an interpersonal or international level, enmity and hostility rule the day. The real challenge is to bring shalom to a troubled world.[78] This prompts two fundamental questions: Whence the source of this peace and how does one make it accessible to others?

The source of peace is not a mystery. Scripture is crystal clear: the Lord himself is the fountainhead of peace.[79] Peace surrounds his throne like the living creatures of Rev 4:8 that constantly praise his name. The hallmark of God's presence on the human plane is peace among his chosen people.[80] In both its OT and NT usage, peace refers to a state of well-being and can thus serve as a synonym for salvation. The great Isaianic prophecy concerning the coming son of David includes this throne name "Prince of Peace" (Isa 9:6), and to this should be compared the contemporaneous utterance of Micah, "the one who is to rule in Israel (Messiah) . . . shall be the one of peace" (Mic 5:5). The Apostle Paul leaves no doubt where peace may be found: "For he [Christ] is our peace" (Eph 2:14).

Being a peacemaker is challenging; it is also not optional. God desires for human beings to dwell together in peace; it follows, therefore, that God's children should desire the same for their fellow human beings.[81] The difficulty lies in the execution. How do the children of God make peace in a warring world? There is no simple answer. No one formula fits all. Each conflict carries its own complexity. From a purely human point of view, being a peacemaker sometimes seems to be mission impossible and success owes more to luck than skill.[82]

This, however, forgets the source of peace. If experiencing peace with God and therefore peace with fellow humans is purely a divine gift, then the

---

78. "References to peace (usually *eirēnē*) in the teaching of Jesus and the Gospel writers can be fully appreciated only in the light of the Hebrew concept of *šālom*, Jewish expectations concerning the coming kingdom of peace and the violence of first-century life in Israel" (Geddert, "Peace," 604).

79. Lev 26:6; Num 6:26; Ps 29:11; John 14:27; Rom 1:7.

80. Luke 2:14.

81. "The reference is to those who disinterestedly come between two contending parties and try to make peace. These God calls His sons because they are like Him" (Foerster, "εἰρηνοποιός").

82. "Peacemaking will sometimes be unsuccessful (Mt 10:34–37)" (Geddert, "Peace," 605).

way to implement peacemaking must surely involve invoking divine grace.[83] As Jesus once pointedly reminded his disciples, "For mortals it is impossible, but not for God; for God all things are possible" (Mark 10:27). He also told them, "All things can be done for the one who believes" (Mark 9:23). To adapt a famous saying of William Carey, "Expect great things from God; attempt great things for God."[84] Peacemakers are risk takers.

Being a peacemaker is closely linked to the other Beatitudes. In other words, a peacemaker is surely one who possesses an uncommon measure of humility, penitence, meekness, righteousness, mercy, and allegiance to God. As we imitate our heavenly Father, the necessary conditions to create peace necessarily create a climate conducive to peace and reconciliation. It may also safely be predicted that another Beatitude, the eighth and final one Jesus mentions, will come into play as peacemakers seek to bring peace.[85]

Persecuted for Righteousness

The children of God must never lose sight of spiritual reality. The kingdom of God has invaded the kingdom of the Dark Lord and, although the ultimate outcome is certain, the battle still rages. The powers of darkness resist "the light [that] shines in the darkness" (John 1:5) and "the cosmic powers of this present darkness" (Eph 6:12) "make war on . . . those who keep the commandments of God and hold the testimony of Jesus" (Rev 12:17). According to the Apostle Peter, the devil himself "prowls around, looking for someone to devour" (1 Pet 5:8).

The Master warned his disciples about what was coming: "If the world hates you, be aware that it hated me before it hated you" (John 15:18). It gets even worse: "they will hand you over to be tortured and will put you to death, and you will be hated by all nations, because of my name"(Mt 24:9). The Apocalypse paints a grim picture: the dragon's evil empire, Babylon the great, is "drunk with the blood of the saints and the blood of the witnesses to Jesus" (Rev 17:6).

---

83. Does not Ps 122:6 ("Pray for the peace of Jerusalem") point the way for all peacemaking? The divine initiation in peacemaking is abundantly clear in the NT (Rom 1:7; 5:1; 14:17; 15:13; et al.).

84. The context of Carey's admonition was world missions. He is considered the father of the modern missionary movement.

85. "[P]eacemaking is costly. It involved a cross for Jesus, and it involves a cross for his followers (Mt 10:37–39)" (Geddert, "Peace," 605).

What is especially noteworthy in this warning about persecution is what Jesus doesn't say. He doesn't endorse retaliation; he encourages rejoicing. There is something almost un-American about this! To be sure, Jesus is not addressing national issues here; he is speaking to individual believers.[86] Even so, responding in kind is more to our liking than counting oneself blessed when persecuted. The fact that only this beatitude is elaborated speaks for itself. Clearly, this state of being blessed comes only by careful cultivation of the preceding attitudes. Responding in the manner prescribed by the Master is probably the moment of truth in the seriousness of our commitment to Christ and his kingdom.

Significantly, it's the Apostle Peter who finally gets it. The learning curve for him was difficult to say the least.[87] But in the end, the message of the Master transformed his thinking and he followed his Lord on the Via Dolorosa.[88] A major appeal in Peter's pastoral letter centers on the pattern of the cross as a paradigm for discipleship: "But if you endure when you do right and suffer for it, you have God's approval. For to this you have been called, because Christ also suffered for you, leaving you an example, so that you should follow in this steps" (1 Pet 2:21). Almost certainly, the words of the Master echo in Peter's exhortation to his Anatolian readers: "Do not repay evil for evil or abuse for abuse; but, on the contrary, repay with a blessing. It is for this that you were called—that you might inherit a blessing" (1 Pet 3:9).[89]

Finally, when we suffer for our faith we need to remember that we are traveling in saintly company. The OT prophets knew what persecution for the name of the Lord entailed. Jeremiah, one of the most reviled prophets in the OT, especially comes to mind.[90] According to Jesus, suffering for one's faith requires a steady gaze toward the eschatological horizon: "your reward is great in heaven" (Matt 5:12). Once again, Peter understands how important this is: "Since all these things [the old heavens and earth] are to be dissolved in this way, what sort of persons ought you to be in leading

---

86. I realize that some would take strong exception to this statement. This isn't the place for an in-depth discussion of pacifism. My view is similar to that of Abraham, *Shaking Hands With the Devil*.

87. The Gospel accounts reveal that Jesus' message of non-retaliation did not sink in until after the resurrection and Pentecost (cf. Matt 16:22–23; John 18:10).

88. According to tradition, Peter, at his request, was crucified upside down in Rome. See further Helyer, *Peter*, 296–97.

89. On suffering for the name of Jesus in 1 Pet, see ibid., 162–83.

90. Jer 12:6; 15:15; 20:7–8.

lives of holiness and godliness . . ." (2 Pet 3:11–15). We should probably assume that Jesus' eschatological fulfillment promise gathers up the previous eschatological blessings in one tidy bundle. Perhaps the Apostle John best captures the content: "God will wipe away every tear from their eyes" (Rev 7:16–17).

Conclusion

The Beatitudes embody Jesus' vision of holiness; a vision completely realized when he brings his redemptive program to its grand finale. The Apocalypse portrays the redeemed dressed in white robes made of linen, which represent the "righteous deeds of the saints."[91] The Eight Words function as the building blocks of the kingdom, both now and forever. The rest of the Sermon simply unpacks the ramifications of each beatitude, just like the rest of the book of the covenant elaborates the Ten Words. Jesus' mission statement is but an extension of living out blessedness in a benighted world. Each antithesis assumes the reality and rightness of one or more Beatitudes. The great central section in which Jesus contrasts true and counterfeit righteousness revolves around the Beatitudes. The Lord's Prayer, or better, the disciples' prayer, patterns itself on the Beatitudes—beginning with humility and ending with peacemaking and persecution. And so it is throughout the Sermon.

Holiness is indispensable. The writer of Hebrews puts it most pointedly: "Pursue peace with everyone, and the holiness without which no one will see the Lord" (Heb 12:14). God's revelation on the two mountains, Mount Sinai and the Mount of the Beatitudes, summons his people to a life of holiness. This should be our primary passion. To this end, these two mountains require re-climbing on a regular basis. The view from the top will literally transform our lives.

---

91. Rev 3:4–5; 6:11; 7:9, 13–14; Rev 19:8.

5

Mount Nebo and Mount Gilboa

Understanding the Consequences of Sin

"Pride goes before destruction, and a haughty spirit before a fall." (Prov 16:18)

Introduction

These two mountains were the scene of two significant moments in the history of Israel, one touching, the other tragic. On their respective heights, a leading figure died: Moses on Mount Nebo and Saul on Mount Gilboa. This chapter revisits those episodes and reflects on their theological and pastoral significance. In short, the issue confronting us on Mount Nebo and Mount Gilboa concerns the consequences of sin, and in particular, the primordial sin of pride.

Location

The location of these two mountains is less problematic than Mount Sinai and the Mount of Beatitudes. In both cases, we can be reasonably sure of the general location, even if the precise spot is either disputed or uncertain.

Mountaintop Theology

Mount Nebo

Although Mount Nebo is explicitly mentioned only twice in Scripture, both texts provide helpful geographical reference points:

> Ascend this mountain of the Abarim, Mount Nebo, which is in the land of Moab, across from Jericho, and view the land of Canaan, which I am giving to the Israelites for a possession; you shall die there on the mountain that you ascend and shall be gathered to your kin, as your brother Aaron died on Mount Hor and was gathered to his kin.... (Deut 32:49–50)[1]

> Then Moses went up from the plains of Moab to Mount Nebo, to the top of Pisgah, which is opposite Jericho, and the LORD showed him the whole land.... (Deut 34:1)

According to Deut 32:49, Mount Nebo belongs to a range of mountains called the Abarim ("regions beyond," i.e. Trans-Jordan). This range, identified from the vantage point of someone residing on the west side of the Jordan River, is further placed in its relative position by means of a text from Jeremiah: "Go up to Lebanon, and cry out, and lift up your voice in Bashan; cry out from Abarim" (Jer 22:20). In this passage, mourners are instructed to go to three mountainous areas to the east of the Jordan Valley and lament the impending destruction of Jerusalem. The historical context is the aftermath of King Jehoiakim's death (ca. 598/7 BC). The three regions, listed in order from north to south are: the Mountains of Lebanon, of which Mount Hermon is the highest and most prominent; the mountains of Bashan, punctuated by volcanic peaks of the Golan Heights and situated to the northeast, east, and southeast of the Sea of Galilee; and the Abarim range, lying south of the Wadi Jabbok, in the ancient land of Moab, today part of the modern Hashemite Kingdom of Jordan. The Abarim range, northeast of the Dead Sea, overlooks the plains of Moab about 4,000 feet below to the west in the Jordan Valley. The primary piece of information for locating Nebo is the reference to being "across from Jericho." Standing on the ancient site of Jericho [Tell es-Sultan], on a clear day and looking toward the eastern skyline, one can pick out several peaks in the Abarim

---

1. There are several references to what appears to be a city named Nebo in the Transjordan (Num 32:3, 38; 1 Chr 5:8; Isa 15:2; Jer 48:1, 22). Apparently there was a town called Nebo on the western side of the Jordan as well ("the other Nebo," Num 7:33).

Mount Nebo and Mount Gilboa

range about fifteen miles away as the crow flies. Mount Nebo is almost certainly one of those summits[2].

Mount Nebo should probably be identified with modern Jebel en-Neba, a peak standing 2,740 feet above sea level.[3] Just to the northwest of Jebel en-Neba and connected to it by a saddle lies the slightly lower Râs es-Siâghah. This ridge is probably the summit of Pisgah where "the Lord showed him [Moses] the whole land" (Deut 34:1). Today, Râs es-Siâghah, popularly called Mount Nebo, is visited by hundreds of thousands of pilgrims and tourists annually.

As early as the Byzantine period, a small church displayed a monument commemorating the tomb of Moses. When our remarkable pilgrim Egeria visited the site in AD 384, she makes mention of the memorial, assured by the hermits who lived there that their predecessors had faithfully preserved the location but not the actual tomb.[4] In the fifth century AD, Peter the Iberian visited the site and by then a large church stood over a cave said to be where Moses was buried. A complex of monastic buildings surrounded the church. In the eighth century, the site was abandoned and eventually fell into ruins.

In 1932 the Custody of the Holy Land (a Roman Catholic organization of the Franciscan order) acquired the site. Excavations led by Fr. Sylvester Saller of the Franciscan Biblical Institute and carried forward by Frs. V. Corbo and M. Piccirillo followed. They were able to discern three distinct building phases from the first half of the fourth century to the end of the sixth and beginning of the seventh centuries AD. The lovely mosaics that grace the floors of the Byzantine chapels are alone worth a visit. One of the more arresting features of the site is a modern bronze sculpture created by Giovanni Fantoni symbolizing the bronze serpent mentioned in the wilderness wanderings and typifying the cross of Christ.[5] Of course, pride of place goes to the promenade to the west of the church. On a clear day it affords a panoramic view of the historic Land of Israel and the West Bank.[6]

2. See map 5 in the appendix.
3. The name means either "mountain of the height" or "mountain of Nabu" [a Babylonian god].
4. Wilkinson, ed., *Egeria's Travels*, 121.
5. Num 21:4–9; John 3:14.
6. Here is Egeria's description of the view:
   From the church door itself we saw where the Jordan runs into the Dead Sea, and the place was down below where we were standing. Then, facing us, we saw Livias on our side of the Jordan, and Jericho on the far side, since the height in

Unfortunately, a few modern Christians have searched in vain for something else on Mount Nebo—the mysterious ark of the covenant. This requires explanation. The connection between Mount Nebo and the ark is based on a Jewish tradition recorded in 2 Maccabees (2 Macc 2:4–10).[7] In this text we read that Jeremiah removed the ark shortly before the destruction of the First Temple in 587 BC. Here is the text:

> It was also in the same document that the prophet [Jeremiah], having received an oracle, ordered that the tent and the ark should follow with him, and that he went out to the mountain where Moses had gone up and had seen the inheritance of God. Jeremiah came and found a cave dwelling, and he brought there the tent and the ark and the altar of incense; then he sealed up the entrance. Some of those who followed him came up intending to mark the way, but could not find it. When Jeremiah learned of it, he rebuked them and declared: "The place shall remain unknown until God gathers his people together again and shows his mercy. Then the LORD will disclose these things, and the glory of the LORD and the cloud will appear, as they were shown in the case of Moses, and as Solomon asked that the place should be specially consecrated." (2 Macc 2:4–8)

Assuming this account to be sober history, one "arkeologist," an American named Tom Crotser, financed an unauthorized expedition to Mount Nebo in the autumn of 1981 and, under cover of night, broke into the basement of the church. At the end of a long tunnel, he claimed to have discovered the ark and took pictures to prove it. After being pressed to reveal these photos, he did so to a respected archaeologist, Siegfried Horn of Andrews University in Michigan. When Dr. Horn looked at the photos he knew immediately the claim was bogus. The photograph clearly shows a modern nail along the edge of the box alleged to be the ark![8] Scams that claim tangible proof for the truthfulness of Scripture are unhelpful and unnecessary—the

---

front of the church door, where we were standing, jutted out over the valley. In fact from there you can see most of Palestine, the Promised Land and everything in the area of Jordan as far as the eye can see (Wilkinson, ed., *Egeria's Travels*, 121).

7. For background on this document, see Helyer, *Jewish Literature*, 158–66.

8. For an account of this unauthorized excavation and Dr. Horn's response, see Shanks, "Ark of the Covenant."

Holy Spirit testifies to its veracity.[9] In my view, the Jeremiah ark tradition is legendary and the fate of the ark remains shrouded in mystery.[10]

---

9. I have personally known one other American who spent months in the surrounding area trying to locate the ark of the covenant. His name was Vendyl Jones and he claimed to be the original inspiration for the Indiana Jones character in the blockbuster movie, *Raiders of the Lost Ark*. Among other endeavors, Vendyl scoured the caves in the vicinity of Qumran in search of the ashes of the red heifer used by the priests in making the water of purification for ritual defilement (cf. Num 19). He also claimed to have found some of the holy anointing oil and the incense used in the Second Temple rituals. According to some experts, it's just possible the latter claim is true. See Patrich, "Hideouts," 34–35.

10. In 2 Chr 35:3 Josiah is credited with restoring the ark to its place in the holy of holies. Presumably, one of his predecessors had removed it. This is the last reference to the ark being in the First Temple. Second Chr 36:10 says Nebuchadnezzar brought "the precious vessels of the house of the Lord" to Babylon. According to 1 Esdras, a work written in Greek and dating to the second century BC, "they [the Chaldeans] took all the holy vessels of the Lord, great and small, the treasure chests of the Lord, and the royal stores, and carried them away to Babylon" (1 Esd 1:54). But neither text explicitly mentions the ark and so, not surprisingly, Jewish tradition is divided over its fate. The Mishnah recounts a tradition that the ark was hidden beneath the paving stones of the chamber for wood in the temple (*m. Yoma* 6:1–2). According to a talmudic tradition, Josiah hid the ark so it would not be taken to Babylon (*b. Yoma* 53b; *y. Shek.* 6:1; 49c). There are many pious Jews today who believe that the ark is buried beneath the Dome of the Rock. The late rabbi Shlomo Goren, who was the Ashkenazi Chief Rabbi from 1973 until 1983, held this view. In fact, rabbi Goren and rabbi Yehuda Meir Getz, Rabbi of the Western Wall for 27 years, illegally excavated a tunnel leading off to the east from the well-known Western Wall Tunnel. Both men believed they were getting close to the ark when Muslim authorities discovered them. This precipitated a brawl between Muslims and Jews and the Israeli police intervened and sealed off the illegal tunnel with concrete to prevent further violence. One may still see the place where this tunnel begins. Understandably, many religious, Zionist Jews like to pray in this particular area, since it is as close to the holy of holies as one can be and still offer Jewish prayers. Islamic authorities do not permit Jews (or Christians) to pray on the Temple Mount itself, called by Muslims the Haram esh Sharif, "the noble sanctuary." Ironically, Jeremiah himself proclaimed in the Lord's name: "[I]n those days, says the Lord, they shall no longer say, 'The ark of the covenant of the Lord.' It shall not come to mind, or be remembered, or missed; nor shall another one be made. At that time Jerusalem shall be called the throne of the Lord, and all the nations shall gather to it, to the presence of the Lord in Jerusalem . . .'" (Jer 3:16–17). Most interpret this to mean that the ark was forever lost, either before or during the destruction of the First Temple, but some insist that it still exists and will be recovered in the end times. The saga continues and "the fate of the ark is a bigger mystery than its origin" (Davies, "Ark of the Covenant," 224). Of course, fans of *Raiders of the Lost Ark* know exactly where it's located!

Mountaintop Theology

Mount Gilboa

Hundreds of thousands of tourists pass by Mount Gilboa and view it from several different vantage points, but very few ever stand on its summit.[11] This is not owing to its difficult terrain but to time constraints of a ten-day or two-week tour. One must leave the main routes connecting sites like Beth-shan and Megiddo in order to drive up on its summit, taking precious hours away from other more highly valued sites. For those who do get up there, an observation tower just off Route 667 affords a nice panorama of the Jezreel Valley, the Beth-shan Valley, and the central ridge of Samaria. In 1970 a portion of the area was declared a nature reserve and in 2005 even more acreage was added to the reserve. A special treat during the spring is the appearance of purple irises on its slopes.

I need to make another qualification. Even though Scripture mentions a Mount Gilboa, we are really talking about a mountain ridge and not one specific site.[12] David's lament over Saul and Jonathan's death speaks of "you mountains of Gilboa" (2 Sam 1:21). The name means, "mount of the bubbling fountain," probably a reference to the spring En Harod at the foot of its northern slopes. The exact spot where Saul met his demise cannot be determined. The Gilboa ridge, in the tribal area of Issachar, runs southeast to northwest along the southern edge of the Jezreel and Beth-shan Valleys and is connected on its south side to the central highlands of Samaria, the ancestral inheritance of the tribe of Manasseh. The Green Line runs just to the south of the Gilboa range.[13] This ridge, rising to 1,670 feet, is called Jebel Fuqû'ah. On its southern slopes is an Arab village called Jelbôn, still preserving the biblical name of Gilboa.[14]

---

11. See maps 5 and 6 in the appendix.

12. 1 Sam 31:1, 8; 2 Sam 1:6.

13. The Green Line is the demarcation line established in the 1949 Armistice Agreement between Israel and her Arab neighbors and sometimes applied to the cease-fire line between the West Bank and the State of Israel following the Six-Day War in 1967.

14. One of the important aids in the study of the historical geography of the Holy Land is Arabic place names. It is remarkable how often these place names still preserve the equivalent Hebrew names from the Bible. See further Aharoni, *Land of the Bible*, 94–117, and Rasmussen, *Atlas of the Bible*, 204–5.

Narration

Now that you have a general idea where these two mountains are situated, I want to reexamine the narratives recounting the deaths of these two leaders of Israel.

Moses and Mount Nebo

Moses's visit to Mount Nebo is an emotional roller coaster. His heart rejoices as he views with his own eyes the land promised to the patriarchs and reaffirmed to the second generation of Israelites who left Egypt.[15] After forty years of arduous wandering and untold hardships, the mission is almost over. Sadly, Moses is denied admission—so close and yet so far! How bitterly disappointing that he could not even set foot in the promised land. Is this fair? Why does the Lord refuse Moses the privilege of leading his people into their inheritance? As is often the case, there is a backstory that must be taken into account.

Moses's role in salvation history is huge. No human being was granted as many privileges as this man. His legacy as lawgiver and leader is unrivaled—his story is bigger than life.[16] Providentially spared destruction as an infant from an unnamed Pharaoh's genocidal decree, he was adopted, ironically, by Pharaoh's own daughter.[17] He was raised in the Egyptian court and "instructed in all the wisdom of the Egyptians . . . powerful in words and deeds" (Acts 7:22).[18] But he never forgot his Hebrew roots. Intervening on their behalf necessitated an escape from Egypt and exile in the land of Midian.[19] After forty long years, the Lord appeared to Moses near Mount Sinai in a burning bush and commissioned him to go back to Egypt and lead the Hebrews out of slavery and to the promised land.[20] Think of it: a solitary man, and an expatriate felon at that, claiming to represent the God

---

15. Gen 12:7; 13:14–17; 15:18–19; 17:18, et al. and Num 33:50–34:12. Only Joshua and Caleb from the first generation actually enter the land because of their complete trust in the Lord's ability to drive out the inhabitants of Canaan (Num 14:6–9).

16. "Besides Jesus, Moses plays the most important role in Western literature, art and music, and has been the subject of many modern biographies . . ." (Chavalas, "Moses").

17. Exod 1:22—2:1–9; 2:10.

18. For scholarly opinion on the date of Moses and the identification of the Pharoah, see Chavalas, "Moses," 572–73, and Walton, "Exodus, Date of," 258–72.

19. Exod 2:11–15.

20. Exod 3:1—4:17.

of the lowly Hebrew slaves, demands that Pharaoh, virtual dictator of the world's only superpower, release his work force on whose backs the empire was built. Talk about mission impossible, this is it!

A contest, a trial of strength, between the Lord, the God of the Hebrews, and Pharaoh, considered a god in Egyptian ideology, begins in earnest. After ten devastating plagues, Pharaoh relents and allows the Hebrews to leave.[21] Then, changing his mind, he leads his chariot force after them and to its destruction in the waters of the Red Sea.[22] The Hebrews raise their voices in jubilation: "Free at last! Free at last! Thank God Almighty, we are free at last!"[23]

But all does not go well in "that great and terrible wilderness" (Deut 1:19), a region the Hebrews call "this wretched place" (Num 20:5). The wilderness wanderings, lasting thirty-eight long years, are replete with apostasies, complaints, rebellions, and general discontent.[24] Repeatedly, Moses endures complaints and criticism. It's a testament to his commitment to the Lord that he stays the course. One of the most remarkable testimonies to his character and spiritual maturity is the following: "Now the man Moses was very humble, more so than anyone else on the face of the earth" (Num 12:3). Leading that crowd tests his humility to the max!

Counterbalancing the constant carping, Moses is privileged to experience the divine presence in an unprecedented way. Beginning at the burning bush and continuing throughout the great trek across the desert to the borders of Canaan, Moses is privy to direct divine revelation. He alone ascends the holy mountain where the Lord speaks directly to him and gives him the two tablets "written with the finger of God" (Exod 31:18). Furthermore, the glory of the Lord passes before him as he stands in a cleft of the rock on the holy mountain.[25] Moses also has a sort of private prayer chapel outside the camp, called the tent of meeting, but distinguished from the tabernacle.[26] This provides direct access to the Lord's presence during which time "the lord used to speak to Moses face-to-face, as one speaks

---

21. Exod 5:1—12:32.

22. Exod 14:5—31.

23. Taken from Dr. Martin Luther King Jr.'s famous "I Have a Dream" speech, delivered August 28, 1963, at the Lincoln Memorial, Washington DC.

24. Exod 32—33; Num 25; Exod 15:24; 16:2—3, 6—9; 17:3; Num 11:1, 4—6; 14:2—3; 16:13—14; 20:2—5; 21:4—5; Num 13:25—14:4; 16—17; Deut 1:26.

25. Exod 33:18—23; 34:5—9.

26. Exod 33:7—11.

to a friend. Then he would return to the camp . . ." (Exod 33:11). There is another remarkable passage that gives some indication of the unparalleled privilege accorded this man: "When there are prophets among you, I the Lord make myself known to them in visions; I speak to them in dreams. Not so with my servant Moses; he is entrusted with all my house. With him I speak face to face—clearly; not in riddles; and he beholds the form of the Lord" (Num 12:6-8).

So once again I ask, why did the Lord deny entrance to the promised land to this great man of God? The answer lies in a revealing episode, a moment that forces us to reflect on the taproot of sin. After leaving the Mount Sinai area, the Israelites make their way north to the region of Kadesh Barnea.[27] A persistent problem surfaces: "Now there was no water for the congregation; so they gathered together against Moses and against Aaron. The people quarreled with Moses and said, 'Would that we had died when our kindred died before the Lord'!" (Num 20:2-3). When Moses and Aaron go to the entrance of the tent of meeting to beseech the Lord for help, the glory of the Lord appeared and the Lord told Moses: "Take the staff, and assemble the congregation, you and your brother Aaron, and command the rock before their eyes to yield its water. Thus you shall bring water out of the rock for them; thus you shall provide drink for the congregation and their livestock" (Num 20:8).

That's the straw that breaks the camel's back. Moses has tolerated complaining for two years and he's had it up the wazoo. His exasperation echoes that of Rodney Dangerfield: "I don't get no respect!" Moses is ordered to "command the rock" to yield its water. In the first plague upon Egypt, Moses "lifted up his staff and struck the water in the river, and all the water in the river was turned into blood . . ." (Exod 7:20-21). But for the other plagues, Moses was instructed simply to stretch out his staff and announce the plague.[28] A similar procedure was to be followed here. But that is not what Moses does: "'Listen, you rebels, shall *we* bring water for you out of this rock?' Then Moses lifted up his hand and *struck the rock twice* with his staff; water came out abundantly, and the congregation and their livestock drank" (Num 20:10-11 [italics mine]).

The sacred narrative immediately records a divine reprimand: "Because you *did not trust in me*, to show *my* holiness before the eyes of the Israelites, therefore you shall not bring this assembly into the land that I

27. Num 20:1; 33:36; Deut 1:46.
28. Exod 8:5, 16; 9:22; 10:12, 21.

have given them" (Num 20:12 [italics mine]). Moses tries to wring personal respect and admiration out of his whining people with a wondrous display of power. He seeks strokes for saving the lives of the Israelites. In short, this towering giant succumbs to an ancient nemesis, the sin of pride. Pride is essentially exaggerated self-esteem and self-importance. Moses might well be forgiven for thinking that his fellow Israelites should have treated him better. In fact, most modern Christians probably think the Almighty didn't give Moses a fair shake—he got the short end of the stick! This disparity between the Lord's reaction and our own requires a closer look. But before doing so, let's revisit Saul's death on Mount Gilboa.

Saul and Mount Gilboa

As is the case in Moses's death on Nebo, an important backstory explains Saul's death on Gilboa. That story is set in a protracted war with the Philistines. In fact, the elders' choice of Saul as the first king of Israel represented a frantic attempt to stave off domination by these relative newcomers to Canaan. Sometime in the twelfth century BC, various Greek tribes in the Aegean were driven from their ancestral homeland by Dorian invaders. Among these displaced persons were the Philistines who boarded their long boats and sailed east to Egypt and the eastern littoral of the Mediterranean. Some of them settled along the coast of Canaan from Dor (just south of Haifa) in the north to Gaza in the south. Once they established a beachhead, they began to penetrate into the Shephelah, the low foothills between the coastal plain and the central hill country of Judah and Samaria to the east. The hill country was the heartland of the Hebrew tribes, protected on the west by the Shephelah and on the east by the desert. It's precisely in the Shephelah where conflict between the Philistines and Hebrews first erupts.

One can appreciate the strategic concerns of the Philistines. Having a memory of being dispossessed from their ancestral homeland, the Philistines feel psychologically vulnerable with only a narrow coastal enclave. Understandably, they wish to establish a permanent residency in Canaan and having the Hebrews to the east above them on the central mountain ridge does not contribute to a feeling of security. Already in the book of Judges, we read of clashes between the Hebrews and Philistines. The Samson stories are set in the Shephelah where these two people groups cautiously encounter each other and then jostle for control.[29] Samson grew up

---

29. Judg 13–16.

in the Danite village of Zorah, within eyesight of Gath, one of the five major Philistine cities.[30]

By the time of Saul, the Philistines have penetrated all the way to the central ridge, the heartland of Hebrew settlement. We read of Philistine garrisons in Gibeath-elohim (probably the same site as Geba) and in Michmash.[31] It's a geopolitical reality in this land between that whoever controls the central mountain ridge is in the driver's seat to control Canaan, and the Philistines are very much aware of it. That's where Saul comes into the picture. The old tribal confederation was fragile, woefully inadequate to deal with the peril of the tightly structured and militaristic Philistines. Rejecting the theocratic leadership of the judges, the people clamor for a monarch, a military leader able to unify the tribes and stem the tide of Philistine hegemony.[32] Remarkably, Saul acts like a monarch and proceeds to do precisely that. He and his small core of elite soldiers, led by his charismatic son Jonathan, seize the initiative and drive the Philistine outposts off the central ridge.[33] Saul also inflicts military defeats on the surrounding Moabites, Ammonites, Edomites, and Arameans.[34]

But the wheels begin to fall off the Saulide cart. The sacred historian provides us with one of the most remarkable political biographies in the OT. When Saul first appears in 1 Samuel, he is an unassuming young man devoid of political ambition and overweening ego; in fact, he suffers from an inferiority complex.[35] Many Israelites openly express doubts about his ability to cope with the crisis.[36] Initially, Saul confounds his critics and delivers some crushing blows to oppressive neighbors, especially the vaunted Philistine military machine.

Unfortunately, flaws in Saul's character and commitment to the Lord begin to surface.[37] On one occasion, Saul disobeys the prophet Samuel's direct order and personally offers a sacrifice before a major engagement.

---

30. Josh 13:3.

31. 1 Sam 10:5; 13:3, 5

32. 1 Sam 8:19–20; 9:16. For further background on this critical period of Israelite history, see Helyer, *Yesterday*, 169–70, 192–99.

33. 1 Sam 14:1–46.

34. 1 Sam 14:47–48.

35. 1 Sam 10:22; 15:17.

36. 1 Sam 10:27.

37. "Saul remains a complex and enigmatic figure, at once a hero and villain" (Youngblood, *1 Samuel–2 Kings*, 291).

Mountaintop Theology

For this he is roundly rebuked.[38] But some time afterward, Saul disobeys another direct, divine command by sparing Agag, king of the Amalekites, and by permitting the Israelite troops to take the best of the spoils.[39] This is not baseball—there will be no third strike and you're out! Samuel announces the Lord's rejection of Saul as king.[40] However, rather than retire from office and give way to another, Saul clings to power. Indeed, Samuel is reluctant to anoint a new king because he fears Saul's reaction.[41] Saul determines to perpetuate his dynasty through his son Jonathan. This leads him in a maniacal effort to eliminate the rising star David as a threat to Jonathan's succession. Unfortunately, war on two fronts seriously undermines his kingdom's ability to confront the Philistine crisis.

The greatest disaster for Saul occurs when the Spirit departs from his life.[42] All his early successes were achieved by the power of the Spirit. Now, spurned by the Lord and bereft of the Spirit, he vainly clings to his throne. The deformation is chilling and complete—the dark side takes over and Anakin becomes Darth Vader. Lord John Acton's adage, "Power tends to corrupt, and absolute power corrupts absolutely," plays itself out. All dissenting voices are stifled, including that of the crown prince Jonathan. David is caricatured as a criminal and relentlessly pursued in the Judean wilderness. Saul's raging paranoia and his increasingly severe manic-depressive bouts undermine his ability to rule. The upshot is that Saul paints himself into a corner. When David defects and becomes an apparent vassal of Achish, the Philistine king of Gath, Saul's best hope for deliverance is gone. He and his sons must face the Philistine menace by themselves. The fate of the Israelite kingdom hangs in the balance.

The Philistines settle on a simple but effective strategy: dissect the Israelite kingdom, control the central lines of communication and confine the Hebrews to their hill country enclaves. Accordingly, they mobilize their forces at Aphek on the coastal plain and travel northward along the coastal highway into the Jezreel Valley.[43] This broad valley, slicing through the central mountain ridge from the Mediterranean on the west to the Jordan

---

38. 1 Sam 13:13–15; 1 Sam 13: 8–12.
39. 1 Sam 15:1–9.
40. 1 Sam 15:10–31.
41. 1 Sam 16:2; 19:22.
42. 1 Sam 16:14.
43. They mobilize at the same spot as they had when they defeated the Israelites in the days of Eli and captured the ark (1 Sam 4).

Mount Nebo and Mount Gilboa

Valley on the east, is a natural boundary between the northern and southern tribes. Saul has no choice; he must respond to this gambit if he is to stave off Philistine domination.

Saul mobilizes his forces and moves northward up the central ridge towards the Jezreel Valley. The stage is set for a winner-take-all clash. The stakes couldn't be higher. And Saul couldn't be more alone. Samuel has died and the Lord refuses to answer Saul's requests for guidance and help.[44] In his desperation—and in defiance of his own earlier ban on sorcery—he turns to the dark side and consults a medium.[45] Note the irony in Samuel's earlier denunciation of Saul: "For rebellion is no less a sin than divination . . ." (1 Sam 15:23). This bizarre encounter with Samuel only reinforces his sense of impending doom: "the Lord will give Israel along with you into the hands of the Philistines; and tomorrow you and your sons shall be with me; the Lord will also give the army of Israel into the hands of the Philistines" (1 Sam 28:19).[46]

Saul initially positions his troops on the heights of Gilboa—the northern slopes of Gilboa are quite steep and inaccessible for chariots.[47] The high ground is the only advantage he possesses in the impending clash. When the Philistines camp at the village of Shunem (Arabic *Sôlem*), Saul moves his army down off the heights to the southern edge of the Jezreel Valley and camps at a spring near the town of Jezreel (Arabic *Zer'în*).[48] The battle probably takes place on the level ground between the two camps and one can easily surmise what happens.[49] The Philistines, with their chariot corps, overwhelm the Hebrews, who retreat back to the Gilboa ridge. Unfortunately for Saul and his army, the western approaches to the Gilboa range gently incline and permit easy access to the summit ridge.[50] The Philistines

---

44. 1 Sam 28:3, 6.

45. 1 Sam 28:9. See Goss, "What is the Occult?"

46. 1 Sam 28:19. This passage raises a long-standing exegetical and theological problem: Did the witch of Endor actually conjure up Samuel? Did the Lord allow Samuel to appear at this dramatic moment in Saul's life? Was the appearance fraudulent or was it something that took place entirely in Saul's deranged mind? In my view, Samuel actually appeared to Saul by special divine permission.

47. Saul adopts a strategy similar to what Gideon employed many years earlier against the Midianites (Jdg 7:8).

48. 1 Sam 19:1.

49. In this regard, the confrontation is similar to an earlier engagement in which Saul camped over against the Philistines in the Elah Valley (1 Sam 17:1–3).

50. My reconstruction of the battle of Gilboa follows that of Rainey, "Jezreel." I take

in hot pursuit cut off and surround the Hebrews. Saul, like Custer, makes his last stand. One by one, his sons, including Jonathan, his right-hand man and crown prince, fall before the Philistine onslaught.[51] Saul knows it's over. Rather than be taken alive and tortured by the Philistines, he decides to end his life by falling on his sword.[52]

When David hears the news, he is deeply affected. He composes a moving tribute to Saul and Jonathan. In the course of this composition he utters a curse on the mountains of Gilboa. It's worth noting that no subsequent event in the OT is recorded as having taken place on these mountains.[53]

The Theological and Pastoral Significance of These Two Episodes

So, what do these two stories have in common? They both point to a deadly sin that gets little attention and reflection in our day. And yet it continues to sabotage and subvert the lives of countless believers and nonbelievers alike. This sin is Satan's dirty little secret. It's time to shine a little light into a dark corner of our souls.

The taproot sin that produces a profusion of pernicious plants is pride. Unfortunately, this is easily overlooked as the ultimate culprit. In fact, readers of this chapter may query whether I have correctly identified pride as the underlying problem in the case of both Moses and Saul. After all, the sacred historians offer their own analysis of what went wrong for both leaders and in neither case do they mention pride. Rather, Moses is indicted because he did not trust in the Lord and show his holiness before the Israelites.[54] Fur-

---

this opportunity to pay tribute to my former teacher for his remarkable knowledge of the historical geography of the Holy Land. He passed away on February 19, 2011.

51. 1 Sam 31:2.

52. In 2 Sam 1, an Amalekite claims to have finished off a dying Saul. He probably fabricated the story in order to receive a reward from David. In any case, there is deep irony in the fact that an Amalekite was at the scene of Saul's death, inasmuch as it was Saul's failure to kill the Amalekite king Agag and all the Amalekite sheep that led to Saul's rejection (1 Sam 15:1–23). David has absolutely no sympathy for the Amalekite's alleged deed and orders him executed (2 Sam 1:15–16; cf. 1 Sam 24:6–7; 2 Sam 3:26–38; 3:9–12). Unbeknownst to the Amalekite, in the lead-up to the battle of Gilboa, Amalekite raiders attacked David's settlement at Ziklag and carried off the women and children. David tracked the raiding party down and wreaked vengeance upon them (1 Sam 30:1–20). Let's just say the Amalekite chose the wrong person and the wrong time to seek a reward!

53. 2 Chr 10:1, 8 only refers back to Saul's defeat.

54. Num 20:12.

thermore, Samuel says Saul was "little in [his] own eyes" (1 Sam 15:17) and that his sin was one of disobedience, rebellion, stubbornness, and rejection of the word of the Lord.[55] Yes, this is so. But the sacred historians merely identify the noxious fruits that poisoned the victim, not the taproot that produced it. And that is our task—time for a taxonomy of sin.

If we identify pride as essentially a desire for self-exaltation, an unwarranted assessment of one's importance, a shifting of ultimate confidence from God to self, then a good case can be made that we are dealing with "the beginning of all sin."[56] In this negative sense, pride lies at the core of disloyalty and disobedience. To be sure, there are a few instances in Scripture where pride is a positive thing. For example, the land of Israel, viewed as God's gift to his people, can be referred to as "the pride of Jacob" (Ps 47:4) and "parents are the pride of their children" (Prov 17:6 [NIV]). More clearly still, the Lord himself is portrayed as highly exalted and majestic in glory.[57] God is the one person in the universe who never overestimates his worth!

For the rest of us, however, the temptation to value ourselves more highly than we ought and more highly than others is a constant danger. In Paul's words, "I say to everyone among you not to think of yourself more highly than you ought to think, but to think with sober judgment, each according to the measure of faith that God has assigned" (Phil 2:3–4).[58] In dealing with a fractious congregation at Corinth, Paul asks a question we all need to ponder: "What do you have that you did not receive? And if you received it, why do you boast as if it were not a gift?" (1 Cor 4:7). We read it, we hear it, we may even repeat it like a mantra; but we repeatedly fail to act on it. At the very core of our being lies a persistent impulse to prefer self to others and, though it pains us to say it, to prefer self to God. How did this come about?

---

55. 1 Sam 15:19, 22–23; 28:18. Saul's inferiority complex ("I am only a Benjaminite, from the least of the tribes of Israel, and my family is the humblest of all the families of the tribe of Benjamin," 1 Sam 9:21) doesn't mean he was immune to pride—quite the contrary. He desperately sought affirmation and praise because he felt this was really what he deserved. He was, after all, "a handsome young man" who "stood head and shoulders above everyone else" (1 Sam 9:2).

56. "The beginning of human pride is to forsake the Lord; the heart has withdrawn from its Maker. For the beginning of pride is sin, and the one who clings to it pours out abominations"(Sir 10:12–13a).

57. Exod 15:7; Job 37:4; Isa 2:10.

58. Cf. Gal 5:26; 1 Cor 10:4; 1 Pet 5:5.

Mountaintop Theology

I begin with the beginning, the story of Adam and Eve's primal disobedience in the garden of Eden.[59] This Hebrew narrative masterpiece allows us to analyze what went wrong.[60] Behind the serpent we detect the schemes of Satan. His appeal to the woman, following an injection of doubt about God's character and a flat denial of God's word, lies in this startling claim: "for God knows that when you eat of it your eyes will be opened, and you will be like God" (Gen 3:5). Can you think of anything more intoxicating than possessing power on a par with God? The world lies at your feet! The first couple begin to imagine charting their own course, without having to trust in God's gracious provision—to be "masters of the house."[61] This is heady business! And it's utter foolishness. In the words of the Apostle Paul: "they became futile in their thinking, and their senseless minds were darkened, claiming to be wise, they became fools" (Rom 1:21–22).

The first couple disobey a direct command of God, but before they actually eat the forbidden fruit, sin is already present, because their wills have already inclined away from God and decided on a contrary choice.[62] The Apostle James, perhaps reflecting on Gen 3, analyzes temptation this way: "one is tempted by one's own desire, being lured and enticed by it; then, when that desire has conceived, it gives birth to sin, and that sin, when it is fully grown, gives birth to death" (Jas 1:14–15). And what is "one's own desire"? In the context of James's epistle, it is that which stands over against the will of God.[63] So, what then is sin? It's hard to improve on the answer found in the *Book of Common Prayer*: "Sin is the seeking of our own will instead of the will of God, thus distorting our relationship with God, with other people, and with all creation."[64] This comes very close to defining pride, since pride places self on a pedestal and prefers self to God. For this

---

59. Gen 3.

60. See Helyer, *Yesterday*, 66–69.

61. An allusion to a jaunty song written by Herbert Kretzmer in the Broadway production of *Les Misérables*.

62. "Our first parents fell into open disobedience because already they were secretly corrupted; for the evil act had never been done had not an evil will preceded it. And what is the origin of our evil will but pride? For 'pride is the beginning of sin.' And what is pride but the craving for undue exaltation? And this is undue exaltation, when the soul abandons Him to whom it ought to cleave as its end, and becomes a kind of end to itself" (Augustine, *City of God* 14.13).

63. Thus one may desire many things that are quite acceptable in God's sight. For example, "Take delight in the Lord, and he will give you the desires of your heart" (Ps 37:4). "[I]n your right hand are pleasures forevermore" (Ps 16:11).

64. *Common Prayer*, 848.

reason, I identify pride as the taproot of virtually all other sins. No wonder many church fathers placed it first in the list of the seven deadly sins.

Pride, however, probably reared its ugly head long before the garden of Eden. Many ancient interpreters, and some modern as well, ascribe the fall of Satan to the sin of pride. The famous taunt song of Ezek 28:1–19 describes a Canaanite king puffed up with his own self-importance. Behind this imagery lurks the Dark Lord himself, the angelic being who "was the signet of perfection, full of wisdom and perfect in beauty, [who was] in Eden, the garden of God" and who was "with an anointed cherub as guardian" and who resided "on the holy mountain of God" (Ezek 28:14). Though initially created as blameless, "iniquity was found in [him] . . . and [he] sinned" (Ezek 28:15). The cause of this sin is clearly stated: "Your heart was proud because of your beauty" (Ezek 28:17).[65] A comparable taunt song about a Babylonian king in Isa 14:12–14 may also depict Satan's pre-creation fall from grace. This tyrant's overweening sense of self-importance certainly fits Satan's profile: "I will ascend to heaven; I will raise my throne about the stars of God; I will sit on the mount of assembly on the heights of Zaphon; I will ascend to the tops of the clouds, *I will make myself like the Most High*" (Isa 14:13–14 [italics mine]). The Apostle Paul likely had these passages in mind when he warned Timothy about appointing bishops who were recent converts, since they "may be puffed up with conceit and fall into the condemnation of the devil" (1 Tim 3:6). To these archetypal stories I add brief snippets from two other sad stories in Scripture where pride leads to destruction.

The Pharaoh of the Exodus is a classic example of a person brought low by pride. It certainly didn't help matters that Egyptian ideology viewed Pharaoh as a god, the incarnation of the divine Amon Re. This radically wrong assumption led him to resist the true and living God until his nation lay literally in ruins.[66] Lest we think it unfair that the Lord should harden Pharaoh's heart, note that it's not until the fifth plague that the Lord steps in and hardens Pharaoh's heart.[67] Up till this point, Pharaoh hardens his own heart. Pride prods him to exalt himself above the Lord: "Who is the Lord, that I should heed him?" (Exod 5:2). Pharaoh has an opportunity to repent

---

65. According to Waltke, "the imagery fits Satan quite well" and "the lament for this Edenic king provides an account of the origin of evil in the created world" (*OT Theology*, 274).

66. Exod 7–14.

67. Exod 9:12; cf. Rom 1:24, 26, 28.

but refuses. Repentance is essentially recognizing that we have a problem that only the Lord can help us with, and then casting ourselves upon his mercy and grace. The problem is that pride blinds us to this truth.[68] No wonder Jesus said, "Truly I tell you, unless you change and become like children, you will never enter the kingdom of heaven" (Matt 18:3).

For all his virtues, King David was not immune to vices. His affair with Bathsheba illustrates what can happen when we succumb to self-centered pride.[69] In David's case, passion led to adultery, then murder, then a royal coverup. When the prophet Nathan exposes this sordid affair, he cuts right to the heart of the matter: "Why have you despised the word of the Lord, to do what is evil in his sight?" (2 Sam 12:9). In short, David conveniently ignored the Deuteronomic law of the king, especially the warning about "neither exalting himself above other members of the community nor turning aside from the commandment..." (Deut 17:20). Success and power led him to think he was exempt from the constraints placed upon everyone else.[70] This delusion is an occupational hazard for politicians at all times and all places, as regularly confirmed by the news media.

But pride doesn't affect only the high and the mighty; it messes with all of us. Nowhere is this more evident than in the Wisdom literature of the OT: Psalms, Proverbs, Ecclesiastes and Job. This portion of the canon waves a red flag about the danger of pride. The sages of Israel drew upon a rich repository of careful observation and reflection about the human condition. What they realized was alarming: pride wreaks havoc across the entire spectrum of society. Pride deceives us into thinking God doesn't really take note of our wrongful deeds. It also incites strife with our neighbors.[71] We seem never to learn what is virtually axiomatic: "When pride comes, then comes disgrace" (Prov 11:2, NIV) and "a person's pride will bring humiliation" (Prov 29:23).

---

68. When confronted by the Lord, Cain essentially denies his problem and seeks to deal with it by himself. Needless to say, he completely fails. The narrator reveals Cain's fundamental spiritual problem: "Then Cain went away from the presence of the Lord" (Gen 4:16).

69. 2 Sam 11.

70. The report card for all the kings of Israel and Judah shows a failing grade in this regard. See, e.g., Uzziah (2 Chr 26:16: "But when he had become strong he grew proud, to his destruction.") and Hezekiah (2 Chr 32:25: "But Hezekiah did not respond according to the benefit done to him, for his heart was proud. Therefore wrath came upon him and upon Judah and Jerusalem.").

71. Psa 10:4; Prov 13:10.

Mount Nebo and Mount Gilboa

I return to Moses and Saul. Jesus lays out a principle that surely applies to both leaders. "From everyone to whom much has been given, much will be required; and from the one to whom much has been entrusted, even more will be demanded" (Luke 12:48). Moses received remarkable privileges and powers; Saul received kingship and initial success. The Lord expected great things of both men. Whereas Moses achieved nearly everything he was commissioned to do, Saul had limited success and, in the end, failed miserably. Both, however, experienced bitter disappointment at the end of their lives. I have argued that in both cases the ultimate culprit was self-centered pride. To be sure, Saul's collapse was more catastrophic than Moses. Nonetheless, pride was a stumbling block for both men. Moses sought admiration and respect; Saul desperately craved honor and praise ("honor me now before the elders of Israel" [1 Sam 15:30; cf. 1 Sam 18:7–9]). And so do all of us.

It can be stated without fear of contradiction that every Christian must wrestle with self-centered pride. Furthermore, if we are placed in positions of authority and responsibility, the danger increases exponentially. As the old adage goes, "the higher they rise, the harder they fall." Here is the Apostle Peter's pastoral counsel for all those who exercise leadership roles in ministry:

> And all of you must clothe yourselves with humility in your dealings with one another, for "God opposes the proud, but gives grace to the humble." Humble yourselves therefore under the mighty hand of God, so that he may exalt you in due time. Cast all your anxiety on him, because he cares for you. Discipline yourselves, keep alert. Like a roaring lion your adversary the devil prowls around, looking for someone to devour. Resist him, steadfast in your faith. (1 Pet 5:5–9)

This is sound advice for all followers of Jesus. As the Apostle Peter reminds his readers (and that now includes us!) Christ left us an example that we "should follow in his steps" (1 Pet 2:21). Self-giving love is the antidote to self-centered pride. The Apostle Paul portrays the pattern of life to which we are called: "Let the same mind be in you that was in Christ Jesus, who, though he was in the form of God, did not regard equality with God as something to be exploited, but emptied himself, taking the form of a servant . . ." (Phil 2:5–7). The cruciform life must constantly shape our thinking: "May I never boast of anything except the cross of our Lord Jesus Christ, by which the world has been crucified to me, and I to the world"

(Gal 6:14). Isaac Watts captures the spirit of Peter and Paul's exhortation in this marvelous hymn:

> When I survey the wondrous cross
> On which the Prince of glory died,
> My richest gain I count but loss,
> And pour contempt on all my pride.
>
> Forbid it Lord, that I should boast,
> Save in the death of Christ, my God;
> All the vain things that charm me most—
> I sacrifice them to His blood.

6

Mount Ebal and Mount Carmel

Understanding Culture and Compromise

"Choose this day whom you will serve." (Josh 24:15)
"How long will you go limping with two different opinions?" (1 Kgs 18:21)

Introduction

Once again we climb two mountains whose location is not disputed.[1] In fact, Mount Carmel is one of the most visited mountains in the land of Israel, being a favorite stop for tour groups. In contrast, Mount Ebal, situated in the West Bank and not far from the Palestinian city of Nablus, is rarely visited by tourists. Unfortunately, the area has been the scene of sporadic violence between Palestinian militants and the Israeli Army. This, along with the time constraints of a limited tour, account for infrequent visits.

Our interest centers on two landmark events in the history of biblical Israel that took place either on the summit or beneath the shadow of these mountains. In each instance, a towering figure from Israel's storied past confronts his people with an ultimatum: "Choose this day whom you will serve" (Josh 24:15) and "If the Lord is God, follow him" (1 Kgs 18:21). These figures are Joshua and Elijah and their challenge to the Israelites of their

---

1. See map 6 in the appendix.

days reverberates in our own. The climb in this chapter is all about staying the course and refusing to compromise our commitment to the Lord.

Locating Our Mountains

Mount Ebal

Mount Ebal is closely connected geographically and historically with Mount Gerizim, a twin peak directly opposite and to the south, and with the ancient city of Shechem that nestles below and between them in a valley.[2] Today, the modern city of Nablus engulfs Tell Balâta, which is almost certainly ancient Shechem. In light of a momentous event that took place on its summit, Mount Ebal will serve as shorthand for this general area.

Mount Ebal is a well-recognized landmark in the hill country of Samaria and affords a panoramic view of the land.[3] Its Hebrew name means "bald mountain," perhaps reflecting the fact that relatively little vegetation grows on its southeastern sector. Rising to a height of 3,080 feet above sea level, Ebal stands like a sentinel over the east-west valley pass between it and its counterpart, Mount Gerizim. The ancient site of Shechem was the first recorded place Abram pitched his tent in the land of Canaan (at "the

---

2. William M. Thomson, a missionary who spent forty-five years in Syria and Palestine, describes this area as follows:
> By some convulsion of nature, the central range of mountains running north and south was cleft open to its base at right angles to its own line of extension, and the deep fissure thus made is the vale of Nâblus, as it appears to one coming up the plain of el Mûkhna from Jerusalem. The valley is a least eighteen hundred feet above the level of the sea, and the mountains on either hand tower to an elevation of about one thousand feet more. Mount Ebal is on the north, Gerizim on the south, and the city between. (*The Land and the Book*, 2:138)

3. Travelers in the nineteenth century comment on the excellent view from the summit of Ebal. Thomson's narrative captures the vista:
> Here we are at last upon the summit, and the prospect, in all directions, is indeed vast and wonderfully varied, and we see it to great advantage through the transparent atmosphere of this brilliant morning.
>
> Being considerably higher than Gerizim, the range of vision is much more extensive, and reaches to many parts not visible from the top of that mountain. It includes not only the entire province of Samaria, from the shores of the Mediterranean on the west to the Jordan valley on the east; and from Esdraelon [Jezreel] northward to the border of Judah, and far beyond it towards Jaffa and Jerusalem on the south; but also all of Galilee, upper and lower, to Jebel Jermûk, west of Safed, and the mountains north of that to the range of goodly Lebanon; while beyond Jordan, eastward and northward, the whole land of Gilead and of Bashan, up to snow-capped Hermon, are distinctly seen. (ibid., 152–53)

oak of Moreh") after his long trek from Haran in northern Iraq. "Then the Lord appeared to Abram, and said, 'To your offspring I will give this land.' So he built an altar to the Lord, who had appeared to him" (Gen 12:7). Not surprisingly, Shechem figured prominently as an important site in the subsequent history of Israel.[4]

Mount Carmel

Mount Carmel, like Mount Gilboa, is a mountain ridge rather than an isolated peak. The Carmel ridge is one of the most distinctive and prominent landmarks in the land of Israel. Indeed, it was known to many ancient mariners who navigated the eastern Mediterranean. Egyptian merchants sailing along the shores of Canaan even had a nickname for this promontory, calling it "the Nose of the Gazelle's Head."[5] Today, driving north on highways 2 or 4 from Tel Aviv to Haifa, one glimpses the Carmel ridge looming large on the horizon and immediately appreciates the well-chosen Egyptian appellation.[6]

The entire Carmel range, running in a northwest-southeast direction, is about thirty miles long and effectively cuts off the coastal plain by extending right out to the sea.[7] To the south the coastal plain is known as the Plain of Sharon and to the north the Plain of Acco. The northwest promontory is 470 feet high and farther to the southeast the ridge reaches its highest elevation at 1,742 feet. The ridge formed the southern boundary of the tribe of Asher and the northern boundary of Manasseh. The name refers to a garden land or orchard, no doubt owing to its favorable location and elevation. Since its heights benefit from generous amounts of precipitation (twenty-eight to thirty-six inches per year) on its fertile red-brown soil—the famous *terra rossa*—abundant vegetation abounds. This feature figures prominently in the background of the story to be developed shortly. First, however, we take up the chronologically prior story of Joshua on Mount Ebal.

---

4. Gen 33:18; 35:4; 37:12–14; Jos 20:7; 21:21; 24:1, 25, 32; 9:1–57; 1 Kgs 12:1; 12:25.
5. Aharoni, *Land of the Bible*, 99, 125.
6. See maps 5 and 6 in the appendix.
7. In fact, the Carmel ridge is divided into three distinct regions. Starting at the northwest end, we have the Carmel headlands, then the lower central basin, and finally, at the southeast end, the Umm el-Fahm arch (Baly, *Geography*, 180–83). The Carmel headlands, the focus of our attention in this chapter, is about thirteen miles long.

MOUNTAINTOP THEOLOGY

Historically Understanding Our Mountains

Ebal Traditions

Mount Ebal twice was the scene of a national assembly during the illustrious career of Joshua. The first came early on in the invasion of Canaan; in fact, it followed the destruction of the city of Ai—only the second of three cities the Israelites actually burned to the ground, the other two being Jericho and Hazor.[8] The initial attack on Ai was unexpectedly repelled, a circumstance traced to the deceit of Achan who snatched some of the forbidden plunder and hid it in his tent.[9] After dealing swiftly with this breach of faith, Joshua employed some deception of his own, a military ruse in which Ai was completely destroyed.[10] Perhaps Joshua felt that a public covenant renewal ceremony was needed in order to solidify commitment by all the tribes and to rally support for the covenant obligations. At any rate, he temporarily postponed the invasion and led a pilgrimage to Mount Ebal. There he built an altar to the Lord and "offered on it burnt offerings to the Lord and sacrificed offerings of well-being" (Josh 8:30–31) ("fellowship offerings," NIV, or "peace offerings," KJV). Then Joshua "wrote a copy of the law of Moses" on stones in the presence of the Israelites (Josh 8:32).[11]

It was not a coincidence that Joshua chose Mount Ebal as the place for a covenant renewal ceremony. Besides its sacred associations going back to Abraham, Moses had explicitly commanded that a covenant renewal ceremony be held at this historic location.[12] As per instructions, the tribes of Israel stood in two groups facing the ark of the covenant, which was surrounded by priests down in the valley between the two peaks. Half of the tribes stood on the slopes of Gerizim and the other half on the slopes of Ebal.[13] The tribes standing on the Mount Ebal side represented the curses

---

8. Josh 8:30–35; 6:24; 11:11. A still unresolved chronological problem concerns the date of the conquest. See Meier, "History of Israel," for an overview.

9. Josh 7:1, 20–21.

10. Josh 7:10–26; 8:1–29.

11. Joshua either plastered over the altar stones and inscribed the words of the law on them (Josh 8:32) or had specially prepared, plastered stones on which he wrote (Deut 27:2–3, 8).

12. Deut 11:26–30; 27:4–8.

13. The tribes of Simeon, Levi, Judah, Issachar, Joseph, and Benjamin stood on Gerizim and the tribes of Rueben, Gad, Asher, Zebulun, Dan, and Naphtali stood on Ebal. Acoustical experiments by a number of explorers and travelers have confirmed the reliability of the biblical account (see, e.g., McGarvey, *Lands of the Bible*, 506–8). As

that would befall them for disobedience and those on the Gerizim side represented the blessings that would accrue from obedience (Deut 27:11–14). After the Levites sounded out the content of a specific curse or blessing, the appropriate tribal grouping responded with a loud "amen." Makes you wonder how the tribes who uttered the curses felt! A more dramatic setting for reaffirming the Sinai covenant can scarcely be imagined.

The second national assembly also took place at Shechem, in the shadow of Mount Ebal, at the end of Joshua's storied and successful career.[14] The tribes had secured a foothold in the hill country from Galilee to the Negev; but much land remained unconquered.[15] Sensing a weakening of commitment to the Sinai covenant, Joshua summons the tribes for another renewal ceremony. Especially revealing is his command to "put away the foreign gods that are among you, and incline your hearts to the Lord, the God of Israel" (Josh 24:23).[16] The climactic moment centered on Joshua leading the people in a covenant renewal ceremony. According to the sacred historian, Joshua "made statutes and ordinances" for Israel and added these to the already existing "law of God." Then he erected a large stone "under the oak in the sanctuary of the Lord" (Josh 24:25–26), the same place where Abram first pitched his tent and built an altar.[17] The stone served as an enduring witness to Israel's covenant with the Lord. We hear echoes of the inaugural covenant ceremony at Mount Sinai. Just like the Exodus generation who loudly proclaimed, "all the Lord has spoken we will do, and we will be obedient" (Exod 24:7), so too, the conquest generation loudly asserts, "we will serve the Lord! . . . We are witnesses" (Josh 24:21). Sadly, it turns out to be a broken vow.

The reader may wonder if the altar and stone at Shechem may still be seen today. The short answer is no. What may be seen are the foundations of a Middle Bronze Age city wall, a gate complex, and the foundations of a temple, identified by the excavator, G. Ernest Wright, as the temple of Baal-berith and El-berith where the usurper Abimelech burned alive a

---

can clearly be seen from aerial photographs and on-site inspection, the facing slopes of Gerizim and Ebal have matching, natural amphitheater-shaped contours.

14. Josh 24.

15. Josh 13:1–7.

16. This recalls Jacob's demand that his family "put away the foreign gods that are among you" (Gen 35:2). The setting of this story is also at Shechem and follows the infamous Dinah affair.

17. Gen 12:6–7.

thousand men and women.[18] There is even a broken, freestanding stone at the entrance to this temple that recalls the one Joshua set up, but, alas, the surviving portion lacks an inscription.

There is, however, something rather extraordinary that has come to light on Mount Ebal itself. We already knew from earlier explorers and pilgrims that a Byzantine church once stood on its heights and there was a long-standing tradition that John the Baptist was buried on Mount Ebal.[19] A surface survey in 1980 revealed ancient ruins at *el-Burnat* ("the hat"), on the northeastern slope of Ebal.[20] In 1982, Adam Zertal excavated these remains and uncovered a double enclosed structure.[21] He identified it as a cultic installation with altar, ramp, and surrounding wall (*temenos*). In the layers of fill, within an area eventually identified as the altar, he found numerous animal bones, all of them kosher, that is, permissible to eat and offer as a sacrifice according to the Mosaic law.[22] No pig bones whatsoever turned up. At first Zertal was puzzled by the layers of fill. Then he realized that the fill was deliberately placed there in fulfillment of the biblical requirement that the altar be hollow.[23] This construction method has parallels to Assyrian altars. Associated pottery clearly dated to the early Iron Age, a period generally assigned to the Israelite settlement of the hill country. Two Egyptian scarabs also correlated with this dating.[24]

Zertal believes he may have found the ancient altar erected by Joshua on Mount Ebal. As you might expect, many in the archaeological community have registered emphatic disagreement with Zertal's interpretation; others have taken a wait and see attitude. It's a pity current conditions do not encourage tourists to visit the site and recount Joshua's covenant

---

18. Judg 9:4, 46, 49.

19. The connection is not as tenuous as might at first be supposed. John the Baptist carried on a baptizing ministry "at Aenon near Salim because water was abundant there" (John 3:23). Salim is only 5 kilometers east of Nablus.

20. The eastern slopes of Ebal consist of a series of four descending terrace steps. *El Burnat* is on the second such step. In fact, one cannot even see Mount Gerizim from this location, a major objection to identifying this as Joshua's altar.

21. See Zertal, "Joshua's Altar" and "Mount Ebal."

22. Lev 11:1–8.

23. Exod 27:8.

24. A scarab is an image of a dung beetle, held sacred by ancient Egyptians, carved on a gem stone. The image usually included a religious or historical inscription and served as an amulet or seal for the owner. The scarabs Zertal found are dated to the time of Rameses II (thirteenth century BC).

renewal ceremony on Mount Ebal. Many tourists do, of course, visit Jacob's Well and the ancient site of Shechem (Tel Balâta), where Abraham pitched his tent, the blessings and curses reverberated across the valley, and Jesus encountered the Samaritan woman. As always, visiting the actual site brings the Scriptures to life.

Convergence of Traditions

Before turning to the story of Elijah, I draw attention to a connection between Mount Sinai, Mount Nebo, and Mount Ebal. Twice Moses summoned Israel to give exclusive loyalty to the Lord. At Mount Sinai, the generation that crossed the Red Sea was called upon to enter into a special covenant with the Lord. Then, at the end of his life, in the plains of Moab and at the foot of Mount Nebo, just before the invasion of Canaan, Moses challenged the second generation to be faithful and loyal to that covenant. Twice Joshua challenged the Israelites to put away foreign gods and reaffirm their exclusive allegiance to the Lord. The first time was after the crossing of the Jordan River and the taking of Jericho and Ai, as recounted above. The second was a covenant renewal ceremony at the end of his life, at the foot of Mount Ebal. In a symbolic sense, Mount Ebal, like Sinai and Nebo, addresses the nation with the issue of commitment, staying the course.

That prompts a question: Why this emphasis on covenant renewal? Why was it apparently so difficult for Israel to remain loyal to her covenant Lord? Why, at the end of his life, must Joshua implore a new generation to put away foreign gods? Herein lies an important and perennial issue; indeed, one that confronts each new generation of believers. The short answer is that culture constantly threatens to undermine our loyalty to the covenant Lord. We tend to accommodate the gods of our day. This becomes clearer after we revisit another mountain, Mount Carmel.

Mount Carmel Traditions

The story of Elijah's exploits on Mount Carmel is a Sunday school staple. The vivid details of this life and death contest for the hearts and minds of the Israelite nation are still etched in my mind and I never tire of taking students and tourists to the roof of the monastery at Mukhraqa on Mount

Carmel to relive that dramatic encounter.[25] The view is one of my favorites in Israel. On a clear day, the vista is splendid; before one's eyes so many biblical episodes unfolded. Across the Jezreel Valley, on the Nazareth ridge, the modern city of Nazareth reminds us that this region was where Jesus grew to manhood.

Mukhraqa ("place of burning or sacrifice") is a Carmelite monastery and obviously does not go back to biblical times. Nor can one seriously maintain that it stands on the exact spot where the rival altars once stood. On the other hand, one can affirm with a fairly high degree of probability that the monastery lies in proximity to the biblical location, since the biblical description of the event and the geographical features of the site neatly dovetail.[26]

Understanding the Backstory

In order to comprehend fully what took place on that memorable day, one needs to review the backstory. Why was there such a dramatic contest on this particular location? The answer requires a brief foray into the nature of Canaanite religion. The indigenous peoples of Canaan subscribed to a fertility cult in which their chief deity Baal, a storm god, embodied virility and was portrayed as riding on the clouds in his chariot with lightning bolts in his hand.[27] The land of Canaan lies on the eastern edge of the Mediterranean, a climate zone consisting of two seasons: a hot, dry period lasting from May until mid-October, and a cool, rainy season, typically running from mid-October to April. The dry season rarely has any precipitation

---

25. Murphy-O'Connor captures my sentiments completely: "the episode that has fired the imagination of all succeeding generations is the epic trial of strength between Elijah and the 450 prophets of Baal (1 Kgs 18)" (*Holy Land*, 405). For a firsthand description of the view from the roof of the Carmelite monastery, see Thomson, *The Land and the Book*, 2:241. Father Murphy-O'Connor went to be with the Lord November 11, 2013. His amazing scholarship will be missed.

26. As Murphy-O'Connor states, "site and text harmonize perfectly. From the platform in front of the little Carmelite monastery (built in 1868) one can see the sea (1 Kgs 18:43), and there is a spring, Bir el-Mansoura, just below (18:33). The Qishon brook runs at the bottom of the hill (18:40) in the Jezreel valley (18:45–46). The colourful narrative comes to vivid life when read in this setting" (ibid.). For a lively exposition of the contest on Carmel with accompanying pictures of the site, see Smith, "A Fiery Prophet."

27. Note that in Hebrew psalmody, the poets can depict Yahweh with similar imagery: "Lift up a song to him who rides upon the clouds—his name is the Lord—be exultant before him" (Ps 68:4).

other than the moisture that comes in off the Mediterranean and condenses on the western slopes of Palestine in the form of dew. Needless to say, the vegetation dries up and conditions become quite arid.

As a consequence of such a seasonal pattern, agriculture must adapt to a long period of no precipitation. Irrigation, except in very limited locations, was not an option in the biblical period. If the former and latter rains failed to materialize, crops would be sparse or fail entirely. The former rains (October–December) permitted the farmers to plow up the hard, packed soil and plant their crops. The all-important latter rains (March–April) gave the crops one last boost before harvest stage.

This is where Baal enters the picture. Canaanite ideology and mythology viewed him as a leading player in a divine pantheon of gods, primarily responsible for the nourishing rains that afforded fruitful seasons. This being so, an important aspect of Canaanite liturgy was entreating Baal for the release of life-giving rains. It is even thought by some that Baal functioned as a seasonal, dying and rising god, that is, during the dry summer months, he descended to Mot, the god of the underworld, but then returned to life during the rainy season.[28] Be that as it may, because of Mount Carmel's verdant vegetation, it was considered a place where Baal was powerful and where he "loosed the fateful lightning of his terrible swift sword."[29] There were, in fact, various versions of Baal in different localities. The OT even uses the plural form Baals and mentions a number of place names and personal names that incorporate the name of Baal (e.g., Baal Gad, Baal Hamon, Baal Hazor, Baal Meon, Baal Peor, Baal Perazim, Ishbaal, and Jerubbaal).[30]

Canaanite religion, like other ancient religions generally, was steeped in magic. Magic assumes that human beings can, by certain techniques and rituals, manipulate deities to act on their behalf.[31] A morally degrading side to this ideology was the notion that ritual prostitution stimulated Baal to have intercourse with his heavenly consorts. This was thought to be what produced the powerful storms and their accompanying rains. Consequently, Canaanite sanctuaries involved sacred spaces where priestesses consorted with male worshipers. Once such a ritual takes root, hormones, not ideology, perpetuate it.

---

28. See further Curtis, "Canaanite Gods and Religion," 135–37.
29. From the first stanza of *Battle Hymn of the Republic* by Julia Ward Howe (1861).
30. Judg 2:11; 3:7; 10:6, 10; 1 Sam 7:4; 12:10 et al.
31. This is what sociologists of religion call sympathetic magic, ritualized actions that mimic the divine realm and link it to the human.

Mountaintop Theology

At first glance, one may be surprised that Israelites would stoop to such levels. But on further reflection, the appeal of this world view becomes only too apparent. Israelites knew that they were relative newcomers to the land. The indigenous population had practiced their religion for generations. All of Israel's neighbors subscribed to the view that each people group had its own deities. The sentiment was widespread in the Middle East that one should at least respect local deities, even if one's own were superior. Given the complete dependence of Hebrew farmers and pastoralists upon the annual rainfall for sustenance, it's not surprising that a period of drought could raise questions. What if the local deity was upset with the inhabitants and thus withholding rain? The temptation to "cover the bases" and "tip one's hat" to Baal doubtless arose in difficult times. Perhaps it wouldn't hurt if local custom were occasionally followed. Alas, more than a few succumbed to the inducement, explaining why the Hebrew prophets regularly rail against the detestable cult of the Baals.

This brings up the phenomenon of syncretism, another contributing factor to Israel's recurring problem of apostasy. Religious syncretism melds different traditions forming a new one. In short, the Hebrews flirted with a form of Yahweh worship in which Yahweh began to assimilate the attributes and characteristics of Baal. Remember that already at Mount Sinai, the Hebrews molded a golden calf to represent their invisible God.[32] The strong desire for concrete representation of the deity was difficult to suppress and living among the Canaanites only intensified that yearning.[33] Compounding the problem is the fact that Baal was represented as a young bull. Egypt, where the Hebrews had previously lived for generations, included in its large pantheon Apis the sacred bull. One also thinks of ancient Minoa to the west and the Hindus valley to the east where a god was represented in the form of a bull or cow. Slowly but surely, the faith of Mount Sinai was incorporating the faith of Mount Zaphon, the Canaanite mythical mount where Baal and his heavenly consort resided.[34] As the lines slowly blur

---

32. Exod 32.

33. Archaeological excavations of Canaanite sites in the land of Israel testify to the presence of figurines and amulets portraying fertility gods and goddesses. For a brief article and picture of a stele showing Baal, see Cundale, "Baal."

34. Gerhard von Rad identifies David's incorporation of large tracts of Canaanite territory into the empire as a time during which Canaanite influence grew to dangerous proportions. Jahwism began a gradual process of crumbling. He asks rhetorically, "But were the people still worshipping *Jahweh*? Was it not rather Baal, with his control over the blessings of the world of nature, who was now in their minds? For Baal was

between Baal and Yahweh, the importation of Canaanite rituals, including sacred prostitution, becomes less and less offensive. Add to this the sheer, physical attraction of unrestrained sexual gratification, which one could dignify under a religious cloak, and you have the seeds of spiritual destruction.

Crisis in the Days of Ahab

This is precisely what began to happen in the northern kingdom of Israel. Exacerbating the situation was a zealous champion of Canaanite religion in the person of Queen Jezebel, the daughter of Ethbaal, a Canaanite king. She was a devotee of Asherah or Ashtoreth, the female consort of Baal. The OT contains numerous warnings and admonitions about the wooden poles that were erected at Canaanite high places and that apparently represented this female fertility goddess. Jezebel ruthlessly suppressed the Hebrew prophets and sought to establish a state controlled Canaanite religion, abetted by King Ahab himself. This proved to be a deadly brew and drastic measures were necessary if the true faith of Mount Sinai were to survive. The Lord called a man who was up to the challenge.

Elijah the Champion of the Covenant

Into this national crisis steps Elijah, the champion of the Sinai covenant. Chapters 17–18 of 1 Kings stand at the very center of 1–2 Kings and reinforce the theme that God is in control of history and nature, not Jeroboam's golden calves or Ahab's Baal. 1 Kings 16:31 leads into our story on Mount Carmel: "And as if it had been a light thing for him to walk in the sins of Jeroboam son of Nebat, he took as his wife Jezebel daughter of King Ethbaal of the Sidonians, and went and served Baal, and worshiped him." The Lord calls Elijah to appear at the royal court and announce an extreme drought for the next three years. As suddenly as Elijah appears, he disappears, first hiding out in the Wadi Cherith on the east side of the Jordan, then staying with a widow at Zarephath on the coast of Phoenicia (modern Lebanon) to the north of Israel.[35] The consequences of the drought were devastating

---

nonetheless Baal, even when invoked by the name Jahweh. Or was the object of worship some indeterminate third party who belonged somewhere between the two?" (*OT Theology*, 2:15).

35. Another instance in the OT in which God's grace is extended to Gentiles. Jesus

for both animals and people.[36] The theological significance of this account is apparent: the Lord controls the rain, not Baal. For three years, in spite of appeals to the reputed storm god of Canaan, there is neither rain nor dew. Even on the coast of Phoenicia, a bastion of Baal worship, drought reigns supreme at Yahweh's command.

Contest on Carmel

At the end of the three years, it's time to demonstrate that Baal is impotent, even on the famed and fertile headland of Carmel; nay, even more, he is no god at all. Elijah reappears and confronts Ahab who accuses Elijah of being the "troubler of Israel" (1 Kgs 18:17). Elijah caustically fires back, "I have not troubled Israel; but you have, and your father's house, because you have forsaken the commandments of the LORD and followed the Baals" (1 Kgs 18:18). Elijah quickly follows up with orders to proclaim a national assembly and a test of strength at Mount Carmel. Ahab, himself reduced to impotence by the crippling drought, can only acquiesce.

As already discussed, Mount Carmel had long been venerated in Canaanite tradition as a stronghold of Baal. The "force" was supposed to be strong there. Elijah challenges this ideology head on. To use basketball lingo, Yahweh challenges Baal to a one-on-one game on Baal's home court. Elijah skillfully sets up the terms for this contest. To a disinterested outsider, it might seem heavily stacked in favor of Baal; after all, he has 450 prophets as his attendants; Elijah stands as the solitary messenger of Yahweh. Of course, in reality, Baal is a nothing and Yahweh is everything. Elijah wants this fact to be dramatically portrayed before the eyes of the onlooking Israelites, to say nothing of Ahab and his officials.

The objective in this trial by strength was to determine which deity could cause fire from heaven to set ablaze the sacrificial wood. Remember that Baal was represented as holding lightning bolts in his hand and hurling them to the earth. Surely, on these hallowed heights, he could display his mastery of fire and lightning. Elijah insists that the prophets of Baal go first, since they are so numerous. This clever stratagem allows Elijah to expose to full view the futility of this fertility cult. As the prophets of Baal frantically perform their ritualistic actions designed to induce Baal to action,

---

refers to her story in his Nazareth sermon, much to the displeasure of the Jewish listeners (Luke 4:25–30).

36. 1 Kgs 17:12; 18:5.

Mount Ebal and Mount Carmel

Elijah is unsparing in his derision and sarcasm. This rises to a pitch when Elijah taunts them: "Cry aloud! Surely he is a god; either he is meditating, or he has wandered away, or he is on a journey, or perhaps he is asleep and must be awakened" (1 Kgs 18:27). The expression "he has wandered away" is probably best rendered "he is using the toilet," or "he is relieving himself"![37] At first the prophets of Baal invoke him through stereotyped formulas and liturgies. This proves ineffective. Then they perform a ritual dance around the sacrifice, whipping themselves into an ecstatic trance and uttering gibberish.[38] As Elijah mocks them, they increase the intensity of their appeals and frenzied dancing. Still to no effect. Finally, they resort to extreme measures; they begin slashing themselves with swords and lances so that their blood flowed as they raved about the sacrifice.[39] The sacred historian laconically and with great effect simply says, "there was no voice, no answer, and no response" (1 Kgs 18:29).

As the time for the evening offering drew near, Elijah calls a halt to the Canaanite charade, and takes center stage. His preparations are simple, solemn, and stringent. As required by the Mosaic law, he gathers twelve unhewn stones, representing the twelve tribes of Israel, and builds an altar. After digging a trench around the altar, he lays the wood and places the pieces of the bull on the altar. Before entreating the Lord to answer by fire, he takes special pains to forestall any charges of fraud and trickery. He requests that four jars of water, three times (thus a total, once again, of twelve) be poured out on top of the sacrificial pieces, the wood and the altar. Then as the hour of the evening sacrifice arrived, he simply prays: "Let it be known this day that you are God in Israel . . ." and that "this people may know that you, O Lord, are God, and that you have turned their hearts back" (1 Kgs 18:36-37). The response is spectacular. Everything on and

---

37. CEV, NLT, and GNB.

38. Rhythmic actions that induce ecstasy and euphoria are well-documented in various religious groups. One thinks of the whirling dervishes of the Islamic Sufi sects.

39. Bloodletting is a long-standing technique used in pagan religions. The point is to demonstrate one's utter devotion to the deity. This manipulative approach to the deity is still practiced in various religions today. In fact, not far from ancient Sidon, each spring the Muslims celebrate the martyrdom of a revered holy man. All Muslim males from young boys to aged men allow an imam to slice their foreheads with a straight edge as they make their way in procession to the local mosque as a demonstration of their depth of devotion to Allah. Alas, Christianity is not immune to such excesses, especially in certain parts of the world where, during Holy Week, individuals allow themselves to be nailed briefly to a cross. In my view, such actions are neither acceptable nor commendable—they betray pagan influence and should be abandoned.

Mountaintop Theology

around the altar is totally consumed by the fire of the Lord, including the stones! The impact on the audience is instantaneous and spontaneous: the people fall on their faces and loudly proclaim, "The Lord indeed is God; the Lord indeed is God" (1 Kgs 18:19).

This extraordinary, divine intervention is not without precedent. In fact, it is the third time fire from the Lord consumes a sacrifice. The first was the climactic conclusion of a ceremony on the eighth day following a seven day period of consecration for the sanctuary and priests at Mount Sinai.[40] Here is the account: "Moses and Aaron entered the tent of meeting, and then came out and blessed the people; and the glory of the Lord appeared to all the people. Fire came out from the Lord and consumed the burnt offering and the fat on the altar; and when all the people saw it, they shouted and fell on their faces" (Lev 9:23–24). The second occurred when David built an altar on the threshing floor of Arunah the Jebusite, on the summit of Mount Zion (Moriah), and presented burnt and peace offerings: "He called upon the name of the Lord, and he answered him with fire from heaven on the altar of burnt offering" (1 Chr 21:26). This altar became the site of the First Temple built by Solomon.[41]

It's worth mentioning that on the Day of Pentecost, the birthday of the church, a fiery phenomenon manifested itself: "And suddenly from heaven there came a sound like the rush of a violent wind, and it filled the entire house where they were sitting. Divided tongues, as of fire, appeared among them, and a tongue rested on each of them. All of them were filled with the Holy Spirit and began to speak in other languages, as the Spirit gave them ability" (Acts 2:2–4). In contrast to the incoherent babbling of the prophets of Baal, the apostles proclaim "God's deeds of power" in the various languages of the first century AD (Acts 2:8–11). In short, one may typologically connect the events of Mount Sinai, Mount Zion of David's day, Mount Carmel, and Mount Zion of Pentecost in a remarkable trajectory of divine intervention and revelation.[42] The three OT events involved either the ratification or renewal of the old covenant of Mount Sinai and the

---

40. Lev 8–9.

41. 2 Sam 7:1–13; 24:18–25; 1 Kgs 5:1–6.

42. I distinguish Mount Zion in David's day from the scene of Pentecost because in the intervening years between David and Pentecost, the true location of Mount Zion was lost and it was mistakenly relocated on the western hill, just outside the present Old City of Jerusalem.

NT counterpart was the inauguration of the new covenant of the heavenly Mount Zion, about which I will say more in the last chapter of this book.[43]

Seizing the momentum, Elijah orders the execution of the 450 prophets of Baal.[44] But the contest is not finished—the problem of drought still remains. Can Yahweh bring the life-giving rains he promised in the Sinai covenant?[45] Elijah goes back up to the summit from which one can see the Mediterranean. Seven times Elijah dispatches his servant to scan the skies while he "bowed himself down upon the earth and put his face between his knees" (1 Kgs 18:42). After the seventh request, the report comes back: "Look, a little cloud no bigger than a person's hand is rising out of the sea" (1 Kgs 18:44).[46] Elijah quickly orders Ahab to hightail it for the palace at Jezreel—a cloudburst is on the way. In another supernatural feat, Elijah runs before the chariot of Ahab all the way to Jezreel, a distance farther than a mini-marathon, about sixteen miles. Alas, there was no one to clock Elijah, which is too bad, since his time would doubtless still stand as a world record![47]

Space limitations require that I break off the story here and return to the main point of this chapter. Before doing so, however, I must at least mention that in the aftermath of Jezebel's death threat against Elijah and his subsequent flight, it's not without theological significance that Elijah retreats to Mount Sinai, the scene of the original covenant ratification. After a theophany reminiscent of Moses's experience,[48] Elijah is recommissioned to combat the Canaanite cult of the northern kingdom. In short, Ahab and Jezebel's days are numbered. Elisha will succeed Elijah and continue the struggle.[49] These two prophets call out a remnant of the faithful who refuse to bow the knee to Baal. Eventually, the northern kingdom succumbs because of their covenant unfaithfulness and is destroyed by Assyria.[50]

---

43. Heb 12:22; Gal 4:24–27.
44. Cf. Exod 22:20; Deut 18:20.
45. Deut 11:11–12, 14.
46. The number seven is not a mere coincidence. One remembers the siege of Jericho and the seven-day circumlocution of the city followed by a seven-fold circuit on the seventh day prior to its destruction. If Jericho represented the first clash between Canaanite and Yahwistic religion, Carmel marks another critical encounter in an ongoing struggle for dominance.
47. For more details on this extraordinary race, see Helyer, "Come What May."
48. 1 Kgs 19:11–14.
49 1 Kgs 19:15–18.
50. 2 Kgs 17:1–23.

Theological Significance of Mount Ebal and Mount Carmel

These two mountains and the momentous events that transpired on their summits or below their heights address a common human problem. In the words of the hymn writer, "Prone to wander—Lord I feel it—Prone to leave the God I love."[51] A major factor in this tendency to wander lies in the powerful attraction and seduction of our culture. Both Testaments warn the people of God that they must, in certain, specified ways, be separate from the culture in which they live and move and have their being.[52] How on earth can this be done? Judging from the scriptural narrative, not easily and not without great commitment and sacrifice.

Earlier in our chapter on Mount Sinai and the Mount of Beatitudes, we examined the biblical teaching of holiness. At the core of this concept lies loyalty, complete allegiance and faithfulness to the covenant obligations of our sovereign Lord. This is true of both the old and new covenants.

Joshua and Elijah summoned Israel to unswerving loyalty. Jesus agrees: "No one can serve two masters" (Matt 6:24). Simply stated, the believer can't straddle the fence; there is no middle ground. Scripture reminds readers that the stakes are high in the spiritual struggle between the dark side and the kingdom of God. Redemptive history records the consequences of compromising commitment to the one, true and living God—the low lights of salvation history.[53]

Contemporary Application

A major challenge for Christian commitment flows directly out of the stories we've just considered. The ancient Canaanite fertility cult never really disappeared. In fact, it is very much alive and well in our modern culture. "Sex makes the world go 'round." This clever slogan captures both the mood and credo of contemporary culture whether in developed or undeveloped nations. Sex sells and pop culture, social media, and the advertising industry know it. The entertainment industry keeps chipping away at social acceptability standards and the result is 24/7 sexual bombardment. What

---

51. From the hymn "Come, Thou Fount." Lyrics by Robert Robinson (1735-1790).

52. Lev 26:12-15; Ezek 37:21-23; Isa 52:11; Rom 12:1-2; 13:12-14; 1 Cor 5:9-13; 6:9-20; 2 Cor 6:13-7:1; Gal 5:17-21; Eph 2:1-10; 1 Thess 4:3-8; 2 Tim 3:1-9; Heb 13:5-6; 1 Pet 2:11-12; 1 John 1:6-10; 2:15-17.

53. A point repeatedly made in the so-called Deuteronomic History, i.e., the books Judges-2 Kings.

would have been totally unacceptable by the general public forty years ago, now hardly raises an eyebrow. This steady exposure is like a narcotic; it is highly addictive and Christians are not immune.

Committed Christians find themselves in a difficult situation. On the one hand, we are convinced that sexuality is a gift from the Creator to be celebrated and enjoyed within marriage between a man and a woman. On the other hand, we are concerned because illicit sex threatens to undermine the creation order and Christian ethical standards based upon Scripture and tradition. It is no secret that growing numbers of Christians cohabit, that divorce rates are entirely too high, that addiction to pornography is escalating—even among pastors—and that lesbian, gay, bisexual, and transgender (LGBT) lifestyles are increasingly gaining social and legal acceptability and even viewed as normal in some Christian circles.

The NT speaks unequivocally on this point and Paul's exhortation to the Thessalonians may be paralleled in many other passages: "For this is the will of God, your sanctification: that you abstain from fornication; that each of you know how to control your own body in holiness and honor, not with lustful passion, like the Gentiles who do not know God . . ." (1 Thess 4:4–5).[54] Even the pragmatic argument of the ancient Israelites justifying their participation in Canaanite fertility rites finds its counterpart in our own day with its pragmatic, though quite erroneous, claim that sexual experimentation is entirely normal and even desirable for healthy psychological development.

A case in point is my concern that Canaanite religion has slipped in through the back door of our churches. One of the most contentious aspects of modern church life is contemporary Christian music. Convictions and preferences run deep and objectivity is difficult. I want to establish as much common ground and consensus as possible. Certainly, Christians can and ought to appreciate a wide range of music and worship practices.

What I find troubling, however, is the subtle importation of sexual insinuation into the performance. That is, sometimes the *manner* and *style* in which Christian contemporary music is performed subliminally conveys the sexually charged environment of its secular counterpart. There is no objection in principle to adapting popular music and tunes to a sacred setting. This has been done throughout church history with generally good effects. What is problematic, however, are the subtle, sexual innuendos that

---

54. The Greek word *porneia*, translated as "fornication," is used "of every kind of unlawful sexual intercourse" (Arndt and Gingrich, *A Greek-English*, 699).

may also be imported. For example I attended a worship service, with a praise band in which the female lead vocalist was dressed in a skintight outfit. I have seen young men in similar bands imitate the moves of secular rock band guitarists that are overtly sexual in nature. Christian songs sung with sexual overtones mute the spiritual message and spiritual lyrics can't sanctify subliminal sex.

Christian artists and performers may be offended by my criticism and reply that it's my problem not theirs. I refuse to give ground on this issue. I've had enough life experience to know that sexuality is close to the surface and a real and present danger, if not kept on a short leash. Evangelicalism has had far too many sexual scandals splashed across the media to pretend otherwise. The boundaries between spirituality and sexuality can be quickly crossed. Furthermore, whether members of a worship band are consciously aware of this or not is an insufficient reason to permit this kind of behavior. The Dark Lord is a master of deceit and he is having a field day right in the midst of Christian sanctuaries. "The desire of the flesh, the desire of the eyes, and pride in riches" (1 John 2:16) are not just quaint phrases; they depict powerful drives, especially in a sex-sated society such as our own. This must be firmly dealt with and monitored by pastoral staffs, worship committees, and those charged with the spiritual oversight of the local church. Guidelines should be clearly stated and carefully maintained.

I come to the heart of the issue. Our culture is all about self. Never before in human history has narcissism been so pervasive. This kind of psychological environment wreaks havoc with biblical truth. A little reflection makes it clear that the heart of the NT is self-giving love. The Son of God gave himself for us in order to set us free from servitude to self, sex, and society.[55] Furthermore, our bodies are the temple of the Holy Spirit and in these bodies we are called to minister the redemptive love of Christ.[56] Our culture broadcasts a totally different message. It beckons us to indulge ourselves to the max—to abandon our defenses and let our "darker side give in to the power of . . . the music of the night."[57] In reality, it's a flight into illusion, and ultimately, disillusion. Christians who turn off onto this path are in grave danger of never making it to the finish line. The reason is simple:

55. John 8:32–36; Gal 5:1, 13; Rom 6:6, 18; 8:2; Heb 2:15; 9:15; 1 Pet 2:26.

56. 1 Cor 3:16; 6:19–20.

57. "The Music of the Night," from *Phantom of the Opera*. The lyrics are by Andrew Lloyd Webber, Henry Zachary Stilgoe, and Charles Eliott Hart. The setting of the song is a seduction scene and the lyrics are illustrative of the power of the broader culture to seduce us from a complete allegiance to Christ.

narcissism withers the spiritual life by fostering apathy, indifference, and unbelief. If left untended, this can only lead to rebellion and apostasy.[58]

The link between narcissism and sexual addiction and perversion is undeniable. This all ties back to the reason why it is essential for us to climb Mount Ebal and Mount Carmel. The gods of our day are, when all is said and done, simply variations of what Joshua and Elijah confronted in their time. The Canaanite fertility cult was all about manipulating the deity to get what one wants. In short, Baalism has morphed into narcissism and it's as deadly and addictive as ever. There can be no compromise with this ideology. It must be resisted and not allowed to gain a foothold in one's heart. In Paul's words, "do not let sin exercise dominion in your mortal bodies, to make you obey their passions" (Rom 6:12).

How do we do this? The answer is basically the same as it was in Joshua and Elijah's day: we must choose whom we will serve and put away all false gods. Having made the commitment that Jesus is Lord, we continue to trust him and serve him to the very end. "As you therefore have received Christ Jesus the Lord, continue to live your lives in him, rooted and built up in him and established in the faith, just as you were taught, abounding in thanksgiving.[59] Each new day requires a conscious act of covenant renewal. And so it is until we reach the summit.

---

58. Heb 2:1–3; 3:12–4:11; 6:1–8; 10:26–31; 12:25–29.
59. For further discussion of practical steps, see Helyer, "Proclaiming Christ as Lord."

7

Mount of Transfiguration and Mount of Olives

Understanding the Future

"They will see 'the Son of Man coming on the clouds of heaven' with power and great glory." (Matt 24:30)

Introduction

Two mountains are the setting for three significant events in the life of Jesus. What happened and what he said there are literally of earth-shattering importance, impacting every person who has ever lived or will live on the planet. Simply stated, on these two mountains, Jesus previews and predicts the end of the world as we know it. Eschatology, the study of last things, is the subject of this chapter and the objective of our climb.

Locating the Mount of transfiguration

Traditional Site

Once again, however, the question of identification must be addressed.[1] The traditional location is Mount Tabor (Jebel et Tur), a striking, cone-shaped peak rising to an elevation of 1,843 feet at the northeastern end of

---

1. See maps 5 and 6 in the appendix.

the Jezreel Valley, about six miles southeast of Nazareth and twelve miles to the north of the Gilboa ridge.[2] This was the mountain on which Deborah ordered Barak to assemble 10,000 men from Nahptali and Zebulun in the days of King Jabin the Canaanite and Sisera the commander of his army (Judg 4). Human remains on Mount Tabor reach back to the Neanderthal age (80,000 to 15,000 BC) and it was clearly an important site throughout the biblical period.[3] The prophet Hosea denounces false worship on Mount Tabor in the eighth century BC.[4] The Hasmonean king Alexander Jannaeus (103–76 BC) fortified it and in the First Jewish Revolt against Rome (AD 66–73), Josephus strengthened its defenses.[5] Since Jesus grew up at Nazareth, nearby Tabor would have been a familiar landmark for him, although nowhere does the Gospel tradition explicitly mention Jesus' presence on the summit or slopes of the mountain.[6]

What testimony exists for identifying Mount Tabor as the place where Jesus was transfigured? In AD 326, Queen Helena authorized the construction of a chapel on its summit to commemorate the event. But the identification of Tabor as the Mount of Transfiguration occurs already in a marginal note on Ps 88:13 LXX (89:12 MT) by the church father Origen around AD 200.[7] Eusebius, the fourth-century church historian and resident of Caesarea Maritima, wavered between Mount Tabor and Hermon. The latter should probably not be identified with Mount Hermon in northern Galilee, but with "Little Hermon," the biblical hill of Moreh (Jebel Duhi) located only about five miles southwest of Tabor.[8] The pilgrim of Bordeaux (AD 333) cites the Mount of Olives as the place where this event was celebrated. One wonders if the convenient proximity to Jerusalem entered into the equation. The Jerusalem area ill fits the context of Jesus' transfiguration, so we may safely dismiss this option. Cyril of Jerusalem (AD 348) was the

---

2. See Jung, "Tabor."

3. Josh 19:22; Judg 4:6, 12, 14; 8:18; Jer 46:18; Ps 89:13 and perhaps Deut 33:18–19.

4. Hos 5:1.

5 Josephus, *J.W.*, 4.54–56.

6. See Scharlemann, "Transfiguration, Mount of," and Liefield, "Transfiguration."

7. See Hilhorst, "The Mountain of Transfiguration." Hilhorst translates the comment as follows: "Tabor is the mountain in Galilee on which Christ was transfigured."

8. Judg 7:1. This is the Mount Hermon that Egeria described. See Wilkinson, ed., *Egeria's Travels*, 95–97.

earliest of the church fathers to unequivocally support Mount Tabor,[9] and after Jerome adds his endorsement, the tradition is firmly established.

On its summit, Benedictine monks built the church of the transfiguration in AD 1100, an edifice Saladin pillaged in 1187 and Sultan Bybars completely destroyed in 1263. Not until 1631 were Franciscan monks allowed to occupy the mountain. In 1921–1924 the Franciscans built a basilica with two towers dedicated to Moses and Elijah. The Greek Orthodox also built the St. Elijah Church nearby on top of older Byzantine remains. Most Western Churches and the Eastern Orthodox still celebrate the Feast of Transfiguration in August, a tradition that is sometimes called *Thaborion* ("Tabor feast").

Problems with the Traditional Site

An objection to Mount Tabor as the Mount of Transfiguration comes from the testimony of ancient historians who mention that the mountain was inhabited and fortified with walls in the time of Antiochus III (third century BC) and in the time of the Roman general Pompey (first century BC).[10] We also know that Josephus strengthened the defenses of Itabyrium (the name for the settlement on Mount Tabor) during the First Jewish Revolt against Rome in the first century AD.[11] Most likely, then, during Jesus' ministry, there was some sort of settlement on its summit or slopes. Since Mark says "Jesus took with him Peter and James and John, and led them up a *high mountain apart, by themselves*" (Mark 9:2 [italics mine]), this may call into question Mount Tabor as the authentic location. One should, however, bear in mind William Thomson's assessment:

> A more appropriate site for such a glorious manifestation could not be desired. Nor does the fact that there may have been a fortified city on the summit at that time present an insuperable difficulty. There are many secluded terraces on the north and north-east sides admirably adapted for the scenes of the Transfiguration, and I regret that the early faith in this site has been disturbed.... [The Gospels] contain nothing decisive against the claims of Tabor.[12]

9. Cyril of Jerusalem, *Catecheses* 12.16.

10. Frankel, "Tabor, Mount."

11. Josephus, *J.W.* 2.20.6; 4.1.8. See further Murphy-O'Connor, *Holy Land*, 413 and Schlegel, *Satellite Bible Atlas*, 9–6.

12. Thomson, *The Land and the Book*, 2:327

Another objection arises from the immediate context of the transfiguration, namely, "the villages of Caesarea Philippi" (Mark 8:27; cf. Matt 16:13). Mark places the transfiguration only "six days later" (Mark 9:2) and Luke says "about eight days" (Luke 9:28). But the distance and time are not really a serious problem; it could easily have been accomplished within the stated time frame. Finally, some argue that Jesus' point in traveling to Caesarea Philippi in the first place was to withdraw from the hostile Jewish authorities in Galilee in order to impart private, uninterrupted instruction and revelation to his disciples. But this hardly requires that the ensuing transfiguration took place somewhere other than Mount Tabor.

Mount Meron

Some suggest Mount Meron (Jebel Jarmaq), the highest peak in upper Galilee, about 20 miles across the Rift Valley to the west of Mount Hermon and reaching 3,963 feet. Besides its elevation, this area could account for the presence of both a Jewish crowd and, more significantly, Jewish scribes. Neither of these observations, however, are decisive. Though considerably higher than Mount Tabor, the *relative* height of Mount Meron appears less than that of Tabor because there are other peaks of similar elevation in the region. Tabor, on the other hand, appears as a relatively high mountain because it is surrounded by the low-lying Jezreel Plain. The major problem with Meron is the complete absence of any early Christian tradition locating the transfiguration on Meron.

Mount Hermon

If Mount Hermon be the Mount of transfiguration, we at last climb a "real" mountain. At 9,232 feet in elevation, it towers above the previous mountains we've scaled, standing more than three times higher than Mount Calvary and Mount Moriah, Mount Nebo and Mount Gilboa, Mount Ebal and Mount Carmel—qualifying as a mountain even by North American standards and serving as a splendid setting for a stunning revelation.

What a candidate it is—lofty Mount Hermon decked out in her winter snow is a postcard picture. Local tradition calls it Jebel el-Sheikh ("gray-haired mountain") or Jebel el-Thalj ("mountain of the snow"), " both appropriate appellations. On a clear day—alas, such glorious days seem less frequent than when I lived in Israel back in 1968-69—one can glimpse

Hermon from far away. Travelers and missionaries of former generations provide wonderful descriptions of this majestic mount.[13]

In the OT, it is most often called Hermon, meaning "devoted or sacred place." This points to its religious significance among the pre-Israelite peoples, including the various Amorite and Canaanite peoples. The Sidonians called the mountain Sirion and the Amorites called it Senir.[14] Psalm 29 depicts a violent thunderstorm and earthquake on its heights in which lightning splits the mighty cedars of Lebanon: "The voice of the Lord breaks the cedars; the Lord breaks the cedars of Lebanon. He makes Lebanon skip like a calf, and Sirion like a young wild ox."[15] In the Song of Solomon, the lover longingly entreats his beloved to "Come with me from Lebanon, my bride, come with me from Lebanon. Depart from the peak of Amana, from the peak of Senir and Hermon, from the dens of lions, from the mountains of leopards" (Song 3:8). As late as the nineteenth century, bears were occasionally seen on Mount Hermon.[16] According to 1 Chr 5:23, the members of the half-tribe of Manasseh who lived on the east side of the Jordan are situated "from Bashan to Baal-hermon, Senir, and Mount Hermon." It has been suggested that these names are the three distinct peaks comprising Mount Hermon.[17] Perhaps this is why in Ps 42:6, the Hebrew word for "Hermon" is actually plural, "Hermons." Given the long-standing, religious traditions connected with Mount Hermon, it seems fitting that a remarkable theophany should take place on its slopes or summit.

Objections to Mount Hermon

But Mount Hermon is not without its difficulties. When Jesus and his three apostles come down off the mountain, they immediately encounter the disciples who remained behind and Jewish scribes arguing with them (Mark 9:14). Given the pagan environment of the Caesarea Philippi cult center, would Jews have even been in the vicinity? In reply, one need not assume that the confrontation occurred at or even near the cult center. After all,

---

13. None better than that of the intrepid traveler William Thomson. See *The Land and the Book*, 522–23.

14. Deut 3:9.

15. Ps 29:5–6.

16. Ibid.

17. See Bowling, "Senir." For a description of the three peaks, see Thomson, *The Land and the Book*, 2:519–23. They are about a quarter of a mile apart from each other.

there were *villages* in the district, doubtless comprising mixed populations of Jews and Gentiles, just like at Bethsaida. It would be important that Jewish populations living in such areas have scribal authorities to provide guidance in observing Jewish law. Unfortunately, the following context in Mark 9:30, 33 ("They went on from *there* and *passed through* Galilee. . . . Then they came to Capernaum . . . "[italics mine]) can be harmonized with either Tabor, Meron, or Hermon as the point of departure ("from there"). In short, we are lacking decisive evidence for any of the three candidates.

Conclusion

I confess to my readers that when I began research on this book, Mount Hermon was my preferred choice for the site of the transfiguration. Further investigation has raised doubts.[18] The weight of tradition, reaching back perhaps to the middle and end of the second century AD, has been a significant factor. It wasn't until John Lightfoot in the seventeenth century that Mount Hermon was suggested as the site of the transfiguration. One also suspects that a general Protestant distaste for Latin and Greek "holy sites" entered into the calculus of site identification. At any rate, though I personally prefer closure, I'm leaving this an open question. In the final analysis, Robert Stein is certainly correct: "the biblical writers apparently were not interested in locating exactly *where* this event took place; they were more concerned with *what* took place."[19] But before recounting the what, we describe our matching mountain, the Mount of Olives.

The Mount of Olives

The Geography of the Mount of Olives

Needless to say, there is absolutely no dispute about the location of the Mount of Olives and it has to be one of the most frequently visited mountains in the world.[20] Millions of tourists stand on its heights and gaze with wonder at the breathtaking view of Jerusalem the Golden to the west and

---

18. In April 2014 my wife and I drove up to the summit of Tabor and spent time exploring the chapels and appreciating the vista. Perhaps this was a factor in my wavering support for Mount Hermon.

19. Stein, "Transfiguration," 782 (italics his).

20. See map 2 in the appendix.

Mountaintop Theology

the wilderness of Judea falling off into the great Jordan Rift Valley to the east. Its elevation is a mere 2,700 feet above sea level, but it stands about 200 feet higher than the Old City of Jerusalem lying to its west and thus affords a splendid observation point. One is always aware of this mountain ridge with its distinctive towers on the eastern skyline of the Old City.[21] Once again, we're talking about a mile-long limestone ridge, running north and south and parallel to the Old City, rather than a distinct summit.[22] A mere twelve miles to the east of the ridge, the way the crow flies, lies the Dead Sea, the lowest place on planet Earth at more than 1,200 feet below sea level. Consequently, the Mount of Olives stands some 3,900 feet higher than the Dead Sea and thus seems a lot higher than it actually is to one who is ascending to Jerusalem up the Jericho road.

Har Zetayim in Hebrew means "Mount of Olives." Visitors during the summer months may marvel that olive trees can flourish on this location, but it stands just on the edge of the great Judean Wilderness and receives enough annual precipitation to sustain olives and figs.[23] A short distance to the east, however, one enters a rain shadow, as the moisture bearing winds from the Mediterranean drop their last precious cargo and begin a precipitous descent into the Jordan valley. As the air plummets down the slopes of the wilderness it increases in temperature and actually sucks what little moisture there is out of an already arid landscape.[24] The region between the Mount of Olives and Jericho is a true desert.

---

21. These towers are, moving from north to south, the Hebrew University tower, the Augusta Victoria tower, the Russian Church of the Ascension tower, and the Church of the Pater Noster tower. There are other smaller towers but the ones mentioned dominate the skyline of the Mount of Olives.

22. The ridge is actually divided into five distinct hills (Pfeiffer, *Bible Atlas*, 150–53).

23. Thus, for example, Jesus passed through a village on the eastern slopes of the Mount of Olives called Bethphage, meaning, "House of figs" (Mark 11:1; Luke 19:29; Matt 21:1). This village sits right on the fringe of the desert but still receives enough moisture to sustain fig trees.

24. There is even a mathematical equation that describes this phenomenon. In short, air temperature decreases or increases in proportion to the rise or fall in elevation.

Mount of Transfiguration and Mount of Olives

Redemptive History and the Mount of Olives

David's Ascent

This mountain figures in a memorable scene from the life of David. The setting was Absalom's rebellion.[25] As Absalom's forces swept down upon Jerusalem from Hebron, David had no choice but to evacuate the city. The sacred historian sketches a poignant moment during David's escape: "But David went up the ascent of the Mount of Olives, weeping as he went, with his head covered and walking barefoot; and all the people who were with him covered their heads and went up, weeping as they went"(2 Sam 15:30). Every time I stand on the Mount of Olives and look down the western slopes of Mount Olivet and across to the ancient City of David to the southwest, I remember this low point in the life of David.

Jesus' Descent

But I also remember a later, westward descent from the summit of the Mount of Olives down into the Kidron and across to the Temple Mount. The Son of David, riding on a donkey, crested the summit and began his fateful descent on what we now call Palm Sunday. On March 24, 2013, my wife and I joined thousands of festive pilgrims who walked from the church at Bethphage over the summit of the Mount of Olives and down its slopes to the church of All Nations and across the Kidron Valley up to the church of Saint Anne in the Old City. In Jesus' day, the jubilant crowds, waving their palm fronds and anticipating the long-expected messianic kingdom, burst out in singing; but not Jesus: "As he came near and saw the city, he wept over it" (Luke 19:41).

Typological Link

This typological intersection between David's ascent and Jesus' descent is marked by similarity and contrast: both men wept "on Olive's brow," but for quite different reasons. David was shaken by the consequences of his own sin; the Son of David was shaken by the consequences of his people's sin:

> If you, even you, had only recognized on this day the things that make for peace! But now they are hidden from your eyes. Indeed,

---

25. 2 Sam 15.

the days will come upon you, when your enemies will set up ramparts around you and surround you, and hem you in on every side. They will crush you to the ground, you and your children within you, and they will not leave within you one stone upon another; because you did not recognize the time of your visitation from God. (Luke 19:42–44)

It is fitting that the Mount of Olives should be the site where Jesus prophesies the fate of Jerusalem and the end of the age, and where he was taken up to heaven. But all of that in due course. It's time for our spiritual climb of the Mount of Transfiguration.

Historical Setting of the Transfiguration

Jesus' transfiguration occurs at a moment of crisis and functions as a hinge in all three Synoptic Gospels. Prior to this, Jesus' ministry in Galilee attracts both large crowds and growing opposition. The Pharisees plot with the Herodians how to get rid of this upstart teacher who challenged Pharisaic interpretation of the Torah and threatened the status quo.[26] Jesus warns his disciples about the "yeast of the Pharisees and the yeast of the Herodians" just before leaving the Sea of Galilee area and going up north to the villages of Caesarea Philippi.[27] This predominantly Gentile region provides a temporary respite from the critical and prying eyes of the Pharisees. It also allows Jesus some time alone with his disciples. Seen in hindsight, he is preparing them for his final visit to Jerusalem. Jesus' question to his disciples about his identity is the functional midpoint of all three Synoptic Gospels and the most important question any human being must answer: "But who do you say that I am?" (Mark 8:29; Matt 16:15). Immediately after Peter's great confession, "You are the Messiah, the Son of the living God" (Matt 16:16), Jesus drops a bombshell. "Then he began to teach them that the Son of man must undergo great suffering and be rejected by the elders, the chief priests, and the scribes, and be killed, and after three day rise again" (Mark 8:31). They don't fully understand who this Son of man is and what he must do, especially the part about rising again. What is clear, however, is that the stakes are high: "Those who are ashamed of me and of my words in this adulterous and sinful generation, of them the Son of Man will also

---

26. Mark 3:6; Matt 12:14; 15:1–20.
27. Mark 8:15; Matt 16:5–12.

be ashamed when he comes in the glory of his Father with the holy angels" (Mark 8:38). This warning is the immediate lead-in to what next transpires.

Historicity

According to Mark's gospel, here is what happened:

> After six days Jesus took Peter, James and John with him and led them up a high mountain, where they were all alone. There he was transfigured before them. His clothes became dazzling white, whiter than anyone in the world could bleach them. And there appeared before them Elijah and Moses, who were talking with Jesus. (Mark 9:2–4)

But is this what really happened? Was it real or a dream? Is it a historical account or is it a literary creation by the evangelists in order to make a theological point? I have no hesitation: it was historical, neither a dream nor an invention. Some modern scholars have suggested that the transfiguration account is actually a post-resurrection story read back into Jesus' earthly ministry.[28] This is an unwarranted explanation that undermines the reliability of Scripture. A face value reading of the Synoptic Gospels points to an event that actually happened as described.

Meaning

If we assume the story's historicity, what does it mean? The evangelists Mark and Matthew employ the verb *metamorphoō* in the passive voice, thus describing an action performed upon Jesus. This is almost certainly an instance of what is called the divine passive, that is, an action attributed to God.[29] The basic meaning of the verb in the passive is "to be changed in form." According to leading lexicographers, it is here used "of a transformation that is outwardly visible."[30] Of course the key question is: changed into what? The evangelists describe the change undergone by Jesus in terms of an OT theophany. In fact, a famous divine throne room scene in Dan 7:9 illuminates Jesus' transfiguration: "As I watched, thrones were set in place,

---

28. Stein ("Misplaced Resurrection Account?") argues persuasively against this theory.
29. Nützel, "μεταμορφόω."
30. BAGD, 513.

and an Ancient One took his throne, his clothing was white as snow, and the hair of his head like pure wool; his throne was fiery flames, and its wheels were burning fire...." Here is Mark's description of what happened to Jesus: "There he was transfigured before them. His clothes became dazzling white, whiter than anyone in the world could bleach them" (Mark 9:3). Matthew's depiction is slightly different: "His face shone like the sun, and his clothes became as white as the light" (Matt 17:2). Luke's version reads, "As he was praying, the appearance of his face changed [a different verb in Greek is used] and his clothes became as bright as a flash of lightning" (Luke 9:29). The evangelists apparently believed that for a few moments Christ's divine nature, like the glory cloud of Sinai, shone forth to the inner three, Peter, James, and John.[31]

This latter detail is probably not without significance. Remember that in the Sinai theophany, Aaron, Nabu and Abihu accompanied Moses halfway up the mountain.[32] In fact, a number of details in the Sinai narrative find a counterpart in the transfiguration.[33] Most likely, the evangelists deliberately draw a connection between these two mountaintop theophanies. On the mount of transfiguration, two important figures from Israel's storied past suddenly turn up: Moses and Elijah, both of whom glimpsed the glory of the invisible God on Mount Sinai, appear on the mount of transfiguration alongside Jesus. The great mediator of the Sinai covenant and the great defender and champion of the covenant materialize beside the mediator of the new covenant. Clearly, this is a moment of high drama in redemptive history—the climactic turning point of redemptive history is about to unfold and the kingdom of God will enter its final, decisive stage. The last campaign against the kingdom of the Dark Lord begins in earnest. In the Apostle Paul's words, "The God of peace will shortly crush Satan under your feet" (Rom 16:20). Luke even tells us that Moses and Elijah "were speaking about his departure, which he was about to accomplish at Jerusalem" (Luke 9:31). "Departure" renders the Greek word *exodos*, suggesting that what Jesus accomplishes in redemption may be likened to a second exodus. And it is Luke, with his keen eye for the significance of historical events, who ominously informs us that soon thereafter, "he set his face to go to Jerusalem" (Luke 9:51).

---

31. "It is clear that in this manifestation of Jesus they were somehow suddenly in direct contact with the glory of the divine presence" (Hagner, *Matthew 14–28*, 493).

32. Exod 24:1–2.

33. For particulars, see Hagner, *Matthew 14–28*, 492–94.

Purpose

The transfiguration of Jesus serves two theological purposes. In the first place, it provides dramatic evidence for Christ's deity to the inner three who will soon assume leadership roles in the Jesus movement. Though shaken by the crucifixion, all the apostles experience a remarkable confirmation of their faith by the post-resurrection appearances of the risen Christ. This reinforces the transfiguration revelation and anchors apostolic conviction in reality. Even doubting Thomas is finally on board: "My Lord and my God" (John 20:28). This confession is the bedrock of what it means to be a Christian. Unless one sincerely affirms that "Jesus is Lord" and that "God raised him from the dead" (Rom 10:9–10), there can be no assurance of saving faith.

The second purpose is to instill hope for the future. Jesus is coming again and the second time he comes in glory and power.[34] The brilliant radiance surrounding him on the Mount of Transfiguration is a preview of his grand return as "King of kings and Lord of lords" (Rev 19:16). Toward the end of the Apostle Peter's career, a denial of the second coming of Jesus began infiltrating churches in Asia Minor. Peter emphatically rejects such a departure from apostolic teaching. A key argument in his defense of orthodoxy is an appeal to his experience "on the holy mountain" (2 Pet 1:18). According to Peter, the doctrine of the second coming is not a "cleverly devised myth" but a revelation of "the power and coming of our Lord Jesus Christ" (2 Pet 1:16). In short, the transfiguration of Jesus anticipates his triumphant return and reign, during which time he will "put all his enemies under his feet" and destroy "the last enemy," that is, death (1 Cor 15:25–26).

Theological Significance of the Olivet Discourse

But Jesus did more than preview his second coming; he also provided some basic information concerning the conclusion of redemptive history. For that we must climb the Mount of Olives and sit at the Master's feet. The Olivet Discourse probably occurred on Wednesday of passion week.[35] The Synoptic Gospels place Jesus and his disciples on the Temple Mount where Jesus teaches the people and engages in controversy with the religious au-

---

34. Cf. 2 Thess 1:5–10; Tim 4:1; Heb 9:28.

35. Hoehner, "Chronology." The chronology of passion week is fraught with difficulties. Hoehner covers the various options.

Mountaintop Theology

thorities.[36] As the disciples exit the Temple area, they express wonder at the size and beauty of the stones and buildings.[37] Jesus then stuns them with an unexpected announcement: "Truly I tell you, not one stone will be left here upon another; all will be thrown down" (Matt 24:2). After ascending the Mount of Olives with its magnificent view of the Temple Mount, Peter, James, John, and Andrew privately inquire about this shocking revelation. According to the Gospels of Mark and Luke, they ask two questions: "When will this be and what will be the sign that all these things are about to be accomplished?" (Mark 13:4; Luke 21:7). Matthew's version rephrases Mark's second question: "What will be the sign of your coming and of the end of the age?" This difference in wording has generated considerable scholarly debate about the overall interpretation of the discourse. It boils down to this: Does the passage predict only the destruction of Jerusalem in AD 70, or does it predict both the historic destruction of Jerusalem and a later, separate event, namely, the coming of Jesus in glory at the end of the age?

In my opinion, we have two distinct predictions, one in the near future (AD 70) and the other at an undisclosed time in the eschatological future. On this assumption, I propose to explain Jesus' prophecy that covers the last era of redemptive history.

Prophetic Perspective

All commentators are agreed that the Synoptic Gospels depict Jesus as prophesying a destruction of Jerusalem within the lifetime of the disciples. Some hold that this prophecy is actually an invention of early Christian tradition placed in the mouth of Jesus by the evangelists in order to portray Jesus as a genuine prophet and as the omniscient Son of God.[38] I believe the saying is authentic and that Jesus predicted the temple's destruction about 40 years before it occurred. But I also believe that Jesus predicted more than just the destruction of Jerusalem and its crown jewel, the Second Temple; he also sketched the course of the last era of redemptive history, culminating in his second advent.

Here is my understanding of the flow of the Olivet Discourse using Matthew as the primary text:

36. Mark 11:17–12:44; Matt 21:18–23:39; Luke 20:1–21:4.
37. Matt 24:1. The rabbis remark: "Whoever has not seen Herod's building has not seen a beautiful building in his life" (*B. Bat.* 4a).
38. The technical term for this is *vaticinium ex eventu*, "prophecy after the event."

- Course of the present age: "the beginning of the birth pangs" (24:4–14; cf. Mark 13:5–13)
- Great tribulation featuring the desolating sacrilege of the antichrist (24:15–28; cf. Mark 13:14–23)
- Second coming of Christ (24:29–31; cf. Mark 13:24–27)
- Illustrations and exhortations concerning the second coming (24:32–35; cf. Mark 13:28–37)
- Three parables illustrating the proper attitude and behavior of believers who await the coming (23:45–25:30)
- Reward of the righteous and judgment of the wicked (25:31–46)

Several observations are worth noting. First, Jesus gives neither dates nor diagnostic events whereby one might determine the precise time of his coming.[39] Rather, what we have are general features that characterize life from Jesus' day until the present, a period marked by false messianic claims, wars, famines, earthquakes, and persecution of believers. While certain periods have witnessed greater or lesser frequency and intensity of these phenomena, no discernible pattern or formula enables a prophetic calendar.

Secondly, the only thing that offers a chronological perspective is the statement that "this good news of the kingdom will be proclaimed throughout the world, as a testimony to all the nations; and then the end will come" (Matt 24:14). This implies that the interval will not be as short as the apostles probably thought, that is, during their lifetime.[40] But it also implies that one cannot know for sure when the good news has been proclaimed throughout the world. Given this ambiguity, we must be content with affirming both the certainty and contingency of his coming. That is, he *could* have come at an earlier time and he *may* come during our lifetime. One may rest assured, however, that he *will* come because the Father has a

---

39. Despite the clear statement that "about that day and hour no one knows, neither the angels of heaven, nor the Son, but only the Father" (Matt 24:36 and pars.), many prophecy teachers have nonetheless confidently set dates. Needless to say, they have all proven to be incorrect. Unfortunately, failure has not discouraged the sometimes lucrative business of date setting!

40. Cf. Matt 10:23; 16:26; 1 Thess 4:17; 1 Cor 7:29–31; Rom 13:11–12. But note carefully, the apostles did not teach *when* Jesus would come. A distinction must be drawn between apostolic opinion and apostolic teaching. The latter is infallible; the former is not. For a fuller discussion of this point, see Helyer, *Revelation for Dummies*, 159–73.

fixed plan and date. Consequently, the call for each generation is always the same: "Keep awake therefore, for you do not know on what day your Lord is coming" (Matt 24:42) and the divine promise is immutable: "the one who endures to the end will be saved" (Matt 24:13).

Thirdly, the preceding interpretation dovetails nicely with the opening of the seven seals in the Apocalypse of John.[41] In fact, the first five seals closely parallel Jesus' description of "the beginning of the birth pangs": false messiahs, wars, famines, and earthquakes. The sixth seal ("... for the great day of their wrath has come, and who is able to stand?" [Rev 6:12–17]) probably reflects the next phase of Jesus' discourse, the great Day of the Lord, signaled by the phrase "and then the end will come" (Matt 24:14). The seventh seal apparently includes the culmination of redemptive history in the coming of Christ as "King of kings and Lord of lords" (Rev 19:16). See the table below for a visual demonstration of the parallels.[42]

Event	Olivet Discourse (Matthew)	Seals (Revelation)
False Messiah(s)	24:4	6:1–2 First seal
Warfare and bloodshed	24:7	6:3–4 Second seal
Famine	24:7	6:5–6 Third seal
Earthquakes	24:7	6:7–8 Fourth seal
Martyrdom	24:9	6:9–11 Fifth seal
Cosmic disturbances	24:29	6:12–17 Sixth seal
Coming of the Son of Man	24:30–31	8:1 Seventh seal

The Great Tribulation and Jerusalem

On the basis of the foregoing discussion, I infer that Matt 24:15 refers to the great tribulation that precedes the second coming of Christ. Before Jesus returns, a self-proclaimed "god" will attempt a coup. This is the "desolating sacrilege standing in the holy place" (Matt 24:15) and is performed by none other than the antichrist. This is the same moment mentioned by the Apostle Paul when he told the Thessalonians that the Day of the Lord had not yet occurred because "the lawless one" (i.e., the antichrist) had not yet

---

41. Rev 6:1–8:1.

42. See Helyer, *Revelation for Dummies*, 159–73.

been revealed nor had he taken "his seat in the temple of God, declaring himself to be God" (2 Thess 2:4). In my view, the Apostle John's description of the beast rising out of the sea and demanding to be worshiped also refers to the same occasion.[43]

I assume that Antiochus Epiphanes and his persecution of Jews in the second century BC serves as the prototype of the final "man of lawlessness" who, during the great tribulation, orders a desolating sacrilege, blasphemes the name of God, makes war on the saints, and exercises authority over the earth for forty-two months.[44] The Roman general Titus may have partially fulfilled Daniel's prophecy, but its ultimate fulfillment unfolds in the antichrist of the end times.

There are objections to the view I've just endorsed. Some say the description of this crisis in Matt 24:15-27 fits the historic siege of Jerusalem tolerably well but raises troublesome problems on the assumption that it refers to the antichrist and the great tribulation of the end times. For example, the instructions about fleeing to the mountains and praying that one's flight from Jerusalem not occur on the Sabbath or during the winter seem irrelevant to an eschatological scenario. In reply, however, if one reads the text in light of OT prophetic passages that apparently employ near/far or double fulfillment schemes, most of the details in the Olivet Discourse may be accounted for by assuming that the historical details of AD 70 serve as the lens through which the great tribulation of the end times is projected onto the eschatological screen.[45] Furthermore, most of the details do not fit the historical situation of AD 70: Christians actually fled Jerusalem well before the "desolating sacrilege" because the Roman army had already invested the city with a circumvallation siege wall, preventing anyone from escaping.[46] Thus one can argue that the instructions and warnings of Matt 24:15-29 accord better with the end time tribulation.

---

43. Rev 13.

44. Dan 7:19-28; 8:9-14; 9:27; 11:36-45; Rev 13:5-8. For further background on the Antiochan persecution, see Helyer, *Exploring Jewish Literature*, 113-117.

45. For further description and support for this approach, see Turner, *Matthew*, 566-67.

46. According to a tradition cited by Eusebius, Jerusalem Christians escaped to Pella across the Jordan Valley in what is today the Hashemite Kingdom of Jordan (*Hist. eccl.* 3.5.3).

Mountaintop Theology

Second Coming

Most interpreters understand Matt 24:30–31 as referring to the second advent. According to Matthew's gospel, Jesus mentioned four features that attend his return:

- A mysterious "sign of the Son of Man" heralds his coming. One can only speculate, but perhaps some kind of celestial phenomenon portends his arrival.[47] In this regard the first advent of Christ is instructive. According to Matthew, a "star" signaled the time and place of the king of the Jews' birth.[48] Perhaps something similar announces the second advent of the "King of kings and Lord of lords" (Rev 19:11–16).[49]
- Worldwide mourning, presumably on account of impending judgment, sweeps the planet.
- Christ arrives on the clouds of heaven in a public and glorious demonstration of power.
- Climaxing his return is a worldwide gathering of believers, often called the blessed hope or rapture of the church, orchestrated by angelic agency.[50] There is no mention of a resurrection, so presumably those gathered are living saints. In 1 Thessalonians, Paul distinguishes between believers who have already died before the rapture and those still living when it occurs.[51]

Beyond that, little else of a descriptive nature is communicated about what actually happens at the second coming. The rest of the Olivet Discourse is devoted to exhortations to watchfulness and warnings about failure to heed them. It's instructive that Jesus placed greater emphasis on the ethical

---

47. Before mentioning the coming of the Son of Man, Mark's gospel alludes to several OT prophetic texts that refer to celestial phenomena that attend the Day of the Lord (Isa 13:10; 34:4; Ezek 32:7–8; Joel 2:10, 31; 3:15). These may well be the "sign."

48. Matt 2:1–2, 9–10.

49. Matthew employs the Greek technical term *parousia* to designate Christ's second coming. In the Hellenistic and Roman eras, a *parousia* was sometimes used to refer to an official state visit by an emperor, king, or high-ranking dignitary. These state visits involved established protocol and probably colored the use and understanding of this term as applied to Christ's second coming. See further Helyer, *Witness*, 293–94.

50. Cf. 1 Thess 4:17.

51. 1 Thess 4:13–18.

Mount of Transfiguration and Mount of Olives

and moral implications of his coming rather than on the chronological and historical details, an emphasis that is often overlooked.[52]

The Ascension of Christ

Finally, I draw attention to the location of the last terrestrial event in Christ's life on this earth. According to Luke, Jesus ascended to heaven from the Mount of Olives.[53] "Two men in white robes" announced to the Apostles: "This Jesus, who has been taken up from you into heaven, will come in the same way as you saw him go into heaven" (Acts 1:11). Luke locates this angelic announcement on "the mount called Olivet, which is near Jerusalem, a sabbath day's journey away" (Acts 1:12). This too is rooted in Scripture. The postexilic prophet Zechariah had a vision of the final tribulation that befalls Jerusalem during the Day of the Lord. The city will be attacked by a worldwide coalition and sacked. But just when all seems lost, the Lord himself intervenes and destroys the invading armies. Then comes this extraordinary prophecy:

> On that day his feet shall stand on the Mount of Olives, which lies before Jerusalem on the east; and the Mount of Olives shall be split in two from east to west by a very wide valley, so that one half of the Mount shall withdraw northward, and the other half southward. And you shall flee by the valley of the Lord's mountain, for the valley between the mountains shall reach to Azal; and you shall flee as you fled from the earthquake in the days of King

---

52. There is, however, one item that requires discussion and this is Jesus' solemn assertion: "Truly I tell you, this generation will not pass away until all these things have taken place. Heaven and earth will pass away, but my words will not pass away" (Matt 24:34–35). Once again, the issue touches on one's overall interpretation of the passage. Those who interpret the passage strictly within the scope of AD 70 point to this verse as confirmation of their view and for the inerrancy of Scripture. On their view, Jesus' prediction was literally fulfilled within the lifetime of the Apostles. Furthermore, they insist that any view trying to fit this into an eschatological scenario fails and has a major problem with the truthfulness of Scripture, since Christ did not return to earth during the lifetime of the Apostles; indeed, he still hasn't after nearly 2,000 years. In reply, I hold that a double fulfillment or near/far perspective adequately handles this supposed dilemma. The Second Temple was destroyed in the lifetime of most of the Apostles but, at the time of the end, the ultimate desolating sacrilege will occur shortly before Christ returns to earth. Those alive when that happens will still be living when Christ returns. Thus the saying properly applies to both the first century and end times audiences.

53. Luke 24:50–52; Acts 1:9–12.

> Uzziah of Judah. Then the Lord my God will come, and all the holy ones with him. (Zech 14:4–5)

In short, the Mount of Olives appears to be both the launch pad for the ascension and the touchdown for the second coming!

Before descending from the Mount of Olives, recall Jesus' last instructions to his disciples: "Repentance and forgiveness of sins is to be proclaimed in his name to all nations beginning from Jerusalem. You are witnesses of these things" (Luke 24:47–48). "But you will receive power when the Holy Spirit has come upon you; and you will be my witnesses in Jerusalem, in all Judea and Samaria, and to the ends of the earth" (Acts 1:8). The same point is made in Matthew's gospel, popularly called the Great Commission: "Go therefore and make disciples of all nations, baptizing them in the name of the Father and of the Son and of the Holy Spirit, and teaching them to obey everything that I have commanded you. And remember, I am with you always, to the end of the age" (Matt 28:18–20). It's certainly worth noting that according to an early Christian tradition, the Great Commission of Matthew's gospel took place on none other than Mount Tabor. If this be so, the theological link between these two mountains is grounded in geography and history, a point I've sought to emphasize throughout this book.

The Great Commission stands at the core of Christian discipleship. Believers have an obligation to proclaim the good news to the ends of the earth. Empowered by the Holy Spirit, a great host has sought to do precisely that. Beginning with 120 believers in an upper room in Jerusalem, the Jesus movement has swelled to more than two billion who identify themselves as followers of Christ. It is the most remarkable movement the world has ever known. But the job is still not finished because the Master has not yet returned. The Great Shepherd of the sheep is still seeking lost sheep who must be gathered into the fold. Clearly, the number of the elect is a very large number and their destiny is glorious beyond words.[54] And that brings us to our last climb.

---

54. Rev 7:9.

8

Heavenly Mount Zion

Understanding Our Destiny

"And of Zion it shall be said ... 'This one was born there.'" (Ps 87:5–6)

"But you have come to Mount Zion and to the city of the living God, the heavenly Jerusalem ...." (Heb 12:22)

Introduction

OF ALL THE PRESSING and troubling questions human existence raises, none cries out more urgently for an answer than that of our destiny. In short, what happens to me after I die? A majority opinion throughout recorded history insists that there must be some kind of survival after death. Skeptics may dis this as wishful thinking, but it continues to be the default option for most.

The Bible is unambiguous in this regard: two drastically different outcomes confront each and every human being. In our spiritual mountain climbs together, we have already surveyed God's gracious plan of salvation anchored in the cross and resurrection of Jesus Christ. Persevering faith in him is the only requirement for attaining full and everlasting salvation, loosely referred to in our culture as heaven. Rejection of this option, tragically, leads to ultimate separation from God and therefore all goodness, truth and beauty. In biblical imagery, this option is typically depicted as being cast into a lake of fire.¹ Experienced mountain climbers are well aware of the perils of plunging into crevices or plummeting down the sheer face of a mountain slope. Such a tragedy serves as a graphic image of falling from grace.

My primary purpose in writing this book is to encourage readers who have committed themselves to the Master for the long, difficult climb up Mount Zion. If, however, any reader should consider the entire enterprise a delusion, or decide that the effort is really not worth it, I urge reconsideration—the consequences are too terrible to contemplate. Consequently, my objective on this spiritual climb is to scale the heights of the heavenly Mount Zion and "catch a gleam of glory bright."² I assure you, this is the ultimate experience—an extreme spiritual sport that results in an everlasting high.

Scripture closely links the heavenly Mount Zion with the city on its summit, variously called "the Jerusalem that is above," "the city of the living God, the heavenly Jerusalem," "the city that is to come," and "the Holy City, the new Jerusalem, coming down out of heaven from God." Believers are reminded that their citizenship rests in this celestial city.³ However it is designated, the panorama from this mountain and its summit city is positively breathtaking. It's time to ascend.

Locating Mount Zion

It may seem odd to take up the question of location. After all, is this really a place with geographical coordinates? That Scripture treats it as a real place seems apparent and in some sense the eschatological Mount Zion corresponds to an actual site whose coordinates and history are known. In the history of redemption, the historical Mount Zion and its celebrated city becomes a transcendent reality.⁴ This transformation deserves a book-length study, but space constraints necessitate condensing this fascinating story into a few paragraphs.

---

1. Matt 5:29; 18:8–9; Rev 20:14–15; 21:8.

2. Lifted from the fourth stanza of the hymn *Higher Ground*, lyrics by Johnson Oatman.

3. Rev 21:10; Gal 4:26; Heb 12:22; Heb 13:14; Rev 21:2, 10; Phil 3:20.

4. "The most important city on earth in the history of God's revelation and redemption" (Douglas and Tenney, eds., "Jerusalem," 724).

The site of ancient Jerusalem was, like virtually all cities ancient and modern, determined by geography.[5] Thus a limestone ridge, just off the Judean watershed, protected on three sides by steep valleys and sustained by the presence of a perennial spring called Gihon, afforded a viable place of habitation.[6] Already in the prehistoric era, there is evidence of human occupation near this spring. During the Middle Bronze Age, Canaanites dwelt on the site and the ancient city first appears in historical records, in *The Execration of Asiatic Princes*.[7] The Egyptian name for the city, *Urushalim*, is similar to the Hebrew name, *Yerushalayim*. In addition, for the first time, we have evidence of a well-fortified city with defensive walls, towers, and water system. Portions of these may be seen today in the City of David excavations. This was the city that the patriarchs knew and where Melchizedek lived.[8] At most, it consisted of about ten to twelve acres of densely populated living space.[9]

During the Amarna Age (fourteenth century BC), it was a relatively important city in the hill country of Canaan. From correspondence between Egypt and Canaan, called the El Amarna Texts, we learn that the name of one of Jerusalem's kings was Abdi Heba.[10] In the days of the judges (thirteenth–eleventh century BC), a people group called the Jebusites occupied the site and called it Jebus.[11] During the conquest of Canaan, Joshua defeated a coalition of kings headed up by Adoni Zedek, the king of Jerusalem.[12] The Israelite tribes, however, were not able to capture the city itself. Long after the settlement of the Israelite tribes, the Jebusites still controlled their city—a foreign enclave in the center of the Hebrew heartland. The Jebusites called a fortress just below the summit, Zion, perhaps meaning

---

5. See map 2 in the appendix.

6. 1 Kgs 1:33, 38, 45; 2 Chr 32:30; 33:14.

7. These texts are magical curses uttered upon Egyptian enemies. Pottery bowls inscribed with the names of enemies were smashed in a symbolic gesture depicting their destruction. Apparently, a not very cordial relationship existed between Pharaoh and the king of Jerusalem at the time! See Pritchard, *ANET*, 329.

8. Gen 14:18. Salem is a variant of Jerusalem (Ps 76:2).

9. For a discussion of early habitation on the site, see Ben-Dov, *Historical Atlas*, xii–42, and Reich, *Excavating*, 279–90.

10. In the Canaanite dialect of the Amarna Letters, the city is named *Ur-salimmu*. For two letters mentioning Jerusalem by name, see Pritchard, *ANET*, 488–89 (EA, No. 287 and 489, EA, No. 290).

11. Jdg 19:10–11; 1 Chr 11:4.

12. Josh 10:1–5.

"stronghold." The summit was probably Mount Moriah that we discussed earlier in chapter two. King David ended this untenable political situation in about 1000 BC when he captured the fortress and city.[13] He took up residence there and named it the City of David. In the OT, the name Zion is still frequently used to refer to the entire city, but its primary name is Jerusalem.[14]

From this time forward, Jerusalem becomes more than merely a Middle Eastern city, the capital of the united monarchy and later of the kingdom of Judah; it takes on a life of its own. How could it be otherwise? It was, after all, the city the Lord chose for the house that bears his name.[15] As we will see shortly, prophet and psalmist extol its virtues.

After the disastrous division of the kingdom in the days of Rehoboam and Jeroboam I (931 BC), Jerusalem remained the political center of the southern kingdom of Judah.[16] This situation continued until the collapse of Judah and the destruction of Jerusalem in the days of Nebuchadnezzar the Neo-Babylonian (586 BC).[17] Against all odds, the exiled people of Judah staged a remarkable return to their ancestral homeland and, like the proverbial phoenix, Jerusalem rose again from its ashes. For several centuries, Judah remained an insignificant province in the vast empire of Persia and the Hellenistic kingdoms created by the successors of Alexander the Great.

Remarkably, during the second century BC, after a protracted, armed conflict, a priestly family called the Hasmoneans (better known as the Maccabees) gained political independence from the Seleucid Empire and, from about 142 BC until 63 BC, an autonomous Jewish nation flourished in the ancestral homeland.[18] Jerusalem was, of course, the political and religious center of this little kingdom. This period of independence came to a violent end in 63 BC, when the emerging superpower Rome incorporated the Hasmonean kingdom into its empire as a bulwark against the Parthians on the eastern frontier.

---

13. 2 Sam 5. David apparently gained entrance into the city through the Canaanite water system connected to the Gihon spring. See Ben-Dov, *Historical Atlas*, 40–45, 59–62, and Meyers, "Jerusalem," 550–52.

14. See Na'aman, "Interchange Between Bible and Archaeology," 57–61, 68 and Ben-Dov, *Historical Atlas*, 42–55.

15. 1 Kgs 8:44; 11:32, 36; 14:21.

16. 1 Kgs 12.

17. 2 Kgs 25.

18. For further background on this era, see Helyer, "Hasmoneans."

Heavenly Mount Zion

The Jewish people could not shake off the shackles of Rome. Twice they tried, in AD 66–70 (the First Jewish Revolt) and in AD 132–135 (the Second or Bar Kochba Revolt), both times with disastrous consequences, resulting in destruction and expulsion. Though there never was a time from the second until the nineteenth centuries AD, when at least some Jews resided in the Holy Land, and only a few periods when they were completely barred from Jerusalem, they were nonetheless aliens and strangers, not citizens and masters, in their ancestral homeland. Not until the modern era, with the reestablishment of the State of Israel in 1948, has an independent Jewish state come into existence and taken its place among the family of nations.

Transforming Jerusalem

I break off the story at this point in order to draw attention to a remarkable phenomenon. Already in the eighth century BC, Hebrew prophets began prophesying about a glorious restoration of Israel and its crown jewel, Jerusalem. These idyllic pictures of a new Jerusalem no doubt played a significant role in the reestablishment of the modern state of Israel; but they have also been instrumental in shaping Christian eschatology. Jesus and his apostles weave these prophetic sketches of a new Jerusalem into the tapestry depicting God's final destiny for his redeemed people. That is what I want you to see as we climb the heavenly Mount Zion.

Isaiah's Tale of Two Cities

Our story begins in the eighth century BC during a time of political crisis. The powerful Assyrian Empire (modern Syria and Iraq) was flexing its military might and seeking to control the Middle East from the Euphrates all the way to the Nile. Standing in its way, of course, are the two small Hebrew kingdoms of Israel and Judah. This natural land bridge, "the land between," was a stepping stone on the way to Egypt and a target in the cross hairs of Assyrian aspirations.

In the midst of this crisis, God raised up a spiritual giant in the person of Isaiah son of Amoz. Isaiah's message to his fellow countrymen was a "bad news, good news" report. On the one hand, the short-term future of Judah and Jerusalem was very bleak. "Your country lies desolate, your cities are burned with fire; in your very presence aliens devour your land; it is desolate, as overthrown by foreigners, and daughter Zion [a figurative appellation for Jerusalem] is left like a booth in a vineyard, like a shelter in a cucumber field, like a besieged city" (Isa 1:7–8; cf. 3:1–4:1). But the long-term future of Jerusalem was incredibly bright; indeed, "the mountain of the Lord's house [Mount Zion] shall be established as the highest of the mountains, and shall be raised above the hills; all the nations shall stream to it" (Isa 2:2). The transformation is stunning. How can this be? The short answer is: for his own glory and by his sovereign power, working through his mysterious, obedient servant—the NT identifies this servant as Jesus of Nazareth—the Lord redeems and restores Jerusalem so that the faithless city of unrighteousness "shall be called the city of righteousness, the faithful city" (Isa 1:26).[19]

This reversal of fortune for Jerusalem is a major theme in prophetic literature. Since space prevents a full discussion, I allow Isaiah, the prince of the prophets, to be our primary tutor; he best captures the paradox of the two Jerusalems: a historical city of dross and an eschatological city of refined silver.[20] Throughout his literary masterpiece, Isaiah continually juxtaposes these contrasting cities; indeed, his magnum opus may well be called a "tale of two cities."[21] Perhaps nowhere is this startling contrast more apparent than in Isaiah 54:11–14:

> O afflicted one, storm-tossed, and not comforted, I am about to set your stones in antimony, and lay your foundations with sapphires. I will make your pinnacles of rubies, your gates of jewels, and all your wall of precious stones. All your children shall be taught by the Lord, and great shall be the prosperity of your children. In righteousness you shall be established; you shall be far from oppression, for you shall not fear; and from terror, for it shall not come near you.

No phrase as aptly describes the more than 3,000-year history of this city since David's conquest than the opening words: "afflicted, storm-tossed, and not comforted." Today, portions of the Old City of Jerusalem rest upon nearly ninety feet of ruble from previous iterations of this storied city. If only the stones and bones of the buried past could cry out, what a wail of

---

19. See Isa 42:1–4; 49:1–6; 50:4–9; 52:13–53:12; 61:1–4; Acts 8:26–38; Phil 2:6–8; 1 Pet 2:21–25.

20. Isa 1:22, 26.

21. The allusion is to Dickens' novel by the same name. Of course, Dickens borrowed the idea from Augustine and the Bible!

Heavenly Mount Zion

lamentation would be heard! Ironically, no currently existing city on earth has endured as many sacks and sieges as this "city of peace." Archaeologists and historians estimate that the city has been besieged twenty-six times and razed to the ground thirteen times. The three most horrific were the destructions by Nebuchadnezzar in 586 BC, the Roman general Titus in AD 70, and the Crusaders in AD 1099.[22] Astonishingly, Isaiah quickly moves beyond the historical travails and portrays a bejeweled and blessed city. Flashes of this future Jerusalem recur throughout Isaiah's marvelous poetry. Here are some selections:

> Whoever is left in Zion and remains in Jerusalem will be called holy, everyone who has been recorded for life in Jerusalem . . . . Then the LORD will create over the whole site of Mount Zion and over its places of assembly a cloud by day and smoke and the shining of a flaming fire by night. Indeed over all the glory there will be a canopy. It will serve as a pavilion, a shade by day from the heat, and a refuge and a shelter from the storm and rain. (Isa 4:3–6)

> Then the moon will be abashed, and the sun ashamed; for the LORD of hosts will reign on Mount Zion and in Jerusalem, and before his elders he will manifest his glory. (Isa 24:23)

> On this mountain the LORD of hosts will make for all peoples a feast of rich food, a feast of well-aged wines . . . . (Isa 25:6)

> And the ransomed of the LORD shall return, and come to Zion with singing; everlasting joy shall be upon their heads; they shall obtain joy and gladness, and sorrow and sighing shall flee away. (Isa 35:10)

> For the LORD will comfort Zion; he will comfort all her waste places, and will make her wilderness like Eden, her desert like the garden of the LORD; joy and gladness will be found in her, thanksgiving and the voice of song. (Isa 51:3)

---

22. Christians are generally unaware of the horrendous massacre perpetrated by the army of Christendom that captured the city from the Muslims. The Jewish community was annihilated in the aftermath since they assisted the infidels and were viewed as "Christ-killers." It is one of the darkest chapters in a tragic history of Christian anti-Judaism. See Rausch, *Legacy of Hatred*, 27.

> Awake, awake, put on your strength, O Zion! Put on your beautiful garments, O Jerusalem, the holy city; for the uncircumcised and the unclean shall enter you no more. (Isa 52:1)

> Arise, shine; for your light has come, and the glory of the LORD has risen upon you.... Your gates shall always be open; day and night they shall not be shut... they shall call you the City of the LORD, the Zion of the Holy One of Israel... I will make you majestic forever, a joy from age to age... you shall call your wall Salvation, and your gates Praise. The sun shall no longer be your light by day, nor for brightness shall the moon give light to you by night; but the LORD will be your everlasting light, and your God will be your glory. (Isa 60:1, 11, 14–15, 18–19)

> For I am about to create new heavens and a new earth; the former things shall not be remembered or come to mind. But be glad and rejoice forever in what I am creating; for I am about to create Jerusalem as a joy, and its people as a delight. (Isa 65:17–18)

These prophecies of a glorious New Jerusalem on Mount Zion from Isaiah may be amplified and augmented by many other prophetic voices.[23] But another influential contribution to this theme arises from the cadences of Israel's hymnody. Listen to these selections from the book of Psalms that celebrate the transcendent character of Mount Zion and Jerusalem:

> Great is the LORD and greatly to be praised in the city of our God. His holy mountain, beautiful in elevation, is the joy of all the earth, Mount Zion, in the far north,[24] the city of the great King. Within its citadels God has shown himself a sure defense.... Walk about Zion, go all around it, count it towers, consider well its ramparts; go through its citadels, that you may tell the next generation that this is God, our God forever and ever.... (Ps 48:1–3, 12–14)

> Out of Zion, the perfection of beauty, God shines forth. (Ps 50:2)

> On the holy mount stands the city he founded; the LORD loves the gates of Zion more than all the dwellings of Jacob. Glorious things

---

23. Jer 31:38–40; 32:36–33:26; Ezek 40:1–4; 48:30–35; Joel 3:1, 16–21; Zeph 3:14–20; Zech 8:1–8; 14:3–21.

24. This is a nice touch because in Canaanite mythology Mount Zaphon ("North Mountain") was reputed to be the residence of Baal. Yahweh on Mount Zion displaces this supposed god on his mountain.

are spoken of you, O city of God . . . . And of Zion it shall be said, "This one and that one were born in it; for the Most High himself will establish it. The LORD records, as he registers the peoples, 'This one was born here.'" (Ps 87:1–3, 5–6)

Those who trust in the LORD are like Mount Zion, which cannot be moved, but abides forever. (Ps 125:1)

For the LORD has chosen Zion; he has desired it for his habitation: "This is my resting place forever; here I will reside, for I have desired it." (Ps 132:13–14)

What is clear beyond question in passages like these is the transcendent dimension of this otherwise rather un-noteworthy city—a spiritual element elevates the historical city to ethereal heights. And it is precisely this spiritual aspect that looms large in the NT.

Theological Significance of Mount Zion/Jerusalem

The OT descriptions of Jerusalem's future glory are taken up and transposed into a higher key by NT authors who depict the ultimate goal of Christian pilgrimage as the heavenly Mount Zion crowned by the magnificent city of Jerusalem. And when it comes to a description of the heavenly Mount Zion, pride of place unquestionably belongs to the Apostle John—his vision of this majestic summit city is unrivalled.

John's Tale of Two Cities

John's Apocalypse features his own version of a tale of two cities.[25] Like Isaiah's visions, a sharper contrast can scarcely be imagined. The first city is depicted as a debauched prostitute clothed in scarlet and purple, gorging herself on the blood of martyrs and sitting on seven mountains.[26] The second city appears as a resplendent bride arrayed in "fine linen, bright and pure" and situated on "a great high mountain."[27] John portrays the first city, the "great whore," in imagery recalling imperial Rome, nestled on its well-known seven hills. His readers no doubt discerned behind the description

25. Rev 17–22.
26. Rev 17:1–17.
27. Rev 19:7–8; 21:2, 10.

of this depraved figure Rome's cruel tyranny.[28] The second city is a radiant bride, a symbol of the redeemed people of God and the city in which she dwells. The great high mountain, though not named, must be Mount Zion. These two, contrasting cities are designated respectively as "Babylon the great" and "the new Jerusalem." Our interest in the rest of this chapter is with the latter.

King Jesus Returns to Jerusalem

In the Sermon on the Mount, Jesus refers to historical Jerusalem as "the city of the great King" (Matt 5:35). But when King Jesus returns on the Day of the Lord, the eschatological Jerusalem replaces the historical Jerusalem. This transition may be traced in the narrative flow of Christ's three grand entrances in the book of Revelation. The first two entrances, involving the historical Jerusalem, anticipate the transition to the eschatological Jerusalem:

- The first is the throne room scene in which the Lion of the tribe of Judah appears as a "Lamb standing as if it had been slaughtered" (Rev 5:6).

- The second involves the dramatic interlude in chapter twelve in which a heavenly woman gives birth to "a male child, who is to rule all nations with a rod of iron" (Rev 12:5).

---

28. Several features in the description of Babylon the great point to imperial Rome as the lens through which John portrays this notorious city. Depicting cities under the guise of a disreputable woman follows the precedent of OT prophets like Isaiah, Jeremiah and Ezekiel (Isa 23:17–18; Jer 51; Ezek 16). The reference to the blasphemous names almost certainly alludes to the imperial cult that deified deceased Roman emperors like Augustus and Tiberius. Even more decisive is the equation of the seven heads with "seven mountains on which the woman is seated" (Rev 17:9). Rome was renowned for its seven hills. The double reference to seven kings most likely refers to seven Roman emperors, though their precise identification remains a disputed point (Rev 17:9–11). Add to this the mention of great wealth, luxury, oppression, self-indulgence and violence, so characteristic of imperial Rome, and one has a substantial case that Rome is the template for Babylon the great. The OT also employs the figure of a virtuous bride to depict the people of God. Jerusalem, for example, is called "daughter Zion" (Isa 37:22; 62:11) and is depicted as a beautiful bride (Isa 49:18; 54:5; 61:10; 62:5; Ezek 16:7–14; Hos 2:16–20). By incorporating this well-used figure, John reflects his Jewish background and his continuity with the OT prophets.

- The third entry ushers in the new Jerusalem and settles once and for all the question: Who's in charge? The Lamb is both "The Word of God" and "King of kings and Lord of lords" (Rev 19:13,16). The first title identifies Christ as the creator of all things and the communicator of all truth concerning God.[29] The second identifies him as the one who truly reigns over all creatures great and small. In short, he shares the sovereignty of God almighty.

John's depiction of the second coming of Christ focuses primarily upon the fate of the beast and his massive army drawn from the kings of the earth. The evil hordes fall before the sword of the Lord, symbolizing his sovereign word. In the original creation, Christ speaks a creative word into the chaos and it becomes a cosmos.[30] At the end of redemptive history, Christ speaks a word of judgment upon the forces of chaos and then creates a new cosmos.

Note carefully that there is no hint in the book of Revelation, or, for that matter, the entire NT, that believers actually participate in a violent war against their oppressors.[31] Vengeance belongs to the Lord and he effortlessly dispatches his enemies at the appointed time. Their defeat is pictured in terms of a banquet for birds consisting of the flesh of the vanquished hosts. This grisly supper stands in marked contrast to the gala supper celebrating the marriage of the Lamb and his bride. The two suppers, like the two cities, symbolize radically different outcomes for humanity. Whether one feasts with the Lamb on Mount Zion or is feasted upon by the birds on Mount Magedon[32] depends entirely upon one's allegiance.

The Heavenly Mount Zion Comes to Earth

That brings us to the heart of this chapter and the climax of both the book of Revelation and the Bible. John attempts, as best he can, to convey the

---

29. Cf. John 1:1–3, 14–18.

30. Gen 1:1–2:3; John 1:1–3; Col 1:16–17; Heb 1:2–3.

31. This stands in marked contrast to the Essene community at Qumran who anticipated a forty-year war against Belial (Satan) and the sons of darkness (all who were not members of their community!) in which they fully participated. See Wise, Abegg, and Cook, *Dead Sea Scrolls*, 150–72.

32. This is a literal rendering of the word Harmagedon (NRSV) or Armegeddon (NIV) in Rev 16:16. The word alludes to the historic site of Megiddo where a number of decisive battles were fought.

overwhelming impact of a new creation crowned by a holy city and a cloistered garden. Fittingly, Rev 21–22 serves as the capstone of biblical revelation and can be considered a kind of Grand Central Station toward which all tracks of biblical revelation converge.

A New Earth

John tantalizes us with a glimpse of the new earth. This peek, however, prompts a very important observation: the final location for the redeemed is not way out there, but very much right down here. That is to say, the ultimate destination in redemptive history is a new earth crowned by a new Jerusalem on Mount Zion. Popular culture, including many Christians, tend to view the final state as completely celestial—the Bible teaches otherwise: God created us as physical-spiritual beings adapted for life on this planet and that is precisely where he intends for us to live in the age to come. A new earth appears out of the ashes of the old and a new Jerusalem descends upon it like a beautiful bride.

An important corollary to this observation is the insistence that matter matters; all creation was originally pronounced "very good" (Gen 1:31) and so it shall always be in the new creation: "See, I am making all things new" (Rev 21:5). Among other things, that means our bodies play a vital role in redemptive history and a continuing role in the eschatological consummation. In them we offer ourselves as "living sacrifices" (Rom 12:1), constitute a "temple of the Holy Spirit" (1 Cor 6:19), and, in our redeemed bodies, carry out our original commission: "have dominion" over God's good creation (Gen 1:26–30). And this time, we get it right! Gnostic visions of the final state in which the body plays no role are erroneous and unsatisfying.[33]

A recurring question concerns the precise nature of the new heavens and new earth. Does the Bible teach that God will create an entirely new order or does he renew and refurbish the old one? This issue has generated more heat than light and is probably not deserving much passion. One can

---

33. Gnosticism was a Christian heresy that stressed privately revealed knowledge. At the heart of this so-called knowledge was a fundamental dualism between spirit and matter, the later deemed as inferior and unnecessary. The aim of redemption in Gnosticism was to escape matter. Christianity teaches that God sanctifies matter as an everlasting habitation for the spirit.

Heavenly Mount Zion

find passages in the OT that imply the eternal nature of the created order.[34] On the other hand, one can find passages that imply the need for a radically new creation.[35] For what it's worth, I incline to the view that God will create a radically different world order with significantly different physical properties. My principal argument is that sin has so permeated our present world order that nothing short of a radically new creation would be fitting for a people clothed with imperishable, glorious, powerful, spiritual bodies like that of Jesus Christ.[36] But either way, we can be sure the new creation will be a thing of perpetual amazement, beauty, and joy.

John's tantalizingly brief description of the new earth rapidly recedes from view, replaced by an awe-inspiring scene. The holy city, the new Jerusalem, descends to the new earth like a massive space station from *Star Wars*. What follows constitutes a climactic moment in redemptive history, a focal point of mystical contemplation and aspiration: "God himself will be with them" (Rev 21:3).

New Tabernacle

How does one even begin to comprehend such a thing? John does the best he can by using language recalling the ancient tabernacle in the wilderness of Sinai. In describing the descent of the holy city, John uses the Greek word meaning "to tabernacle," deliberately recalling that tripartite structure consisting of a courtyard and sanctuary divided into a holy place and a most holy place. The last-named room was a perfect cube of ten cubits (fifteen feet), in which resided the ark of the covenant. Surmounting the lid like sentries stood two cherubim facing each other with outstretched wings. Above this lid, called the mercy seat, the divine presence (called the Shekinah in Jewish tradition) shimmered in a translucent cloud. Only the high priest was allowed access to the most holy place, and that only once a year on the solemn day of Yom Kippur. On that day, the high priest sprinkled the blood of a bull on the mercy seat with his finger seven times for his own sins, and did the same with the blood of a goat for the sins of Israel.[37] As the

---

34. Ps 78:69; 89:37; 104:5; 125:1; Jer 31:35–36.
35. Isa 65:17; 66:22; Rom 8:18–25; 2 Pet 3:10–13.
36. 1 Cor 15:42–49.
37. Lev 16:11–16.

book of Hebrews emphatically insists, Jesus has fulfilled this symbolic ritual by offering himself once for all as a sacrifice for sin.[38]

End of a Long Journey

John's description of the holy city brings us full circle back to the story of creation. In the garden of Eden, the first couple enjoyed unhindered communion with the Creator. After their disobedience, the guilty couple were expelled and excluded from the garden. Fellowship with God was now constrained and life must be lived east of Eden under a curse. Redemptive history can be likened to a tortuous journey back to the garden and the immediate presence of God; or, in keeping with the primary metaphor used in this book, an arduous climb to the summit of heavenly Mount Zion.

In the early stages of redemptive history, God occasionally revealed himself to patriarchs and matriarchs through dreams, visions, and visitations. Following the exodus, God provided the people of Israel with tangible evidence of his presence by means of the tabernacle and its mysterious ark of the covenant overshadowed by a pillar of cloud by day and a pillar of fire by night.[39] Even so, access was guarded and limited—falling considerably short of the fellowship experienced in the garden.

Redemptive history centers on the mystery of incarnation in which the eternal Son took on human flesh and "lived among us" (lit. "tabernacled among us" [John 1:14; cf. 1 Tim 3:16]). Having taken on human flesh, the Lamb of God made "the atoning sacrifice for our sins, and not for ours only but also for the sins of the whole world" says the Apostle John (1 John 2:2).[40] To be sure, the present age brings us much closer to the Father by means of the indwelling Christ and the Holy Spirit who take up residence (lit. "tabernacle") in each believer.[41] In fact, Jesus reminds his disciples: "Whoever has seen me has seen the Father" (John 14:9). Paul makes the same point: "the light of the knowledge of the glory of God in the face of Jesus Christ" (2 Cor 4:6). The writer to the Hebrews exhorts his readers "to enter the sanctuary by the blood of Jesus and "to approach with a true heart in full assurance of faith" (Heb 10:19, 22).

---

38. Heb 7:26–28; 9:6–14, 24–28; 10:11–25.
39. Exod 13:21; 19:9; 33:9; 40:34–38.
40. Cf. Heb 1:3; 2:10–18; 7:26–8:6; 9:11–28.
41. John 14:18–31; 16:12–17:25.

Heavenly Mount Zion

But the writer of Hebrews also reminds us: "here we have no lasting city, but we are looking for the city that is to come" (Heb 13:14). In Rev 21–22, anticipation gives way to celebration as John depicts a glorious homecoming, the finish of a long journey and the end of a lengthy climb, in which the distance between God and his people completely disappears: "They will see his face, and his name will be on their foreheads" (Rev 22:4). This climactic encounter is often called the beatific vision and fulfills the Master's promise to the pure in heart, "they will see God" (Mat 5:8).

New Bride

John employs another striking metaphor to describe the splendor of the moment—he likens the new Jerusalem to "a bride adorned for her husband" (Rev 21:2). Weddings are grand occasions in all cultures and Jewish weddings are no exception. Family jewels and heirlooms bedeck the bride and no effort or expense is spared to enhance her beauty and charm.[42] Of course, in John's description, the bride is dressed in fine, white linen, as befitting a virgin and symbolizing her status as the bride of Christ, resplendent in the righteousness of Christ made possible through his atoning work on her behalf.

New City

The centerpiece of chapter 21 is a virtual tour of the new Jerusalem. Here are some highlights:

Materials and Measurements

The material splendor of the celestial city immediately grabs John's attention. It radiates with the glory of God like the Shekinah cloud above the ark of the covenant and resembles the qualities of jasper and crystal, imagery adapted from the OT.[43] In fact, John's description resonates with the tones and tenor found in Isaiah's visions and the Psalmists' praises. The measurements of the city clearly convey symbolic meaning. The city stands foursquare, a perfect cube with dimensions stretching 1,500 miles in each

---

42. Isa 61:10; Jer 2:32.
43. Exod 39: 8–14; Isa 54:11–12; Ezek 18:13; cf. Rev 4:3.

direction.⁴⁴ This gigantic cube, a virtual holy of holies, portrays a redeemed society radiating the holiness of God. At last the central command of Leviticus is completely realized: "You shall be holy, for I am holy" (Lev 11:44–45; 19:2; 20:7).⁴⁵ The immense size of the city confirms that the number of the redeemed is very large.⁴⁶

Walls and Gates

Surrounding the city are massive walls towering 144 cubits (approximately 225 feet) high. The imagery conveys a sense of sublime security. Safe in the arms of Jesus captures the sentiment. Underlying the walls are foundations consisting of twelve different gemstones, perhaps placed in an alternating pattern around the entire perimeter. The foundation stones recall the breastplate of the high priest of ancient Israel and signify the presence of all the tribes of Israel, here representing all God's redeemed people. The gates are especially noteworthy in that each is "a single pearl" (Rev 21:21). This image has become commonplace in popular culture and many immediately recognize the expression "the pearly gates." Capping John's captivating description is the well-known image of the street paved with "pure gold, transparent as glass" (Rev 21:21). Just as the bars in the ancient tabernacle were covered with gold and the four primary pieces of furniture, the lamp stand, the table for the bread of the Presence, the altar of incense, and the ark of the covenant, were overlaid in gold, so too, main street new Jerusalem reflects the inestimable value of the holy city.

Outstanding Features

Perhaps the most remarkable features of the new Jerusalem are the things not present:

- No Temple. Given that the tabernacle and the First and Second Temples played such an instrumental role in redemptive history, this omission is unexpected. John provides a completely satisfying explanation. There is no need because God is immediately present with his people.

---

44. Rev 21:16.
45. Cf. Heb 12:14; 1 Pet 1:16.
46. Rev 5:1; 7:4, 9.

Heavenly Mount Zion

The NT actually anticipates this outcome by picturing the redeemed people of God as already comprising a spiritual temple.[47]

- No night or darkness. After the initial chaos of Gen 1:2, God introduces light and separates it from darkness so that earth now experiences the regular alternation of night and day. Not so in the new Jerusalem—perpetual light and day reign and no remnant of chaos remains. The source of this radiant illumination is the glory of God pervading both city and people. Because evil is absent, there is no need to shut the city gates (Rev 21:25). This is just another way of expressing the absolute perfection and security of this magnificent municipality. "Nothing unclean will enter it nor anyone who practices abomination or falsehood, but only those who are written in the Lamb's book of life" (Rev 21:27). How could it be otherwise? As Ezekiel foresaw, "the name of the city from that time on shall be, The Lord is There" (Ezek 48:35).

- No curse. Here one recalls the tragic consequences of the first act of human disobedience in the garden of Eden. In John's climactic vision, God's curse on sin and disobedience is finally lifted: the accursed serpent (a symbol of Satan) is forever banished and punished; the curse of all mourning, crying, and pain departs; the curse on the ground is replaced with unparalleled fruitfulness; and the curse of death is reversed as symbolized by the water of life and tree of life.

The new Jerusalem exceeds the wildest expectations of John's first readers. One must remember that the great cities of the empire were hardly like a modern metropolis with its massive infrastructure and conveniences. Rome reeked—literally. Travelers knew they were within a few miles of the city simply by their noses! If you are squeamish about sanitation, forget any romantic notions about how wonderful ancient Rome must have been. Today one stands in awe of the architecture of the Pantheon, Coliseum, and the Forum, but most people in ancient cities lived in squalid tenements with raw sewage coursing through the streets and no interior plumbing or heating other than extremely dangerous charcoal burners that had to be vented through the windows. Crime, disease, violence, and the constant danger of devastating fires stalked the inhabitants. Unwanted infants, usually females, were left on the street as garbage. The misery index for most residents was extremely high.[48] And most Christians belonged to this social

---

47. 1 Cor 3:16–17; 6:19; Eph 2:19–22; 1 Pet 2:4–10; Rev 1:6; 3:12.
48. Of course, we shouldn't forget that modern megacities have huge slums with

group. But even for the aristocratic citizens of Rome, life in the city was no picnic. It is said that Nero constantly burned incense and perfumed his palace and one can certainly understand why! All this to say, the new Jerusalem is a dream come true. The things that made life in ancient cities a hell on earth have vanished and in their place appears an urban utopia. That leads to the final touch of John's stunning portrait of the holy city.

A New Garden

An extraordinary garden lies at the very heart of the new Jerusalem. I have elsewhere commented on the significance of this feature:

> How fitting that John finishes with an enchanted garden. We walk back in time, as it were, to the celebrated garden of Eden—except this timeless garden exceeds in every way the glories and splendor of that primeval garden. The eschatological garden is nothing short of perfection and beggars by comparison the royal gardens of imperial Rome. Gracing the garden is a crystal clear river coursing "from the throne of God and of the Lamb through the middle of the street of the city" (Rev 22:1–2). The tree of life flanks both sides of the river producing twelve kinds of fruit and leaves for the healing of the nations. Paradise imagery conveys the blessedness of eternal life, fulfilling to the nth degree the mission of Jesus: "I have come that they may have life, and have it abundantly" (John 10:10). The integrity and security of the enchanted garden are fail-safe: "Nothing accursed will be found there any more" (Rev 22:3). All the redeemed enjoy equal access to the water of life, the tree of life, and the source of all life, God himself. Not a whiff of class, ethnic, gender, national, racial or social elitism and prejudice may be detected in a place where each individual's name is written in the Lamb's book of life and each bears God's own name written on their foreheads. At last, justice and mercy for all prevails and both the sanctity of persons and the value of community are forever honored and preserved in the New Jerusalem.[49]

---

appalling conditions.

49. Helyer and Cyzewski, *Good News*, 99.

Heavenly Mount Zion

Theological Importance of the Heavenly Mount Zion

So why is it important to focus on the heavenly Mount Zion today? How does this impact and influence my life now? The short answer is: visualizing it helps me through the tough times and strengthens my resolve to stay the course and finish the climb. As Eliphaz the Temanite observed, "human beings are born to trouble just as sparks fly upward" (Job 5:7). Sometimes this trouble is so overwhelming we sink into dark despair. We feel like the psalmist who cried out in his adversity: "How long, O Lord? Will you forget me forever? How long will you hide your face from me? How long must I bear pain in my soul, and have sorrow in my heart all day long? (Ps 13:1–2). Another Psalmist almost renounced his faith in the Lord. It seemed that he was plagued and punished every morning, whereas his arrogant, wicked neighbor was enjoying the good life (Ps 73). That is, until he considered ultimate outcomes. These couldn't be more drastically different: the unbeliever will fall to ruin and be swept away by terrors, but God will receive the believer into glory. That realization prevented the psalmist from stumbling and slipping; it made all the difference and so it will for all who climb Mount Zion. As the Apostle Paul reminds the Roman Christians, "I consider that the sufferings of this present time are not worth comparing with the glory about to be revealed to us . . . [for we] will obtain the freedom of the glory of the children of God" (Rom 8:18, 21). The Apostle Peter agrees. He exhorts his readers, who were undergoing various trials, unjust suffering, and a "fiery ordeal" (1 Pet 4:12), to remember: "the end of all things is near" (1 Pet 4:7). And what will that end entail? Nothing short of "eternal glory in Christ" awaits every successful climber of heavenly Mount Zion (1 Pet 5:10). In the words of the gospel song, "it will be worth it all, when we see Jesus."[50]

The Apostle Peter adds a further dimension to this hope that shapes our lives. In his second epistle, Peter describes the dissolution of the present heavens and earth and the coming of the new on the day of God. He says that this hope in a place where "righteousness is at home" serves as a powerful incentive to live holy and godly lives now (2 Pet 3:11). In other words, visualizing our ultimate objective assists in our present quest for holiness and godliness. Olympic athletes routinely practice visualization before competing, imagining themselves flawlessly performing their particular event—and so should all climbers of Mount Zion. And remember,

---

50. Lyrics by Esther Kerr Rusthol.

successful climbs are those in which the focus is always on the summit, not the way back down. As the old hymn has it, "I'm pressing on the upward way, New heights I'm gaining every day—Still praying as I'm onward bound, 'Lord plant my feet on higher ground.'"[51] Onward and upward!

As I said at the outset of this chapter, making the summit of heavenly Mount Zion is an experience beyond words. A former student of mine served an internship high in the Himalaya Mountains. For the first week, cloud cover obscured everything. The next morning, when she got up and walked outside, the clouds had lifted. She literally could not speak—the sight was so overwhelming it brought tears to her eyes. The impact of the heavenly Mount Zion will be exponentially more breathtaking. One can only bow in wonder and praise before the throne and before the Lamb and join the angelic hosts in singing: "Amen! Blessing and glory and wisdom and thanksgiving and honor and power and might be to our God forever and ever! Amen" (Rev 7:12).

---

51. Oatman, *Higher Ground*.

Bibliography

Abraham, William J. *Shaking Hands With the Devil: The Intersection of Theology and Terrorism*. Downers Grove, IL: InterVarsity, 2012.
Aharoni, Yohanan. "Kadesh-Barnea and Mount Sinai." In *God's Wilderness: Discoveries in Sinai*, edited by Beno Rothenberg, 117–82. London: Thames and Hudson, 1961.
———. *The Land of the Bible: A Historical Geography*. Translated by A. F. Rainey. Philadelphia: Westminster, 1967.
Aharoni, Yohanan, and Michael Avi-Yonah. *The Macmillan Bible Atlas*. 3rd ed. New York: Macmillan, 1993.
Anati, Emmanuel. *The Mountain of God*. New York: Rizzoli, 1986.
Andersen, H. G. "Sinai, Mount." In *ZPEB* 5:447–50.
Arndt, William F., and Wilbur Gingrich. *A Greek-English Lexicon of the New Testament and Other Early Christian Literature*. 4th ed. Chicago: University of Chicago Press, 1957.
Bahat, Dan. "Does the Holy Sepulchre Church Mark the Burial of Jesus?" *BAR* 12 no. 3 (1986) 26–45.
Bailey, Lloyd, R. *Noah, the Person and the Story*. Columbia, SC: University of South Carolina Press, 1989.
Baly, Denis. *The Geography of the Bible*. New York: Harper & Row, 1957.
Barkay, Gabriel. "The Garden Tomb—Was Jesus Buried Here?" *BAR* 12 no. 2 (1986) 40–57.
Ben-Dov, Meir. *Historical Atlas of Jerusalem*. New York: Continuum, 2002.
Beit Arieh, Itzhaq. "The Route Through Sinai: Why the Israelites Fleeing Egypt Went South." *BAR* 15 no. 3 (1988) 23–37.
Beitzel, Barry J. *The New Moody Atlas of the Bible*. Chicago: Moody, 2009.
Blocher, Henri A. G. "Original Sin." In *DTIB* 553–54.
Bowling, Andrew. "Senir." In *ZPEB* 5:338.
Branch, Robin. G. "Rainbow." In *DOTP* 667–68.
Brisco, T. V. "Exodus, Route of the." In *ISBE* 2:238–41.
Brueggemann, Walter. *Theology of the Old Testament: Testimony, Dispute, Advocacy*. Minneapolis: Fortress, 1997.
Chavalas, Mark W. "Moses." In *DOTP* 570.
Cundale, A. E. "Baal." In *ZPBD* 1:430–33.
Curtis, Adrian H. W. "Canaanite Gods and Religion." In *DOTHB* 135–37.
Cyril of Jerusalem. *Catecheses. Nicene and Post-Nicene Fathers* vol. 2, 7:12.16. Edited by Philip Schaff. Peabody, MA: Hendrickson, 1996.

Bibliography

Daane, J. "Sinner." In *ZPEB* 5:444–47.
Davies, G. Henton. "Ark of the Covenant." In *IDB* 1:222–26.
Davies, G. I. "Sinai, Mount." In *ABD* 6:47–49.
Delling, Gerhard. "τέλειος." In *TDNT* 8:74.
Douglas, J. D. and Merrill C. Tenney, eds.; rev. Moisés Silva. "Jerusalem." In *ZIBD* 724–32.
Eichrodt, Walter. *The Theology of the Old Testament*. 2 vols. Translated by J. A. Baker. Philadelphia: Westminster, 1961.
Enns, Peter. "Exodus Route and Wilderness Itinerary." In *DOTP* 272–80.
Foerster, Werner. "εἰρηνοποιός." In *TDNT* 2:419.
Frankel, Raphael. "Tabor, Mount." In *ABD* 6:304–5.
Frantzman, Seth J., and Ruth Kark. "General Gordon, The Palestine Exploration Fund and the Origins of 'Gordon's Calvary' in the Holy Land." *Palestine Exploration Quarterly* 140 no. 2 (2008) 1–18.
Franz, Gordon. "Is Mount Sinai in Saudi Arabia?" *Bible and Spade* 13 no. 4 (2000) 101–14.
Garland, D. E. "Blessing and Woe." In *DJG* 79.
Geddert, Timothy J. "Peace." In *DJG* 604–5.
Geissler, Rex. "Affirming Agri Dagh." Paper presented at the annual meeting of the Near East Archaeological Society. San Diego, California, November 15, 2007.
Goss, Leonard G. "What is the Occult?" In *The Apologetics Study Bible*, edited by Ted Cabal, 450. Nashville: Holman, 2007.
Hagner, Donald A. *Matthew 1–13*. WBC 33A. Dallas: Word, 1993.
———. *Matthew 14–28* WBC 33B. Dallas: Word. 1995.
Har-El, Menashe. "The Exodus Route in Light of Historical Geographical Research." *Ariel* 44 (1977) 69–84.
Harrison, R. K., and J. K. Hoffmeier. "Sinai." In *ISBE* 4:525–28.
Hauck, F. "μακάριος." In *TDNT* 4:368.
Hays, Richard B. *The Moral Vision of the New Testament*. New York: HarperOne, 1996.
Helyer, Larry R. "Abraham's Eight Crises: The Bumpy Road to Fulfilling God's Promise of an Heir." *BRev* 11 no. 5.(1995) 20–27, 44.
———. *The Book of Revelation for Dummies*. Hoboken, NJ: Wiley, 2008.
———. "'Come What May, I Want to Run': Observations on Running in the Hebrew Bible." *NEASB* 48 (2003) 1–12.
———. *Exploring Jewish Literature of the Second Temple Period*. Downers Grove, IL: InterVarsity, 2002.
———. "The Hasmoneans and the Hasmonean Era." In *The World of the New Testament: Social, Cultural, and Historical Contexts*, edited by Joel B. Green and Lee Martin McDonald, 38–53. Grand Rapids: Baker, 2013.
———. *The Life and Witness of Peter*. Downers Grove, IL: InterVarsity, 2012.
———. "Proclaiming Christ as Lord: Colossians 1:15–20." *Southern Baptist Journal of Theology* 17 no. 3 (2013) 4–18.
———. *The Witness of Jesus, Paul and John: An Exploration in Biblical Theology*. Downers Grove, IL: InterVarsity, 2008.
———. *Yesterday, Today, and Forever: The Continuing Relevance of the Old Testament*. Salem, WI: Sheffield, 2002.
Helyer, Larry R., and Edward Cyzewski. *The Good News of Revelation*. Eugene, OR: Cascade, 2014.
Hesiod. *Theogony*. In *The Homeric Hymns and Homerica*. Translated by Hugh G. Evelyn-White. Loeb Classical Library 57. Cambridge, MA: Harvard University Press, 1914.

Bibliography

Hilhorst, Ton. "The Mountain of Transfiguration in the New Testament and Later Tradition." In *The Land of Israel in Bible, History and Theology: Studies in Honour of Ed Noort*, edited by Jacques van Ruiten and J. Cornelius de Vos, 317–38. VTSup 124. Leiden: Brill, 2009.

Hill, Jonathan. *What Has Christianity Ever Done For Us? How It Shaped the Modern World*. Downers Grove, IL: InterVarsity, 2005.

Hoehner, Harold W. "Chronology." In *DJG* 118–22.

Horn, Siegfried H. "What We Don't Know About Moses and the Exodus." *BAR* 3 no. 2 (1977) 22–31.

Hunt, J. H. "Noah." In *DOTP* 605–11.

Jung, Kurt Gerhard. "Tabor." In *ISBE* 4:713–14.

Kertelge, Karl. "δικαιοσύνη." In *EDNT* 1:328–29.

Lewis, Jack P. "Flood." In *ABD* 2:798–804.

Liefield, Walter, L. "Transfiguration." In *DJG* 835.

Mare, W. Harold. *The Archaeology of the Jerusalem Area*. Grand Rapids: Baker, 1987.

Mattingly, Gerald. "Sinai." In *HDB* 956–57.

McGarvey, J. W. *Lands of the Bible*. Philadelphia: Lippincott, 1879.

Meier, Sam A. "A History of Israel I: Settlement Period." In *DOTHB* 425–34.

Meyers, Carol. "Jerusalem." In DOTHB 550–52.

Murphy-O'Connor, Jerome. *The Holy Land: An Oxford Archaeological Guide from Earliest Times to 1700*. 5th ed. Oxford: Oxford University Press, 2008.

Na'aman, Nadav. "The Interchange Between Bible and Archaeology: The Case of David's Palace and the Millo." *BAR* 40 no. 1 (2014) 57–61.

Naudé, Jackie A. "קדש." In *INDOTTE* 3:879.

NoahsArkSearch.com. http://www.noahsarksearch.com

Nützel, Johannes, M. "μεταμορφόω." In *EDNT* 2:415.

Patrich, Joseph. "Hideouts in the Judean Wilderness." *BAR* 15 no. 5 (1989) 34–35.

Peterson, Eugene H. *The Message: The New Testament Psalms and Proverbs*. Colorado Springs: Navpress, 1995.

Pfeiffer, Charles F. *Baker's Bible Atlas*. Grand Rapids: Baker, 1961.

Porter, Stanley E. "Hero or Thief? Constantine Tischendorf Turns Two Hundred." *BAR* 41 no. 5 (September/October 2015) 45–53.

Rai, Raghu, and Navin Chawla. *Faith and Compassion: The Life and Work of Mother Teresa*. Rockport, MA: Element, 1996.

Rainey, Anson F. "Jezreel." In *ISBE* 2:1059.

Rainey, Anson F., and R. Steven Notley. *The Sacred Bridge: Carta's Atlas of the Biblical World*. Jerusalem: Carta, 2006.

Rasmussen, Carl G. *Zondervan NIV Atlas of the Bible*, 204–205. Grand Rapids: Zondervan, 1989.

Rausch, David A. *A Legacy of Hatred: Why Christians Must Not Forget the Holocaust*. Grand Rapids: Baker, 1990.

Reich, Ronny. *Excavating the City of David: Where Jerusalem's History Began*. Jerusalem: Israel Exploration Society, 2011.

Reuven, Peretz, "Wooden Beams from Herod's Temple Mount: Do They Still Exist?" *BAR* 39 no. 3 (2013) 40–47.

Ringma, Charles. *Whispers from the Edge of Eternity*. Vancouver, BC: Regent College, 2005.

Ritmeyer, Leen and Kathleen. *Jerusalem at the Time of Jesus*. Nashville: Abingdon, 2004.

Bibliography

———. *Secrets of Jerusalem's Temple Mount*. Updated and enlarged ed. Washington, DC: Biblical Archaeology Society, 2006.

Scharlemann, Martin H. "Transfiguration, Mount of." In *ISBE* 4:888-89.

Schlegel, William. *Satellite Bible Atlas: Historical Geography of the Bible*. Israel: Schlegel, 2011.

Shanks, Hershel. "Frank Moore Cross—An Interview, Part 1: Israelite Origins." *BR* 8 no. 4 (1992) 23-32, 61-62.

———. "Tom Crotser Has Found the Ark of the Covenant—Or Has He?" *BAR* 9 no. 3 (1983) 66-69.

Smith, David. "A Fiery Prophet." *The Jerusalem Post Christian Edition* 92 (2013) 22-25.

The Book of Common Prayer. New York: Oxford, 1990.

Stein, Robert H. "Is the Transfiguration [Mark 9:2-8] a Misplaced Resurrection Account?" *JBL* 95 (1976) 79-96.

———. "Transfiguration." In *Evangelical Dictionary of Biblical Theology*. Grand Rapids: Baker, 1996.

Thielman, Frank. *Theology of the New Testament*. Grand Rapids: Zondervan, 2005.

Thomson, William M. *The Land and the Book*. 2 vols. New York: Harper, 1882.

Turner, David L. *Matthew*. BECNT. Grand Rapids: Baker, 2008.

US Department of Justice. http://www.bjs.gov/content/content/pub/pub/pdr/htuc8008.pdf.

Von Rad, Gerhard. *Old Testament Theology*. 2 vols. New York: Harper & Row, 1965.

Waltke, Bruce, K. *An Old Testament Theology*. Grand Rapids: Zondervan, 2007.

Walton, John. "Exodus, Date of." In *DOTP* 258-72.

———. "The Flood." In *DOTP* 322.

———. "Sons of God, Daughters of Man." In *DOTP* 793-98.

Wilkins, Michael J. *Matthew: The NIV Application Commentary*. Grand Rapids: Zondervan, 2004.

Wilkinson, John, ed. *Egeria's Travels*. London: SPCK, 1971.

Wilson, John A. "The Execration of Asiatic Princes." In *ANET* 329.

Wise, Michael, Martin Abegg, Jr., and Michael Cook. *The Dead Sea Scrolls*. New York: HarperCollins, 1996.

Wood, Bryant. "Beneath the Surface: An Editorial Comment." *Bible and Spade* 13 (2000) 98-99.

———. "In Search of Mt Sinai." Associates for Biblical Research Electronic Newsletter. 7.6 1-3.

Wright, Paul. *Greatness, Grace & Glory*. Jerusalem: Carta, 2008.

Youngblood, Ronald F. *The Expositor's Bible Commentary: 1 Samuel-2 Kings*, edited by Tremper Longman III & David E. Garland. Rev. ed. Grand Rapids: Zondervan, 2009.

Zertal, Adam. "Has Joshua's Altar Been Found on Mount Ebal?" *BAR* 11 no. 1 (1985) 26-44.

———. "Mount Ebal." In *ABD* 2:255-58.

Appendix

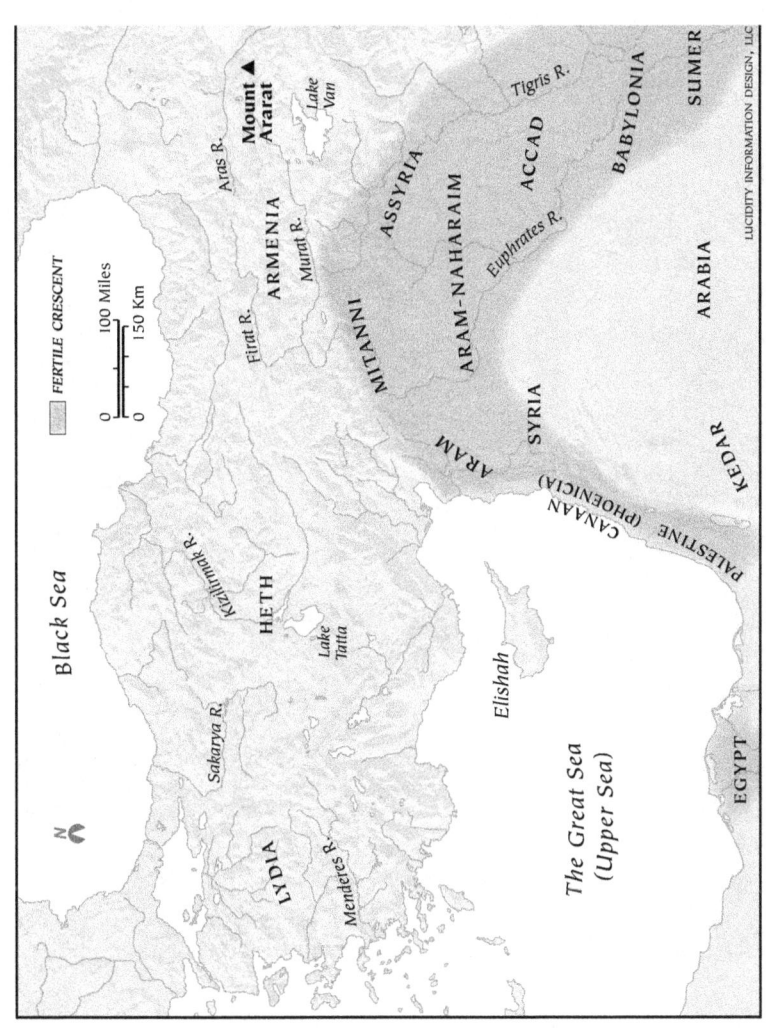

APPENDIX

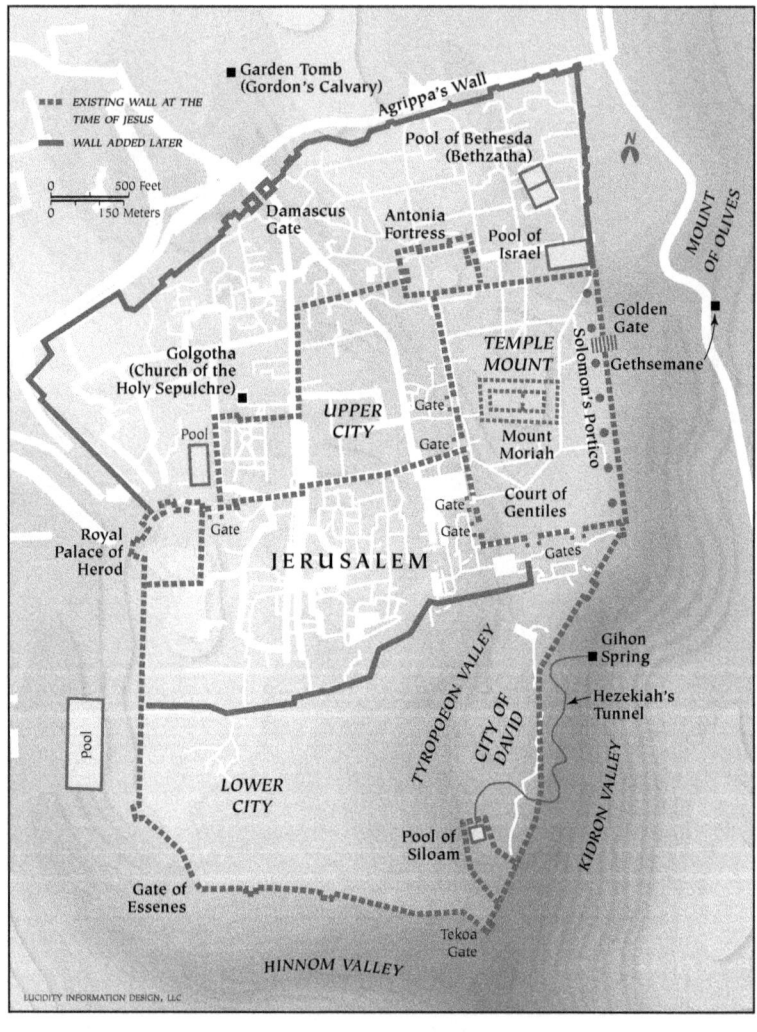

Appendix

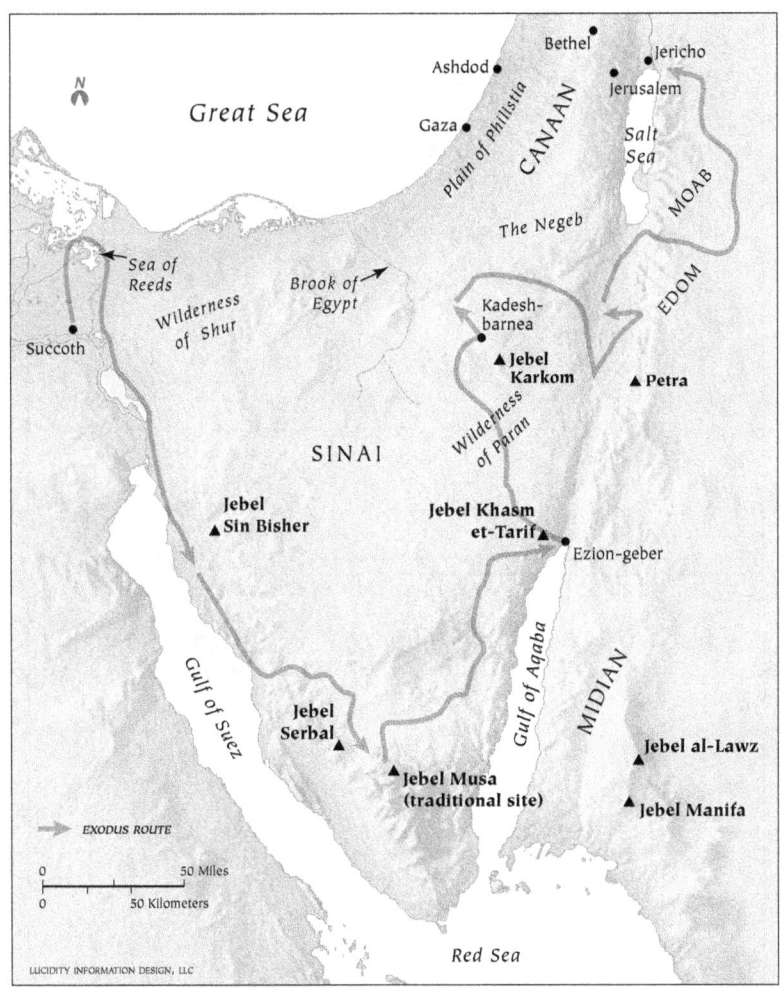

Appendix

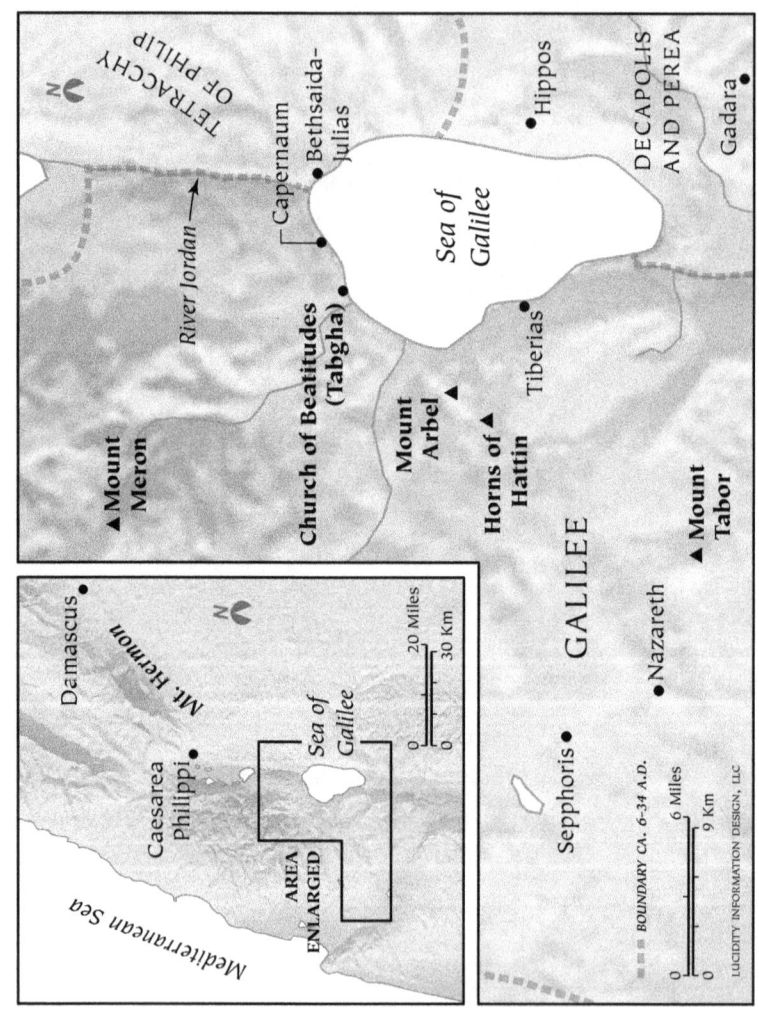

Appendix

APPENDIX

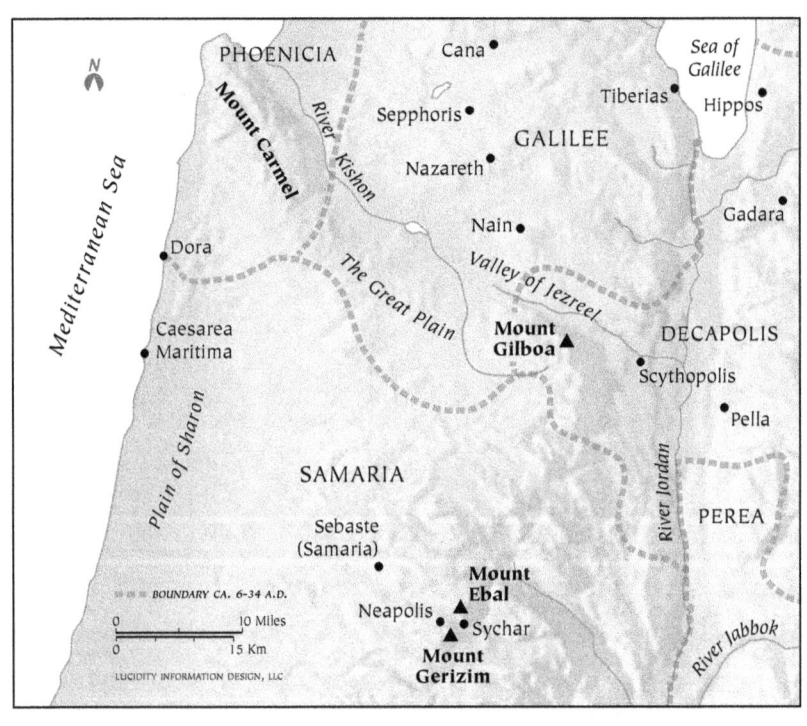

Name Index

Abegg, Martin, Jr., 139n31
Abraham, William J., 69n86
Aharoni, Yohanan, 34, 34n9
Anati, Emmanuel, 45–46, 46n40
Aristotle, 10–11
Arndt, William F., 107n54

Bahat, Dan, 21n23
Bailey, Lloyd R., 2n3
Baly, Denis, 93n
Barkay, Gabriel, 21n23
Beit Arieh, Itzhaq, 45n37
Beitzel, Barry J., 32n3, 33n5, 44n36, 48n48
Ben-Dov, Meir, 131n9, 131n14, 132n13
Blocher, Henri A. G., 4n11
Bowling, Andrew, 114n17
Branch, Robin G., 12n27
Brisco, T. V., 48n47
Brueggemann, Walter, 39–40n23

Carey, William, 68, 68n84
Chavalas, Mark W., 77n15, 77n18
Chawla, Navin, 58n36
Clement of Alexandria, 6
Cook, Michael, 139n31
Cross, Frank Moore, 44
Cundale, A. E., 100n33
Curtis, Adrian H. W., 99n28
Cyril of Jerusalem, 111–12, 112n9
Cyzewski, Edward, 60n51, 146n49

Daane, J., 4n11
Davies, G. Henton, 75n10
Davies, G. I., 48n47
Delling, Gerhard, 54n18
Douglas, J. D., 130n4

Egeria, Etheria or Aetheria, 33, 33n6, 33n7, 52, 73, 73–74n6
Eichrodt, Walter, 36n13, 38n16, 40n25
Enns, Peter, 46n42

Foerster, Werner, 67n81
Frankel, Raphael, 112n10
Franklin, Benjamin, 4
Frantzman, Seth J., 20n22
Franz, Gordon, 44n35, 45n38, 46n40

Garland, D. E., 59n41
Geddert, Timothy J., 67n78, 68n85
Geissler, Rex, 1n2
Gingrich, Wilbur, 107n54
Goss, Leonard G., 83n45

Hagner, Donald, 49n2, 66n74, 120n31, 120n33
Har-El, Menashe, 46n43
Harrison, R. K., 48n47
Hauck, F., 59n41
Hays, Richard B., 57n33
Helyer, Larry R., 6n16, 9–10n23, 16n7, 22n27, 59n40, 60n51, 69n88, 74n7, 81n32, 86n60,

Name Index

105n47, 109n59, 123n40, 124n42, 125n44, 126n49, 132n18, 146n49
Hesiod, 5n13
Hilhorst, Ton, 111n7
Hill, Jonathan, 40n24
Hoehner, Harold W., 121n35
Hoffmeier, J. K., 48n47
Horn, Siegfried H., 32n3, 74, 74n8
Hosea, 63
Hunt, J. H., 6n19

Irenaeus, 6

Jeremiah, 69, 72, 74
Josephus, Flavius, 15n4
Jung, Kurt Gerhard, 111n2
Justin Martyr, 6

Kark, Ruth, 20n22
Kertelge, Karl, 62

Lehman, Frederick M., 29
Lewis, Jack P., 6n16
Liefield, Walter L., 111n6

Mare, W. Harold, 17n9, 18n12, 21n25
Mattingly, Gerald, 48n47
McGarvey, J. W., 94n13
Meier, Sam A., 94n8
Meyers, Carol, 132n13
Mother Teresa, 58n36
Murphy-O'Connor, Jerome, 98n25, 98n26, 112n11

Na'aman, Nadav, 132n14
Naude, Jackie A., 38n19
Notley, R. Stephen, 33n5, 48n47
Nützel, Johannes M., 119n29

Patrich, Joseph, 75n9
Peterson, Eugene H., 49, 57n32
Pfeiffer, Charles F., 116n22
Porter, Stanley E., 34n8

Rad, Gerhard von, 100–101n34
Rai, Raghu, 58n36

Rainey, Anson F., 33n5, 48n47, 83–84n50
Rasmussen, Carl G., 76n14
Rausch, David A., 135n22
Reich, Ronny, 15n4, 131n9
Reuben, Peretz, 18n14
Ringma, Charles, 32n2
Ritmeyer, Kathleen, 17n10, 21n25
Ritmeyer, Leen, 17n10, 21n25

Scharlemann, Martin H., 111n6
Shanks, Hershel, 44, 44n34, 74n8
Smith, David, 98n26
Stein, Robert H., 115, 119n28

Tagbha, Israel, 52, 52n9
Tenney, Merrill C., 130n4
Tertullian, 6
Thielman, Frank, 42n26, 43n32
Thomson, William M., 92n2, 98n25, 112n12, 114n13, 114n17
Tischendorf, Constantin von, 33–34
Turner, David L., 53n13, 125n45

Valerius, Galician monk, 33n6

Waltke, Bruce K., 35n12, 36n13, 37n15, 39n22, 87n65
Walton, John, 2n4, 6n18, 7n20, 77n18
Watts, Isaac, 90
Wilkins, Michael J., 53n11
Wilkinson, John, 20n21, 33n6, 52n10, 73–74n6, 73n4, 111n8
Wise, Michael, 139n31
Wood, Bryant, 47, 47–48n46
Wright, Paul, 33n5

Zertal, Adam, 96, 96n21, 96n24

Scripture Index

OLD TESTAMENT

Genesis

Reference	Page
1–11	2
1:2	145
1:26–30	140
1:31	140
3–9	4
3:5	86
3:14–19	3
3:24	3
4–11	2
4:4	3
4:7	3
4:16	88n68
6:1–13	4
6:4	5
6:6	7
6:8	11
6:11	3, 6
7:19	7
7:21:	7
7:22	7
9:13	1
11:27–25:11	22
12–25	22
12:1–3	22
12:7	77n15, 93
12:10–13:1	23
13:2–18	23
13:14–17	77n15
14:1–16	23
15:18–19	77n15
16:1–16	23
17:18	77n15
18:14	23
18:25	12
19:16	34
19:18	34
20:1–18	23
21:8–14	23
22:1–19	23
22:2	15, 24
22:3	24
22:7	25
22:8	14, 26
23	7
24	23
35:2	95

Exodus

Reference	Page
1–19	35
3:1	44
3:5	36
5:2	87
7:20–21	79
15:11	36
15:13	36
15:22–19	46
16:23	36
19:1	48
19:5–6	38
19:6	37
19:16	34

Scripture Index

Exodus (continued)

19:18	34, 44
19:23	37
20–23	35
20:3	65
24	36
24:7	95
25–40	36
31:18	78
33:11	79
33:18	8
33:19–20	8
33:22	34n10
34:6–7	8

Leviticus

9:23–24	104
11–13	41
11:44–45	144
15	41
17–26	37
19:2	31, 37, 144
20:7	144
20:26	54
21:1–2	41

Numbers

6:6–12	41
6:24–26	38n17
7:33	72n1
12:3	78
12:6–8	79
19:18	75n9
20:2–3	79
20:5	78
20:8	79
20:10–11	79
20:12	80
32:3	72n1
33:1–15	46
33:5–15	48
33:50–34:12	77n15

Deuteronomy

1:2	46, 47
1:19	78
4:20	8
6:5	56
17:20	88
27:2–3	94n11
27:8	94n11
27:11–14	95
32:49–50	72
34:1	72, 73

Joshua

8:30–31	94
8:32	94
24:15	91
24:21	95
24:23	95
24:25–26	95

Judges

4	111

1 Samuel

9:2	85
9:21	85
15:1–23	84n52
15:17	85
15:23	83
15:30	89
18:7–9	89
28:19	83, 83n46
30:1–20	84n52

2 Samuel

1:1–15	84n52
1:21	76
3:9–12	84n52
3:26–38	84n52
12:9	88
15:30	117
24:14	8

1 Kings

6–8	16

Scripture Index

16:31	101
18	98n25
18:17	102
18:18	102
18:19	104
18:21	91
18:27	103
18:29	103
18:36–37	103
18:42	105
18:43	98n26
18:44	105
19:8	47–48n46
19:13	34n10

1 Chronicles

5:23	114
21:13	8
21:26	104

2 Chronicles

26:16	88n70
32:25	88n70
35:3	75n10
36:10	75n10

Nehemiah

9:31	9
13:16	15n4

Job

5:7	147

Psalms

13:1–2	147
25:6	1, 8
29	114
32:5	64
37:11	61
42:6	114
47:4	85
48:1–3	136, 136n24
48:12–14	136, 136n24
50:2	136
51:1	64
68:4	98n27
73	147
87:1–3	137
87:5–6	129, 137
88:13	111
103:12	9
122:6	68n83
125:1	137
132:13–14	137

Proverbs

11:2	88
16:18	71
17:6	85
29:23	88

Isaiah

1:7–8	134
1:26	134
2:2	134
3:1–4:1	134
4:3–6	135
9:6	67
14:12–14	87
15:2	72n1
23:17–18	138n28
24:23	135
25:6	135
35:10	135
37:22	138n28
49:18	138n28
51:3	135
52:1	136
52:11	43
54:5	138n28
54:11–14	134
60:1	136
60:11	136
60:14–15	136
60:18–19	136
61:10	138n28
62:5	138n28
62:11	138n28
65:17–18	136

Scripture Index

Jeremiah

3:16–17	75n10
22	72n1
22:20	72
48:1	72n1
51	138n28

Lamentations

3:22–23	64

Ezekiel

16	138n28
16:7–14	138n28
20:34	43
20:41	43
28:1–19	87
28:14	87
28:15	87
28:17	87
48:35	145

Daniel

7:9	119

Hosea

2:16–20	138n28
6:6	63, 63n63

Micah

5:5	67
7:18	8

Zechariah

14:4–5	128

NEW TESTAMENT

Matthew

4:5	17
5:1–2	49
5:2–12	53
5:3–12	53n13
5–7	55
5:7	63n63
5:8	66, 143
5:12	69
5:13–16	53
5:17–19	35
5:17–48	53
5:18–20	53n16
5:19	54n16
5:35	138
5:48	49, 54
6:1–34	53
6:12	60
6:24	65, 106
6:33	54, 65
7:1–27	53
7:24	53
9:28	59
10	55
10:34–37	67n82
10:37–39	68n85
13	55
16:13	113
16:15–16	118
16:22–23	69n87
16:24–35	66
17:2	120
18	55
18:3	88
21:1	116n23
21:14	18
23:45–25:30	123
24:1–2	18
24:2	122
24:4–14	123
24:9	68
24:13	124
24:14	123, 124
24:15	124
24:15–17	125
24:15–28	123
24:15–29	125
24–25	55
24:29–31	123

Scripture Index

24:30	110
24:30–31	126
24:32–35	123
24:34–35	127
24:42	124
25:31–46	123
28:18–20	128

Mark

7:14–23	42
8:27	113
8:29	118
8:31–32	118
8:38	119
9:2	112, 113
9:2–4	119
9:3	120
9:14	114
9:23	68
9:30	114
9:33	114
10:27	68
11:1	116n23
11:15–17	17
12:29	39
13:4	122
13:5–13	123
13:14–23	123
13:24–27	123
13:28–37	123
15:33	12
15:34	12
15:37	12
16:2	12

Luke

1:49	64
2:22–38	17
2:41–47	17
5:1–11	52
5:8	57
9:28	113
9:29	120
9:31	120
9:51	120
10:33–34	65
10:37	65
12:48	89
19:29	116n23
19:41	117
19:42–44	118
19:47	18
21:7	122
23:46	12
24:47–48	128

John

1:5	68
1:14	142
1:18	66
2:13–25	18
2:19–21	18
3:16	28
3:23n19	95
5:1	18
6:63	53
7:14	18
8:39	28
8:53	29
8:56–58	29
10:10	146
13:21	66
14:9	66, 142
15:18	68
18:10	69n87
19:30	12
20:28	121

Acts

1:8	128
1:11	127
1:12	127
2:2–4	104
2:8–11	104
7:22	77
7:60	60

Romans

1:7	68n83
1:21–22	86
1:24	42

Scripture Index

Romans (continued)

3:25–26	13
5:1	13, 68n83
5:12	4
6:12	109
6:23	42
8:1	13
8:1–2	28
8:18	147
8:21	59, 147
8:31–32	27
9–11	64
10:9–10	121
11:32–33	64
12:1	64, 140
12:8	65
14:17	68n83
15:13	68n83
16:20	120

1 Corinthians

3:21–22	62
4:7	85
5:8	72n1
6:19	140
15:10	58
15:20–21	12
15:25–26	121

2 Corinthians

1:3–4	60
4:6	142
5:21	12
6:17	43

Galatians

4:25	44
5:19	42
6:14	90

Ephesians

2:14	67
4:19	42
6:12	68

Philippians

1:9–10	42
2:3–7	85
2:5–7	89
3:8–9	63

Colossians

3:5	42

1 Thessalonians

1:10	13
4:4–5	107

2 Thessalonians

2:4	124

1 Timothy

1:2	13
3:6	87
3:16	142

2 Timothy

1:2	13

Titus

3:2	61

Hebrews

5:14	43
10:19	142
10:22	142
11:19	29
12:14	36, 70
12:22	129
12:29	9
13:14	143

James

1:8	66
1:14–15	86
3:17	65
4:8	66

Scripture Index

1 Peter

1:3	65
1:14–16	43
2:21	69, 89
2:24	12
3:9	69
4:7	147
4:12	147
5:5–9	89
5:8	68
6:10	147

2 Peter

1:16	121
1:18	121
3:11	147
3:11–15	70
3:13	62

1 John

1:7	43
2:2	142
2:16	108
2:16–17	59

Revelation

3:21	62
4:3	13
4:8	67
5:6	138
6:12–17	124
7:12	148
7:16–17	70
12:5	138
12:17	68
17:6	68
17:9	138n28
17:9–11	138n28
19:11–16	126
19:13	139
19:16	121, 124, 139
21–22	140, 143
21:2	143
21:3	141
21:5	140
21:21	144
21:25	145
21:27	145
22:1–2	146
22:3	146
22:4	66, 143

APOCRYPHA

1 Esdras

1:54	75n10

1 Maccabees

	16n7

2 Maccabees

2:4–8	74
2:4–10	74

Sirach

3:21	28
10:12–13a	85n56

Song of Solomon,

3:8	114

PSEUDEPIGRAPHA

1 Enoch

	5

Subject Index

Abarim (mountain range), 72
Abd al Malik, Caliph, 18, 19n15
Abraham
    covenant, 11
    crises cycle, 23
    Isaac, binding of, 15, 22–27
    name change from Abram, 22n28
    rainbow symbolism, 12
Absalom's rebellion, 117
Acton, Lord John, 82
Adam and Eve, 86, 86n62
Ahab, King, 101
Akkadian account of great flood, 6n19
al Aqsa mosque on Temple Mount, 18–19, 18n13–14, 18n14
al Haram al-Sharif (Noble Sanctuary in Jerusalem), 17
Amalekites, 84n52
El Amarna Texts, 131, 131n10
Amin al-Haj, Mufti of Jerusalem, 18n13
angels, 5–6
Anglican Church, 60n49
anthropopathism, 10
antichrist, 124–25
Antiochus IV resistance (175 BC), 16n7, 125
Araunah the Jebusite, 16
The Arbel (rocky cliffs), 50, 50n4
ark of the covenant, 74–75, 75n9, 75n10, 94, 141, 142
Armenians, 20
art of waiting, 32n2

ascension of Christ, 127–28, 127n52
Atrahasis Epic, 6n19
Augusta Victoria tower, 116n21

Babylon, 16, 68, 75, 137–38, 138n28
Babylonian mythology, 5n13
Bar Kochba Revolt. *See* Second Jewish Revolt
Bashan mountains, 72
beatific vision, 143
being, rather than doing, 31–32, 31n1
being whole, 54, 54n18
binding of Isaac, 15, 22–27
blood
    Christ as sacrifice of atonement, 13
    as cleansing agent, 9
bloodletting, 103n39
Book of Common Prayer, 86
Bordeaux Pilgrims (333 AD), 111
boundaries
    of holiness, 43n32
    ritual uncleanness and, 41
bride, as symbol, 114, 137–38, 138n28, 139, 140, 143
burning bush, 33n7, 36
Büyük Ağri Dağ (Ararat region volcanic mountain), 1

Cain and Abel story, 3
Calvary, etymology, 20
    . *See also* Mount Calvary
Canaanite ideology, 24–25, 41, 94–97, 99

Subject Index

Catherine, Saint, 33
Catholic. *See* Roman Catholic tradition
Chapel of Golgotha, 21, 26
child sacrifices, 24–25
Church of All Nations, 117
Church of Saint Anne, 117
Church of St. Mary, 18
Church of the Beatitudes, 50, 52
Church of the Holy Sepulcher, 19, 19n15, 20–21, 20n20, 21n26, 26
Church of the Multiplication of the Loaves and Fishes, 52
Church of the Pater Noster tower, 116n21
Church of the Primacy of St. Peter, 52
Church of the Transfiguration, 112
City of David, 15–16, 131–32
cleanness, 40–41
Codex Sinaiticus, 33–34
Conder, Claude, 20
confession, 42, 60, 60n49, 60n50, 64
congregational churches, 60n50
Constantine, 20
Copts, 20
Corbo, V., 73
covenant renewal ceremonies, 94–95n13, 94–96, 97
covenants
    Elijah's influence on Mount Carmel, 101–2
    at Mount Sinai, 34
    New covenant, 12–13
    rainbow as sign of, 11–13
    . *See also* Sermon on the Mount theology
Crotser, Tom, 74
Crusaders, invasion of Holy Land, 19, 51, 51n7, 135, 135n22
cultural influences on religions practices
    Canaanite ideology, 98–101, 100–101n34, 100n33
    contemporary application, 106–9
curses
    Adam and Eve, 4, 84

David on Mount Gilboa, 84
Levites, 95
lifting of in new Jerusalem, 145
Custody of the Holy Land, 73

dancing, frenzied, 103, 103n38
David, King, 16, 88
Day of Atonement (Yom Kippur), 40, 141
Dead Sea, elevation of, 116
Decalogue, 36n13
demonic possessions, 5
demonic-human beings, 5
dependency, 58, 58n37
disciples' prayer, 70
Dome of the Rock, 17–19, 17n10, 75n10
double-mindedness, 66

earth, renewed as final location for the redeemed, 140–41
Eastern Orthodox Church, 60n49, 112
Eden, garden of, 142
Eight Words (Sermon on the Mount), 53, 53n12, 70
Eliphaz the Temanite, 147
Episcopal church, 60n49
Ethiopians, 20
Eusebius, on Temple Mount, 18
Evan Almighty (movie), 7
The Execration of Asiatic Princes, 131n7, 147–48
Exodus, structure of book, 35–36, 58n35

fall from Eden, consequences of, 2–4
fallen angels, 5–6
families today, violence in, 3
Fantoni, Giovanni, 73
Feast of Tabernacles, 40
Feast of Unleavened Bread, 40
Feast of Weeks, 40
fire, as symbol of God's promises, 104
First Jewish Revolt (66-74 AD), 52, 111, 112, 133

Subject Index

First Temple (587 BC), 15n4, 16, 18n14, 74, 75n10, 104
flood story, of Noah
    destruction from, 7, 7n20
    Mount Ararat, 1–2
    prequels to, 3–6
    setting of, 2–6
    sign of the rainbow, 11–13
    significance of, 6–13
    sin consequences and, 9–10n23
    wrath of God, 6–9
Franciscan Biblical Institute, 73

garden of Eden, 142
garden of New Jerusalem, 146
Garden Tomb, 19, 20–21
gathered churches, 60n50
Getz, Yehuda Meir, 75n10
Gilgamesh Epic, 6n19
Gnosticism, 140, 140n33
God
    character of, 7
    covenants, 11–13, 34, 101–2
    emotions of, 10
    eternal presence with man, 142–43
    foreshadowing of son's sacrifice, 26, 29
    Holiness of, 9
    immutability of, 10–11
    judgement of sin, 9
    mercy of, 8–9
    promises, 11–13, 22–23, 22n28 (*See also* Sermon on the Mount theology)
    rainbow, as sign of promise, 11–13
    sons of, 4–6
    wrath of, 6–9
Golan Heights, 72
Good Samaritan parable, 64–65
Gordon, Charles, 20–21, 21n22
Goren, Shlomo, 75n10
grace, 13
Great Commission, 128
great floods, 6n19, 9–10n23
. *See also* flood story, of Noah

Greek Orthodox tradition, 20, 112
Greek philosophy, 10
The Green Line, 76, 76n13

Hadrian, Roman emperor, 18
Har Karkom (mountain), 45–46
Haram esh Sharif (the noble sanctuary), 75n10
Har-El, Menashe, 46
Hasmoneans (Maccabees), 16, 16n7, 132
Hebrew University tower, 116n21
Herod the Great, 16, 55
Hesiod, Greek poet, 5n13
Hittite mythology, 5n13
Holiness
    as channel of God's blessing to all people, 38
    Christians and the Old Testament, 41–43
    definition of, 37–38
    expressions of, 39–41
    God as, 9, 38, 38n19
    heart of, 38–39
    Hebrew notion of, 38
    humility, 57–59, 57n34, 58n36
    Jesus and, 56–57, 70
    overview, 31–32
    righteousness and (*See* righteousness)
    Sermon on the Mount, 54–55
    tabernacle and, 37, 37n15
Holiness Code, 37
Holy
    as colloquial expression, 36
    definition of, 38
Holy of Holies, 18
Holy Spirit, as tongues of fire symbol, 104
Horn, Siegfried, 74, 74n8
Horns of Hattin (mountain), 51
humility, 57–59, 57n34, 58n36

incarnation, 142
Isaac, binding of, 15, 22–27
Isaiah, messages to Israel and Judah, 133–37

Subject Index

Islam
   al Haram al-Sharif (Noble
      Sanctuary in Jerusalem), 17
   architectural sites, 19n15
   bloodletting ritual, 103n39
   Jerusalem captured from, 135n22
   Moses as prophet, 35
Israel
   God's mercy on, 8
   as independent state, 133
   Isaiah's message to, 133–37
   kings of, 88n70
   sacrificial cult of, 9
   . See also Jerusalem
Israel-Arab Armistice Agreement
   (1949), 76n13

Jebel al-Lawz, Saudi Arabia, 43–44
Jebel Baqir, 45
Jebel el-Bedr, 45
Jebel el-Sheikh (Mount Hermon),
   113–15
Jebel el-Thalj (Mount Hermon),
   113–15
Jebel en-Neba, 73, 73n3
Jebel et Tur (Mount Tabor), 110–13,
   128
Jebel Fuqu'ah, 76
Jebel Jarmaq (Mount Meron), 113–15
Jebel Katarin, 43
Jebel Khasm el-Tarif, 47
Jebel Manita, 45
Jebel Musa ("mount of Moses"),
   32–34, 43, 48
Jebel Sin Bisher, 46
Jebusites, 131
Jehoiakim, King, 72
Jerome, on Jupiter Capitolinus
   Temple, 18
Jerusalem
   City of David as, 132
   Crusaders capture of from Islam,
      135n22
   First Jewish Revolt (66-74 AD),
      52, 111
   geographic setting, 15–16
   Isaiah's tale of two cities, 133–37

   Jesus' grand entrances, 138–39
   John's tale of two cities, 137–38
   Nebuchadnezzar's destruction of,
      132, 135
   Rome's takeover of, 132–33
   Second Revolt (132-135 AD),
      17n9, 18, 52
   Titus's sack of, 16–17, 135
   transformation of, 133–37
   . See also Israel
Jesus Christ
   association with Second Temple,
      17–18, 17n11
   birth narrative, 55
   crucifixion site, 19–21
   foreshadowing of His sacrifice,
      26, 29
   Holiness and, 56–57, 70
   Jerusalem, grand entrances,
      138–39
   Mount of Olives descent, 117
   pre-incarnate Lord, 29
   religious leaders, controversy
      between, 28–29
   second coming of, 58, 121–28,
      139
   transfiguration of, 119–121,
      120n31
   typological link with Moses,
      55–56
Jewish tradition, 35
Jezebel, Queen, 101
John the Baptist, buried on Mount
   Ebal, 96, 96n19
Jones, Vendyl, 75, 75n9
Josephus, 43, 44
Joshua
   on Mount Ebal, 94n8, 94n11,
      95n16
   Second Temple dedication, 16
judgement
   mercy and, 11
   sin and, 9
Jupiter Capitolinus Temple, 18
justification, 13
Justinian, Byzantine Emperor, 18, 33

Subject Index

kingdom of God
  as both present and future, 58
  character of those who comprise the, 53
  invaded the kingdom of the Dark Lord, 68
  last campaign against the Dark Lord, 120
  spiritual struggle between the dark side and, 106
  strive first for, 54, 65
kings of Israel and Judah, 88n70
Knights Templar, 19
kosher, meaning of, 40

Lebanon mountains, 72
Lightfoot, John, 115
Lord's Prayer, 70
loyalty, 106

Maccabees (Hasmoneans), 16, 16n7, 132
Marcion ideology, 10
marriage, between man and woman, 107
Masis (Ararat region volcanic mountain), 1
Maxentius, Roman Emperor, 33
meekness, 61–62
mercy
  in Beatitudes, 63–65, 64n66
  of God, 8–9
  God's wrath and, 9–11
  on Israel, 8
  judgement and, 11
mercy seat, 141
Mesopotamian stories of great floods, 6n19
Midian, Saudi Arabia, 44
Midianites, 44–45
Mishnah, 57n30, 75
Mosaic law, 35, 38–39, 53–54, 56, 57n30, 95, 95n11, 96, 103
Moses
  Pentateuch, five books of, 55
  pride of, 80, 84, 89
  as prophet, 35

  story of, 71, 73, 77–80, 77n16
  typological link with Jesus, 55–56
Mother Teresa, 58n36
Mount of Beatitudes
  The Arbel, 50, 50n4
  Horns of Hattin, 51
  humility, 57–59, 57n34, 58n36
  hunger for righteousness, 62–63
  Jesus and Holiness, 56–57
  location, 50–53
  meekness, 61–62
  mercy, 63–65, 64n66
  modern site, 50–51
  overview, 49–50
  peacemakers, 67–68, 67n78, 67n81, 67n82, 68n85
  penitence, 59–60
  persecuted for righteousness, 68–69
  pure of heart, 65–66, 66n74
  Sermon on the Mount structure, 53–56
  tradition and history, 51–53
Mount Ararat
  background information, 1–2, 6
  flood story, 2–13
  harmonizing God's wrath and mercy, 9–11
  mercy of God, 8–9
  prequels to the flood story, 3–6
  rainbow sign, 11–13
  setting of the flood story, 2–3
  significance of the flood story, 6
  wrath of God, 6–7
Mount Calvary
  background information, 14, 14n1
  Church of the Holy Sepulcher, 20
  Garden Tomb, 19, 20–21
  Gordon's Calvary, 20–21
  location, 21
  rainbow symbolism, 12
  significance, 21
  theological understanding of, 22–30

Subject Index

Mount Carmel
    description of, 98
    Elijah's influence, 101–5
    historical importance, 97–106
    influence of Baal, 98–101
    location, 93, 93n7
    overview, 91–92
    weather conditions, 98–99
Mount Ebal
    description of, 92n2, 92n3
    historical importance, 94–97, 96n20, 106
    John the Baptist, buried on, 96, 96n19
    Joshua on, 94
    location, 92–93
    overview, 91–92
Mount Gerizim, 92
Mount Gilboa
    location, 76
    overview, 71
    Saul and, 71, 80–84
    theological significance, 84–90
Mount Golgotha. *See* Mount Calvary
Mount Hermon, 72, 113–15
Mount Hor, 72
Mount Magedon, 139, 139n32
Mount Meron (Jebel Jarmaq), 113–15
Mount Moriah
    Antiochus IV resistance (175 BC), 16n7, 125
    background information, 14, 14n1
    binding of Isaac, 15, 22–27
    geographic setting, 15–16
    historical importance, 16–19
Mount Nebo
    ark of the covenant, 74–75
    church built on, 73–74, 73–74n6
    location, 71–75
    Moses and, 71, 73, 77–80
    overview, 71
    theological significance, 84–90
Mount of Olives
    ascension of Christ, 127–28, 127n52
    Bordeaux Pilgrims, 111
    David's ascent, 117
    geographic setting, 115–18, 116n21
    great tribulation and Jerusalem, 124–25
    historical setting, 118–121
    Jesus' ascent, 117
    prophetic perspective, 122–24
    redemptive history and, 117–18
    second coming of the Lord, 121–28
    theological significance, 121–28
    typological link, 117
Mount of transfiguration
    Mount Hermon, 113–15
    Mount Meron, 113
    Mount of Olives, 115–18, 116n21
    Mount Tabor, 110–13
    overview, 110
Mount Pisgah, 72, 73
Mount Seir, 47
Mount Sinai
    description of, 34, 34n9, 34n10
    glory of God and, 8
    Har Karkom, 45–46
    holy ground, 36, 37
    importance of to three monotheistic religions, 34–35
    Jebel Khasm el-Tarif, 47
    Jebel Sin Bisher, 46
    location, 32–34
    Northern Sinai, 45–48
    overview, 31–32
    sacrifice with fire from the Lord, 104
    Saudi Arabia, 43–45
    Sinai revelation, 35–37
    South Jordan, 43–45
    Southern Sinai, 48
    theological significance, 34–41
Mount Tabor (Jebel et Tur), 110–13, 128
Mount Zion
    God's eternal presence with man, 142–43
    Isaiah's tale of two cities, 133–37

Subject Index

Mount Zion (*continued*)
    Jesus returns to Jerusalem, 138–39
    New Jerusalem, 139–146
    overview, 129–130
    theological importance, 147–48
    theological significance, 137–147
    transforming Jerusalem, 133–37
mourning (sorrowing), 59–60
Mukhraqa (Carmelite monastery), 98, 98n26
murder, sin effect of, 3
music, in worship services, 107–8
Muslims. *See* Islam
Mussolini, Benito, 50

Napoleon's soldiers, 50, 50n6
narcissism, in contemporary culture, 108–9
Nebo, city of, 72n1
Nebuchadnezzar, 16, 135
Nephilim ("fallen ones"), 5
new covenant signs
    Beatitudes (*See* Sermon on the Mount theology)
    the Cross, 12–13
    Mount Calvary and, 12
New Jerusalem, 133, 136, 138–146
New Moody Atlas, 44
night and darkness, absent in New Jerusalem, 145
Noah, God's favor in, 11
    . *See also* flood story, of Noah
Northern Sinai, 45–48

Old and New Testaments, typological links, 26–27, 55–56, 104, 105
Old City of Jerusalem, 15
Oral Laws (tradition), 57, 57n30
Orthodox Judaism, 35
Ottoman Sultan, Suleiman the Magnificent, 15

pacifism, 69, 69n86, 69n87
pagan flood stories, 6n19
Palestinian Biblical Topography, 32
peacemakers, 67–68, 67n78, 67n81, 67n82, 68n85
penitence, 59–60
Pentateuch
    five books of Moses, 55
    mentions of Mount Sinai, 32
    Mosaic law, 35
    ritual uncleanness, 40–41
Pentecost, tongues of fire, 104, 104n42
persecution, 68–69
Peter the Iberian, 73
Petra mount in Jordan, 45
Philistines, 80–84
Piccirillo, M., 73
pilgrimage festivals, 40
poor in spirit, 57–59, 57n34, 58n36
pride
    Adam and Eve's, 86, 86n62
    Cain's, 88n68
    effects on everyone, 88, 89
    fall of Satan, 87
    King David's, 88
    kings of Israel and Judah, 88n70
    Moses's, 80, 84, 89
    Pharaoh of the Exodus, 87
    Saul's, 84–85, 85n55, 89
    as taproot of all sins, 84–87, 85n56, 86n62
priests
    calling religious feasts, 17n11
    Holiness and, 37, 38
    on Holy ground of Mount Sinai, 37, 37n15
    money changes and, 17
    politics and, 16n7
    sacrificial offerings, 9
    set apart for special service to God, 38
Promised Land, 77, 77n15
Proto-Sinaitic inscriptions, 45, 45n39
pure of heart, 65–66, 66n74
purity rituals, 40–43

rainbow, as sign of promise, 11–13
Râs es-Siâghah ridge, 73
religious syncretism, 100–101

Subject Index

repentance, 42, 88, 128
righteousness
   holiness and, 36
   hunger for, 54–55, 62–63
ritual uncleanness, 40–41
Roman Catholic tradition, 20, 60n49, 73
Rome, ancient times description, 145–46, 145n48
Russian Church of the Ascension tower, 116n21

Sabbath, 40
sacred seasons, 40
sacrifices with fire from the Lord, 104
sacrificial cult of Israel, 9
sacrificial offerings, 9
St. Elijah Church, 112
Saladin, Ayyubid Sultan, 19, 51n7, 112
Saller, Sylvester, 73
sanctuary, 38, 39–40, 39n22, 39n23
Satan
   fall of, 87
   God's intervention, 7
Saudi Arabia, search for Mount Sinai, 43–45
scarabs, 96, 96n24
Schick, Conrad, 19
second coming of the Lord, 58, 121–28, 139
Second Jewish Revolt (132-135 AD), 17n9, 18, 52, 133
Second Temple
   al Aqsa mosque, cedar beams, 18n14
   controversy between Jesus and religious leaders, 28
   dedication of, 16
   destruction prediction, 122, 127
   Dome of the Rock, 17, 18
   holy oil and incense used in, 75n9
   Jesus dedicated in, 17
   Jupiter Capitolinus, pagan temple, 18
Sermon on the Mount theology
   historical Jerusalem reference, 138
   humility, 57–59, 57n34, 58n36
   meekness, 61–62
   mercy, 63–65, 64n66
   new covenant, Christ and His church, 32
   peacemakers, 67–68, 67n78, 67n81, 67n82, 68n85
   penitence, 59–60
   pure of heart, 65–66, 66n74
   righteousness, 62–63, 68–69
   structure of, 53–56
servant leadership, 61n54
seven, symbolism of, 16, 23, 105, 105n46
seven seals in the Apocalypse, 124
sexual influences on society, 106–9
Shechem, city of, 92, 95, 95n16, 97
Shekinah, 141
signs of God's covenants, 11–13
sin
   of Adam, 4
   after Eden, 2–4
   atonement, 40
   Cain and Abel story, 3
   definition of, 86
   God's Holiness and, 9
   the great flood and, 9–10n23
   judgement and, 9
   of pride (*See* pride)
   by-product of, 42
Sinai covenant, 11
sings of an old synagogue, 38n17
Six-Day War (1967), 76n13
Solomon's temple, 15–16, 15n4
sorrowing (mourning), 59–60
South Jordan, search for Mount Sinai, 43–45
Southern Sinai, 48
spiritual impurity, 42
suffering, 69n89
Sumerian account of great flood, 6n9
supplemental laws, 57
sympathetic magic, 99, 99n31
syncretism, 100–101

Subject Index

Syrian Orthodox tradition, 20

tabernacle
    to describe the descent of the holy city, 141–42
    feast of, 40
    Holiness and, 37, 37n15
    as holy place, 141, 142
Taylor University, 61n54
Temple, absent in New Jerusalem, 144–45
Temple Mount, 15n2, 17, 18–19, 18n13, 18n14, 75n10, 121–22
Templum Domini ("Temple of the Lord"), 19
Ten Commandments (Ten Words, Mosaic law), 35, 36, 38–39, 53, 65
tent of meeting, 78, 79, 104
Thenius, Otto, 20
Thomson, William M., 92
Titans, of Greek mythology, 5n13
Titus's sack of Jerusalem, 16–17, 135
transfiguration of Jesus, 119–121, 120n31
trinity of blessings, 13
Tunguska Event, Siberia, Russia, 7
two suppers, symbolism, 139
typological links, Old and New Testaments
    David and Jesus' ascent from Mount of Olives, 117–18
    fire symbol on Mount Sinai and Pentecost, 104
    Isaac and Jesus, 26–27

Moses and Elijah's covenant flights, 105
Moses and Jesus, 55–56
Mount Sinai and Mount of the Transfiguration, 120

unclean, meaning of, 40
unintentional sins, 40

Valley of the Doves, 50
Valley of the Tyrians, 15n4
vengeance, 139
violence, 3–4
Virgin Mary, 64
visualization, as technique to improve behavior, 147–48

Wadi Jabbok, 72
waiting, art of, 32n2
witch of Endor, 83n46
Wood, Bryant, 47, 47–48n46
worldliness, 66
worship, sacred seasons and, 40
wrath of God
    mercy and, 9–11
    understanding of, 6–9
Wright, G. Ernest, 95
Wyatt, Ron, 43–44, 45

Yom Kippur (Day of Atonement), 40, 141
Young, G. Douglas, 52

Zertal, Adam, 96
Zerubbabel, 16

www.ingramcontent.com/pod-product-compliance
Lightning Source LLC
Chambersburg PA
CBHW031433150426
43191CB00006B/491